THE STUDENT'S GUIDE TO

ARCHAEOLOGICAL ILLUSTRATING

Second, revised edition

Brian D. Dillon, Editor

Archaeological Research Tools, Volume 1
Institute of Archaeology
University of California
Los Angeles

ARCHAEOLOGICAL RESEARCH TOOLS (ART) is conceived as a series of contributions for the practice of archaeology. Manuals for excavation, analysis or publication; glossaries of terms and expressions in English or foreign languages; simple reference works for the field or the laboratory—these are some of the applications for which the series will provide a forum. Scholars and students, professionals and laymen will find ART volumes equally useful in the various aspects of their archaeological practice.

Library of Congress Cataloging-in-Publication Data
Main entry under title:

The Student's guide to archaeological illustrating.

    (Archaeological research tools ; v. 1)
    Bibliography: p.
    1. Archaeological illustration--Addresses, essays,
lectures. I. Dillon, Brian D. II. Series.
CC82.3.S78 1985   930.1'028   85-24066
ISBN 0-917956-38-9

First Edition
        First Printing: March, 1981
        Second Printing: November, 1981

Second, Revised Edition
        First Printing: December, 1985

PREFACE TO THE SECOND EDITION

Response to the initial appearance of this volume was favorable, so much so that two printings were completely distributed during the first year of its existence. The Student's Guide to Archaeological Illustrating was adopted as a training manual in several archaeological laboratory classes at North American Universities and formed the reference nucleus for a scattering of courses and seminars devoted entirely to archaeological illustrating. Through this use and exposure to different practical contexts, shortcomings in the first printing were revealed, and many of these were corrected in the second printing. With distribution of the second printing, demand for the book increased, as did suggestions for improvement, and we resolved to incorporate these in a substantially revised second edition.

The Student's Guide has been completely redesigned for its third printing/second edition so as to make its illustrations clearer and its text more readable. The original chapters have been revised, in some cases expanded, and entirely new ones have been added. Continued use of this book in the classroom, laboratory, and the field will undoubtedly result in further suggestions for expansion or correction, and we welcome these.

Brian D. Dillon

Dedicated to the memory of three great

archaeological illustrators:

Antonio Tejeda, Antonio Oliveros, and Tatiana Proskouriakoff.

TABLE OF CONTENTS

INTRODUCTION

Brian D. Dillon

INTRODUCTION

Brian D. Dillon

The basic training of all archaeologists should be as diverse yet comprehensive as possible. The single most important learning experience that any student can undertake is to plan, carry out, and write up his or her own field project independently from start to finish. The beginner thus learns to do surface exploration, excavation, how to analyze collections, and finally, write reports for publication. The student archaeologist will also discover that accurate recording is his first responsibility regardless of the kind of research being done.

Every archaeologist's education must prepare him for different archaeological situations, and his or her capabilities should be equal to the task of recording different kinds of evidence. This is because archaeology is nothing if not the study of the unexpected, and one seldom, at the beginning of a field project, can accurately predict the kinds of features and artifacts he or she will be working with at its conclusion.

One of the primary reasons why archaeologists identify themselves as "scientific" in their research is that they like to believe that their powers of observation and recording skills are highly developed. Consequently, the more alert an archaeologist is to the details encountered in his research, the greater his need for accuracy and completeness in recording. Although archaeology students are encouraged to write coherently and to take visu-ally informative photographs, it sometimes seems that the need to make careful and accurate drawings is overlooked. This technical ability of making usable drawings should be emphasized, for careful drawings are representations of evidence in graphic, two-dimensional form. Such recording becomes part of the permanent record of work accomplished and results achieved. Archaeological drawings, then, should be an essential part of the recording repertoire, no less so than written descriptions or photographs. Any field worker who neglects this graphic medium is shortchanging not only himself but any future researcher who might need to study the evidence recovered.

The student of material culture, either archaeologist or ethnologist, usually cannot physically examine all original objects needed for any given comparative research task. Consequently, accurate visual representations of specimens are essential. Most archaeology students have plowed through lengthy text descriptions of artifacts or archaeological situations without being able to visualize their form and have wished for the inclusion of illustrations. Illustrations, unlike written or verbal descriptions, can be universally understood and appreciated. They supplement descriptions subject to misinterpretation because of the author's imprecision or choice of language; indeed, sometimes archaeological drawings form the only intelligible portion of a report.

Interpretations stand or fall under the pressures of intellectual advance or historical hindsight, but archaeological evidence, if collected properly and described precisely, can never "go out of style" or be subject to short-lived intellectual fads. Accurate drawings, being a kind of evidence, at minimum may have a useful lifetime far in excess of their accompanying text. At best, they complement outstanding writing and have timeless value (see illustrations in Holmes 1895-1897; Tozzer 1907). Holmes's beautifully illustrated exposition on processes of lithic production/reduction (1919:278-357) has seldom been equaled and stands as one of the best usages of archaeological drafting for all time. We might do well to emulate him today, at a time when many seem to prefer expending miles of typewriter ribbon and reams of computer paper instead of small streams of ink.

This is not to suggest that all archaeological drawings are by nature outstanding or even very good. While careful drawings can add much to a good report and serve as an independent body of evidence useful for comparative purposes, the impact and effectiveness of otherwise good reports is considerably lessened by the inclusion of bad drawings. Illustrations are the most readily visible and immediately noteworthy part of any publication, and it is very easy to spot a bad drawing (much easier, in fact, than it is to identify a poor photograph). A sloppy drawing should lead the viewer to question whether the text itself is not also characterized by a similar lack of polish and care. No matter how exceptional a publication is, it will still seem amateurish if marred by careless drawings or murky photographs. Bad drawings are an embarrassment both to authors and publishers, and it is understandable why many archaeologists tend to feel somewhat uneasy about illustrating their own reports.

Bad drawings can also promote a completely wrong impression about the technology, art style, or even the culture they are supposed to represent; if they are truly execrable, they might even constitute de facto falsification of evidence. A well-known example of this is found in the early recording of low relief plaster friezes at the Maya site of Palenque; Waldeck, described by Ruz L. (1973:18) as an "excellent draftsman, but with excessive imagination" could not resist adding such non-Maya touches as French peasant caps to his renderings of Maya personages (ibid.:fig. 46). Waldeck's drawings were widely copied, and copied by artists who had never visited Palenque. With each successive reworking, the Maya subject matter came to appear more and more similar to the Greco-Roman romantic style that pervaded the time period. Obviously, any interpretations about the meaning of the original archaeological evidence were doomed to failure from the outset because of the unreliability of such illustrations.

Several reasons exist why a considerable portion of the archaeological community does not make use of drawings in reports and publications. Already touched upon is the suggestion that many archaeologists have, at one time or another, attempted line drawings of their finds and were dissatisfied with the results. Unsatisfactory renderings from a casual flirtation with archaeological illustrating are only to be expected, and the person beginning to learn the tricks of the trade should realize that the process is an extremely time-consuming one. Like many other difficult tasks, however, the time expended decreases with practice and through practice proficiency also increases. If a serious commitment is made, producing archaeological drawings can soon become second nature.

A different explanation for eschewing drawings might result from attitudes relative to specialization. In this era of multidisciplinary projects, many beginning archaeologists feel that they might not be able to participate in archaeological research until they have developed a clearly delimited technical specialty. Because of this, more and more students have specialized in narrow fields early in their academic careers, at the expense of broad exposure and general experience. Some may feel that archaeological draftsmanship is the exclusive domain of emotive "artists" and that "scientists" have no business straying outside their chosen specialties.

The average dirt archaeologist, rightly or wrongly, sometimes is discouraged from attempting archaeological illustration, pleading a lack of skill or "artistic insight." Yet then, he or she may opt for photographic representation while laboring under the misconception that this is entirely adequate.

Up until the teens and twenties of this century, when refinements in photographic and chemical technology rendered mass printings of photographs in archaeological reports economically feasible, most reports were illustrated by drawings. This was almost entirely due to the excessive cost of reproducing photograph plates. After the "revolution" in photographic reproduction, drawings were dropped from many reports for a simple reason: authors previously contracting for their illustrations (instead of producing them themselves) now found that the cost of printing a series of photographs was comparable to or cheaper than that of hiring a professional artist. Edweard Muybridge and others in the late nineteenth and early twentieth centuries legitimized photography as a scientific research tool. The camera was now seen, rightly or wrongly, as the most "objective" or unbiased means of graphic recording available to the scientist. By the 1920s, considerably less skill was required to produce photographs than to make drawings, and photography was much more rapid besides. Photographic illustrations consequently supplanted drawings in archaeological publications, and this trend has continued to this day.

The purpose of both photography and line drawings is to reduce a visually perceived subject from three to only two dimensions. All surface irregularities of relief (the projections, depressions, bumps, and dips) that can be experienced through tactile checking of the study specimen must now be placed on a single plane, and distance and depth of perspective must be contracted to but one level. Drawings in many ways are a more informative means of two-dimensional representation than

photographs. The camera can only reveal what is exposed to the lens (or viewfinder), while drawings can depict hidden as well as visible surfaces of the subject through the use of cut-aways, composite views, sectional views, roll-outs and other graphic conventions. In other words, drawings can depict an object as it exists rather than as it is perceived.

Photographs, of necessity, include all imperfections on the surfaces of study objects, whether they are important to the viewer or not. Shadows created through poorly controlled lighting may obscure detail and camouflage a specimen's true appearance. Accidental damage may, when photographed, appear like an intentionally made feature.

Black and white photography, somewhat misleading by virtue of its very name, is primarily concerned with gray tones. Problems of contrast between tones can result in a poor definition between different planes or flake scars on stone tools, between different colors of slip on pottery vessels, and so forth. Textural differences sometimes become merged into a single gray tone in the darkroom, and in many cases it is difficult to determine from a photograph whether a dark area on an artifact results from a shadow cast from afar, an accidental staining, an intentional coloration, or projections or depressions on the object's surface. Much "editing" of photographs is often done in the darkroom before they are acceptable for publication purposes, with dodging, burning, and even retouching necessary before selected details are sufficiently clear for study. In some cases, so many alterations have been made to the prints that one wonders why drawings were not attempted in the first place.

It goes without saying that line drawings are more "subjective" than photographs but the existence of a tradition of "trick photography" and the need to alter many prints in the darkroom to bring out desired features render the photographic medium considerably less "objective" than some presume. Drawings making use of standardized shading conventions provide explanations for doubtful areas at the same time that accurate representations are produced of the overall subject. A drawing represents an artifact in the most favorable conditions of light and darkness, with no details obscured by natural shadows or obliterated by overly harsh lighting. The result is a straightforward, if somewhat idealized and simplified, view of the subject.

Epigraphers have long appreciated the comparative merits of drawings and photographs (see Maudslay 1889-1902) as complementary forms of recording; their use in combination has proved most successful in glyphic decipherment. Most Mayanists are familiar with the legendary description of Sylvanus Morley in the tropical rain forest, drafting glyphic passages from sculpture, his shirt sleeves tied off with handkerchiefs so as to keep the sweat from dripping onto the page, and swatting mosquitos and other assorted insects with his scaled rule. If under normal circumstances a photograph is worth a thousand words, in epigraphic contexts an accurate drawing may well be worth a hundred photographs. This is because a drawing of a hieroglyphic text may have required the study of dozens of different photographic exposures, taken from different angles and under different lighting conditions so as to capture all details present on the surface of the text. While the drawing in this situation reveals what the epigrapher is most concerned with, the photographs should be presented, preferably side by side with the drawings (I. Graham 1967).

Producing drawings is in itself an aid to study, for nothing so forces the observer to concentrate on artifacts or features as having to make accurate renderings of them. Photographic work, of course, demands a similar kind of attention, but of much less intensity than that required for line drawings. In photography the least labor-intensive activity is the actual handling of the specimen or preparation of the feature; the most time-consuming tasks are usually those of controlling the lighting, adjusting the camera, and so forth. In drawing, on the other hand, constant reference to the subject is necessary, and continuous rechecking and measurement is required. In some ways, making a drawing may be compared to doing a replicative experiment, for creating a believable facsimile in two dimensions can lead to insights on function and methods of production.

Drawing a temple pyramid, a stratigraphic profile, or a pottery vessel forces the student to organize his powers of observation and to recognize and record important details. The manipulation of finished drawings can furthermore function as a useful tool in report writing and organization. For basically descriptive reports, it is usually beneficial to complete the illustration section before the text. The illustrations are then ordered in their correct sequence and serve as a writing guide to be followed much as a preliminary table of contents or topical outline. Notes that accompany field or laboratory drawings can be ordered in their logical sequence and may, if complete enough, constitute a preliminary draft of the report in progress. By this organizational method one can not only appreciate but visualize weak points in coverage and remedy faults before writing actually begins.

Like most archaeologists, I never had formal training as an illustrator. I was, however, fortunate enough to have been taught the basics of archaeological illustration in the Lowie Museum at the University of California, Berkeley, by Dr. John H. Rowe and Lawrence Dawson who maintained that neophyte graduate students should not only study artifacts but be able to draw them as well. Some years later I found myself trying to communicate the same information to a half-dozen archaeology students who were learning to draw pottery sherds, ceramic vessels and other artifacts over a six-month period at a field camp in the Guatemalan rain forest. Of the students who sat down to draw, none had any artistic or technical training, yet by the end of the season all were competent archaeological draftsmen and some had become quite expert. More importantly, over 500 accurate drawings had been produced. Our research permit stipulated that few artifacts could be taken back to the home institution for study, therefore all recording and sketching had to be done in the field.

The lack of a suitable written guide to archaeological illustrating became obvious in this field situation, and the genesis of the present volume was the need to collect and describe practical solutions to common drawing problems encountered by most archaeologists. A review of the literature presently available reveals that no single source is adequate to the task of preparing students to graphically record archaeological evidence in whatever form it may be found.

Although one excellent training manual (Joukowsky 1980) includes an entire chapter on artifact drawing, most standard texts on field and laboratory methods in archaeology (see Heizer and Graham 1967; Hester, Heizer, and Graham 1975; Sharer and Ashmore 1979) lack detailed discussions of archaeological draftsmanship. This is surprising, because such texts do have sections devoted to archaeological report writing and photography, and also feature many line drawings of outstanding quality. Some instructors of laboratory analysis classes in archaeology, because of the absence of a suitable guide to archaeological drawing, have utilized the abundant literature on scientific illustration which exists in non-archaeological contexts. Foremost among these sources are Clarke (1940), Isham (1965), Patten and Rogness (1962), Ridgway (1938), Staniland (1953), Wood (1979) and Zweifel (1961).

Most archaeological discussion about illustration is specific to fairly exclusive categories such as mapping (Bryant and Holz 1965), burial recording (Combes 1964), pottery (Kobayashi and Bleed 1971; R. H. Smith 1970; Young 1970), and stone artifacts (Dennison 1973; Van Riet Lowe 1954). Other strictly archaeological treatises on illustrating such as those by Kenrick (1971), Platz (1971) and Rivard (1964) are perhaps too brief to suit the needs of general application. More involved discussions (Brodribb 1971; Piggott

and Hope-Taylor 1965, 1966, 1967; Kowta 1973; Williams 1974) sometimes tend to be parochial. This brief summary indicates that a sizable literature on archaeological illustrating has sprung up during the past decade and a half, yet missing until now is a single guide that exposes the student to a wide variety of archaeological evidence which might be encountered in both field and laboratory contexts.

The present manual, then, attempts to fill this need. It provides suggestions and examples for accurate graphic representations of archaeological evidence based upon the experience of its contributors in both the Old World and the New. Study cases are drawn from the archaeology of hunters and gatherers as well as from that of advanced civilizations. Most of the contributing authors are practicing archaeologists with little or no formal training in art, drafting, or mechanical drawing, and at the time of original writing, most were students. We feel that archaeologists should be able to illustrate their own reports. Because of their familiarity with esoteric artifactual material, archaeologists should be capable of producing better or more accurate drawings than trained artists. The non-archaeological artist, after all, might not fully appreciate the chronological or functional importance of the archaeological specimens in question and/or may also suffer from the need to impart a personal and interpretive style to the rendering.

Archaeological illustrating is more akin to mechanical drafting or medical illustrating than to emotive art, and a formal training in art as taught today on the university level may be a disadvantage for the archaeology student hoping to objectively render prehistoric specimens. This is because the precepts stressed most strongly in art training, the development of a unique "style" and freedom of interpretation, cannot of necessity be tolerated in archaeological rendering. Technical illustrating, be it related to architecture, engineering, botany, or archaeology, uses many of the same tools and techniques as abstract expressionism. The technical illustrator's primary responsibility, however, is to his subject matter rather than to his imagination. The intrusion of personal style in archaeological drawing is to be resisted, unless the constituents of that style are accuracy, fidelity, and objectivity.

This guide is intended for beginning students as well as for professional archaeologists who have hitherto omitted drawings from their reports or engaged the services of non-archaeological artists. In the following pages we suggest that an education in art techniques or in drafting is not a necessary prerequisite to making competent archaeological illustrations, nor is inherited artistic talent or a wide array of expensive tools. All that is required for the production of publishable drawings is an understanding of the subject matter (be it a projectile point, a potsherd, or a parade ground), a few simple tools, a steady hand, and most of all, patience. We hope to demonstrate that one need not be a prodigy to produce good archaeological drawings. The recommendations offered are common sense precautions and prescriptions learned through trial and error, and the skills, tricks and methods described herein can be mastered by anyone.

CHAPTER 1: TOOLS AND TECHNIQUES

Brian D. Dillon

TOOLS AND TECHNIQUES
Brian D. Dillon

Publishable drawings can be produced with very few specialized tools; it is a measure of the archaeological draftsman's flexibility if he can make do with a very simple set. The novice illustrator should begin drawing with only a few tools and then add to his or her stock as the need arises, rather than rush out and buy everything listed in the following pages. The "tool-kit" required for production of rough drawings in the field is considerably smaller than that needed for the creation of final drawings intended for publication. No drawing is ever completed in a single step, and the toolkit should be visualized as only growing increasingly elaborate as each successive drafting task is completed. Drafting tools can be expensive and are sometimes fragile, requiring constant care and maintenance. Some tools will have to be made or modified to suit the individual draftsman, and this cannot be done until basic requirements are completely understood through a process of trial and error.

A comment about field versus laboratory applications is in order at this point. The ideal differs considerably from the real in both contexts, and criteria reflect basically dissimilar priorities and constraints. This is no less true for working methods than it is for the kinds and quantities of tools needed. The first rule is that archaeological draftsmanship should be learned in the lab and then taken to the field. Otherwise, the kinds of frustrations and distractions normally encountered in field situations will complicate the learning process to the point of no return. The field draftsman must travel light, unencumbered by inessential tools and inappropriate working methods. Again it should be stressed that finished drawings are not normally made in the field, but only begun there and completed later in the laboratory. This being the case, copious written notes, sketched comments or trial efforts should accompany the field drawing so that an accurate final version can be made without the original feature or artifact.

The exigencies of fieldwork such as exploration or excavation demand that field drafting tools be portable, durable, and comfortable to use. Over-large or fragile plastic triangles, for example, will probably be discarded after the first 40-kilometer exploratory hike through the desert or rain forest (that is, if they survive), and controlled-flow pens whose ink coagulates under conditions of extreme heat or cold will most likely be inserted into backdirt piles instead of returned to the archaeologist's shirt pocket.

If simplicity is desirable in the field, the reverse is not necessarily the case in the laboratory. Nevertheless, when purchasing drafting equipment, one should try to avoid redundancy and waste, for if one version of a specific kind of tool works well, it does not follow that four slightly different versions will function four times better.

Redundancy in tools and supplies is the surest and most rapid way to exceed whatever drafting budget may be available for any particular project. The best drawings result from the archaeologist's skill, rather than the size of his toolbox. Skill in archaeological illustrating comes from but a single source; practice, and the more the archaeologist draws, the easier drawing becomes. "Easy?" the beginner may exclaim, (with apologies to Dylan Thomas,) "Easy for little Leonardos!" yet, if the neophyte begins with the simple and gradually works toward the complex, he or she will eventually succeed.

DRAFTING PLATFORMS

To produce good drawings, drafting tables and drawing boards need not be expensive. The foremost considerations in selecting a drawing table are that it be at a comfortable height for long hours of work, large enough so that many materials can be spread out, and sturdy enough to provide a steady and secure platform. In most respects, any table and chair combination that allows for comfortable typing is suitable for drawing. The outer edges of the table should not be raised or knurled, as this will inhibit the free movement of drafting tools during drawing.

A certain degree of "give" in the hardness of the table top is preferable, especially for pencil drawing. The effect desired is that of the clearest possible line produced with the least effort or pressure. Too hard a surface will groove the paper, too soft will result in a poor impression from the pencil. Obviously, a textured table top will interfere with any kind of drawing and should be corrected for. A commercial grade hot-press mounting board affixed to the drawing table's top will protect the table and provide a good degree of resilience. For small work, individual pages can be secured inside manila folders with drafting tape, and the folders then positioned as necessary and anchored to the table without damage to the drawing through constant retaping. The folder thus functions similarly to a portable drawing board.

Several small and highly portable drawing tables with either telescoping or screw-mounted legs are available at reasonable cost, but if a field project is making use of standard archaeological surveying equipment, the plane table already in use will make an ideal drawing platform. The simplest boards are without legs and consist of either lightweight and smoothly finished plank sections (avoid plywood unless it is faced with hot-press mounting board), or a section of flat plexiglass of at least 1/4 inch thickness. Glass, although absolutely flat, is too fragile for field application. For extended periods of fieldwork in regions where tables and chairs (or the materials necessary for their construction) are lacking, some kind of stable drawing platform must be created. This need be only a long stick or pole that can serve as a monopod brace for the drawing board. The field archaeological draftsman should be prepared to sit at the base of a suitable tree-trunk or rock with his knees bent and draw for hours with the upper end of the drawing board braced against such a pole socketed in a hole between his feet.

LIGHTING

Proper lighting is as important to the illustrator's comfort as a suitable drawing platform. Insufficient light not only inhibits accuracy but also makes the illustrator tire very quickly; glaring or overly harsh light will do likewise. In most drafting situations, artificial light is preferable to natural light because the former can be standardized and used long before sunrise and after sunset.

In field contexts, drafting is normally done exclusively by available light because of the poor results produced inside dark tents or buildings (Figure 1-1) illuminated by kerosene lamps or candles. Finished sketches are very hard to produce in the field, and the archaeologist should be satisfied with detailed pencil sketches that can be inked when he returns to the base camp or home institution. The draftsman working outdoors should have an overhead shade so that light falling on his drafting board is evenly diffused; umbrellas, tarps, or plywood sections wedged in trees can be used for this purpose. As the day wanes and the direction of sunlight changes, it may prove easier to move the drawing than to reposition the shade or awning every few hours.

The best artificial lighting arrangement consists of a primary, fixed, overhead source and a secondary, movable source. The primary source should expose all parts of the drawing area to light of equal intensity; this can only be accomplished by a fairly bright overhead light. Back and side lighting creates shadows thrown by the illustrator's body or hands and obscures parts of the drawing. While front lighting obviates this problem, it can create another by partially blinding the draftsman.

The function of the secondary light is to provide illumination for specific problems. No line should ever be drawn in shadow, so the illustrator must either rotate his drawing to the best lighting angle for particular strokes or bring his light source to bear directly on the drawing problem at hand. The latter alternative is preferable, for each drawing demands that lines be drawn from many directions. Every time the paper is moved from its anchoring surface, the chances for inaccuracies in repositioning are greatly increased.

The best secondary lighting source is a hooded lamp with a low intensity bulb (40 to 100 watts, incandescent) on a long flexible gooseneck or at the end of fully adjustable countersprung arms. The lamp should be anchored to the table (either clamped or screwed) so that its head can be extended or positioned in any direction without falling over. A fully movable secondary light source may not be available if drawings are made in the field, but it is an absolute necessity for production of finished ink drawings for the publication.

Any time tracings are made, a light source capable of penetrating through at least two thicknesses of work must be found. The usual solution to this problem is the light box, often no more than a pane of glass fixed over a bulb of low

wattage set within a protective container. The glass is sometimes frosted and can be gridded for scaling reductions and to aid symmetrical positioning. In field situations a light box may not be available, but an entirely satisfactory substitute can be provided by a thick pane of glass somewhat larger than the largest paper size to be used. All edges should be carefully covered with several layers of heavy-duty duct tape as a protection against injury, and corners should be reinforced. The glass should be supported at two corners; this enables one side to be lifted above the table, so that its surface is placed at the angle best suited to receive light from the front or side. Light can be accurately directed, if necessary, by positioning a shaving mirror in different positions.

MEASURING AND DRAWING AIDS

CALIPERS. The caliper is the only suitable tool for taking exact measurements of small objects such as chipped stone artifacts or pottery sherds. There are two kinds of calipers: hinged or spreading, and sliding. Both types grip the object between two jaws; the measurement taken is the distance between them. Spreading calipers generally do not have their own scale and must be placed against some other measuring device. Sliding calipers should be graduated in millimeters directly on the shaft. Those with dial indicators are not as durable as the direct-reading variety and can cost much more. Both sliding and spreading calipers should have properly functioning locking screws which render the instrument immobile between its removal from the object being measured and the final recording of the measurement.

RULERS. All tools that will be constantly moved over the paper surface during production of the drawing should be transparent. By being able to see through his tools, the draftsman can determine which parts of the drawing are being touched and avoid smearing or otherwise damaging completed portions. Rulers for archaeological illustrating should be flexible as well as transparent, enough so that the ends can be touched together without

Figure 1-1: A typical field drafting situation, Salinas de los Nueve Cerros, Alta Verapaz, Guatemala. Note handmade tables, available light from right through mosquito netting, and minimal investment in tools and equipment. From left: Millie En Wen Chong, Connie Clark, Rebecca Gonzalez L., and Joyce Olin, rainy season, 1978.

damage. The advantages of flexible rulers over rigid or semirigid ones become obvious when measurements of objects with curved surfaces must be transferred to flat surfaces. The ruler should be marked off both in millimeters/centimeters and in inches. This is because today, while all scientific measurements are made in the metric system, many countries still sell paper sized by inches. The ruler used in constant checking of the drawing should not be so long that it is cumbersome; a maximum length of 12 inches is advisable. Longer measurements can more efficiently be made with a tape measure.

TRIANGLES. A transparent, hard plastic triangle is the workhorse of the drawing table. The majority of simple alignments will be checked with it, and all pencil or ink lines scribed against its edge. Any dent or nick in the triangle's edge impairs its utility as a line guide, so care must be exercised in its use and protection. A 45-90-45 degree triangle with 12-inch sides is the most essential of all triangles for our purposes; it is large enough to allow for parallel or perpendicular lining on most common sizes of drawing paper, its hypotenuse is long enough for layout lining, and yet it is not so large as to be clumsy. If desired, other, smaller triangles or those with different angles may be added, with a 30-90-60 degree 8-inch triangle being the next choice. Most triangles come in a protective plastic envelope or holster, and it is a good idea to keep them there when not in use to protect them from damage and dirt.

A graduated or ruled triangle should be avoided. It is seldom as accurate as a good ruler, is not as handy, and after hard use its ends become blunted; this shortens it overall and results in skewed measurements. Some triangles have recessed or stepped-in edges; these have advantages as well as disadvantages. On the negative side, the edge is half the thickness of the triangle's body, is therefore a weak point, and thus is more easily nicked than the edge of a regular triangle. On the other hand, the recessed edge is preferable for inking lines as it raises the straightedge above the paper surface and thus prevents the ink from seeping under the triangle's surface and smearing.

T-SQUARES. A T-square is not as useful as the triangle in drawing but is most helpful in layout and mounting work. The T-square may be used to create a positive anchor against which other tools may be moved or measurements taken, and if it is to be in constant use in a single position it should be taped to the paper or table. The instrument's true 90-degree angle should be checked periodically by comparison with a large triangle. Because the T-square's two parts often are of different pieces attached to each other rather than a single unit, perfect perpendicularity is hard to maintain under normal use. As this tool is not frequently employed in the process of field drawing, it should be selected for its suitability for layout and mounting. Here, the longer the blade the better, so a T-square with a two-foot or longer blade is desirable. The T-square should have a metal blade rather than a wood or plastic one, because its most common use in layout work is as a straightedge against which cuts are made with the X-acto knife.

PROTRACTORS. A protractor is needed to transfer compass headings to paper in the production of maps and architectural plans, and it is useful in orienting the measured angles or artifact surfaces to baselines or centerlines in the drawing. Two kinds of protractors are commonly used: a one-piece transparent plastic arc or circle, and a two-piece metal version with a movable and locking arm. The plastic type should be limited to a 180-degree span, for a 360-degree protractor is harder to orient to base and centerlines. In use, a penciled dot is made at the correct angle, the protractor is removed, and the starting point and angle are connected by a line scribed along a straight edge. The two-piece model's arm is adjusted to the desired angle and then locked in place with a thumbscrew. The line is then scribed directly against the edge of the arm. Both types have advantages, and the illustrator must decide between greater ease of use and transparency.

SCALED RULES. The scaled rule (or architect's scale) is used in proportional conversions from one size to another or to establish a ratio of reduction. The scaled rule is triangular in cross-section, and with two sides on each of its three faces it can contain up to six different scales. Where the drawing of an object is actual size (100 percent scale) a scaled rule is not necessary; but when large objects or measurements must be converted to a workable size or very small objects are enlarged so as to be more visible, this tool becomes essential. Different scales are expressed either as ratios or as fractions (e.g., 1:250, 1:500 or 1:1000 or 1/8, 3/4) or are simply marked off in multiples of the measuring unit used (inches or centimeters), especially on older models. Depending on the work being done, more than one scaled rule may be necessary. One with a scale of 1:1000 may be needed to produce a map of a large archaeological site, while that same tool will almost certainly not contain a scale of 2:1 which might be needed to enlarge the drawing of a small projectile point.

The scaled rule is almost always used in conjunction with graph paper; when an enlarged or reduced drawing is made, the first thing put down on paper should be the ratio being used. Because normal scales have six different ratios, it is easy for the draftsman to put the tool down to draw a line and then pick it up and mistakenly use the wrong face for the next measurement. A simple solution to this common problem is to make small handles of masking tape on either end of the scale with inked arrows pointing downward to the scale in use. This trick will ensure that the 1:250 scale is never used when the map being made is at 1:2500.

COMPASSES. A compass is not used much in normal archaeological illustrating, except in some cross-section work and in the creation of guides. The compass, if needed, should have locking arms for greater control and should not have a scaled arc. These are notoriously inaccurate, and the only precise way to get a correct radius distance is by placing the points against the ruler and adjusting accordingly, so that the tool serves as a pair of dividers. Dividers are not really necessary for archaeological illustrating but can be useful in simply checking distances on opposite halves of axially symmetrical drawings, comparing finished drawings to preliminary drawings, and sometimes in directly transferring measurements from an object to paper without making a reading.

CIRCLE (DIAMETER) CHARTS. The circle chart is essential for taking rim diameter measurements from pottery sherds but has few other applications. The chart is made by marking off a centerline on a piece of paper in regular increments (usually centimeters) from a starting point, and then drawing concentric circles with a compass using the base point and centerline points as references. Each circle is then marked with a number double the length of its radius; this becomes the rim diameter of the vessel from which the sherd matching that circle is derived.

PARALLEL RULES. The parallel rule is useful in cartographic rendering, architectural reconstructions, and in making penciled base or guidelines on the drawing sheet, but is not necessary for most illustration jobs. The maximum distance possible between the two rules is governed by the length of the swing arms, so the rule has to be fairly long to be effective. Twelve inches should be considered the minimum length, and the rule should be made of transparent plastic.

CONTOUR GAUGES. Contour gauges are either of the sliding rod type or the flexible line type. In both cases the tool is pressed against the surface of an object and a negative impression of its contour is left upon the gauge. The proportions of the original surface can then be roughly traced by placing the gauge over the drawing paper, but this should not be done to the exclusion of taking careful measurements by other methods.

FRENCH CURVE. The French curve is a plastic pattern available in a variety of sizes and is used as an aid to connect separate points on a drawing with curved lines. Most curves in archaeological draftsmanship will be drawn only after a long series of measurements have been taken; thus, the French curve will probably not be used very frequently.

PLASTIC TEMPLATES. Thin plastic sheets with punched-out circles, ovals, triangles, or rectangles in a variety of standard sizes are very useful in archaeological drawing. These tools are most commonly employed in map drafting, where, for example, a certain size of rectangle may be used to indicate excavation units, a specific triangle size, the site datums, and so forth.

BASIC MATERIALS

DRAWING SHEETS. There are two kinds of drawing sheets; paper and plastic. Each one has advantages and disadvantages; the archaeological illustrator should be familiar with both. Special artists' paper is not necessary and in some cases may not even be suitable for archaeological illustrating, but most cheap (e.g., typing) paper should definitely be avoided. Only paper with a high rag content should be used because cheap wood pulp papers vary in their ink absorption rate and are not sufficiently white. The paper should be no lighter than 16 lb., but not so thick that it cannot be folded and refolded without damaging the surface, or so dense that it is not transparent over a light box.

More important than its weight is the paper's surface finish, which should be uniformly smooth and hard so that frequent erasures will not mar it or cause individual fibers to become separated. Textured surfaces should be avoided, as these create problems for precise inking, interrupt the continuity of line, tend to pick up dirt and smudges more easily, and resist erasure more than smoothly finished sheets. Textured surfaces, or those which are poorly woven or overly soft, will often snag the pen point and cause it to skip or plow. Too-soft paper will also allow ink to seep away from the desired line into gaps between fibers; this destroys the crispness of the line and leaves it with a fuzzy border.

Plastic sheeting, generally called drafting film, is sold under a variety of specific names such as acetate or mylar. It can be obtained either clear or frosted in a variety of thicknesses. Plastic sheeting has two great advantages over paper: it is completely transparent (which is extremely useful both in mapmaking over a scaled grid sheet and in making finished tracings with the aid of a light box), and mistakes in ink can be corrected simply by scraping with an X-acto knife. On the other hand, most plastic does not take erasing with rubber as well as paper does, and some kind of smear is almost always left. Inking can create additional problems: some inks will not bond to the plastic surface and may remain wet almost indefinitely. Ink does not seep into the material as it does with paper and thus sometimes can flake off. Some pens may actually chisel small strips from the surface and create ink-filled canals that run and smear easily. Unlike paper, plastic sheeting cannot be folded and refolded without cracking or otherwise becoming damaged. It also tends to stretch or distort more than paper, and easily picks up grease and dirt because of a nearly constant static charge across its surface. For any kind of reduction or for submission as camera-ready work, drawings on plastic sheeting must be mounted over a bright white base board.

The best drawing material for archaeological use, be it artifact drafting at an enlarged scale or cartography at a greatly reduced scale, is the "Fade-Out" graph paper marketed by the Clearprint Company. Grids are available in a variety of metric and English sizes in nonphoto blue and therefore do not reproduce photostatically or photographically. The paper itself is transparent, which facilitates tracing, and can be folded without damage. It comes in pads of fifty sheets, with the most popular sizes being 8.5 by 11 and 11 by 17 inches. Clearprint paper with fadeout grid is also available in wide rolls; this is ideal for map drafting or large-scale drawings that will be considerably reduced.

PENCILS. Hard lead pencils are of little use in archaeological illustrating. This is because they do not leave much of an impression on the paper unless pressure is applied, yet this usually grooves the surface. A soft lead pencil, if misused (held vertically over the page or pressed too hard) will also groove the paper. Grooving cannot be erased and will sometimes appear darker than the ungrooved surface surrounding it, and will make the pen skip and the ink run during the final inking. A selection of medium-soft to soft pencils should be purchased and experimented with until the most suitable one for the job at hand is found.

A dull or blunt pencil will not give a uniform line, cannot be guided as easily as one with a sharp point, and will broaden the line continually until fine detail is obliterated. Consequently, the pencil should be kept as sharp as possible at all times. Pencils can be sharpened either to a conic or to a wedge (chisel) point; the former is best for freehand drawing while the latter is more suitable for scribing against a straightedge. To achieve either, first put a conic point on the pencil with a regular sharpener, then use a secondary sharpener to hone all sides for a conical point, or two opposing sides for a chisel point.

A common secondary sharpener is a sandpaper point file, usually with a light wood backing. These should be avoided as they wear down the pencil quickly if used frequently, and also tend to throw off quite a bit of carbon dust that can get picked up accidentally and transferred to the drawing. The best secondary sharpener for honing the pencil point is simply a piece of tough textured paper. Institutional grade washroom paper towels are ideal for the purpose, and their surface is irregular enough that a point can be kept quite sharp. All carbon removed from the point in this fashion stays on the paper and does not reappear during the final stages of drawing.

PEN AND INK. Felt-tip pens, magic markers, fountain pens, and especially ball-points should never be used for making final illustrations. Only two types of pen are suitable for archaeological drawings, for only these can produce the required quality and consistency of line and can be completely controlled at all times. The older of these two pen types is the "pen holder" (or nib pen, dip pen, "metal quill pen"), while the newer is the "reservoir" (or self-cleaning or "piston") pen. The reservoir pen carries a large quantity of ink inside its body and has a weighted wire that passes through its tubular tip; shaking the pen drives the pistonlike weight back and forth, and the wire effectively cleans the tip from the inside of the point. Reservoir pens normally feature interchangeable points so that a wide variety of line widths can be produced using the same pen body or bodies. The best reservoir pens are made by Staedtler (the Marsmatic 700), Koh-I-Noor (Rapidograph) and Castell; many are sold in sets of three, five, or seven, each with different point widths commonly ranging from .25 mm to 1.0 mm.

The reservoir pen is used for 90 percent of all inking jobs and the nib pen usually only for filling in large areas all black. One disadvantage of nib pens is that they frequently need to be dipped to recharge the amount of available ink, and they are more likely to drip ink onto the drawing or onto the draftsman's fingers than a reservoir pen.

A piece of scratch paper of exactly the same grade and surface as that of the drawing paper should be kept handy at all times during inking. The pen should be tried on it before any new attempt is made at inking the drawing. This will catch blots and get the ink flowing smoothly. No pressure should ever be exerted on a reservoir pen, as the weight of the implement itself should be enough to produce a uniform line. If gravity and the pen's own weight are not sufficient for the necessary line, the pen is malfunctioning and needs attention. Pressure on a reservoir pen will create inkblots, make the pen drag or snag on the paper, and even bend or break the tip. No pen that has been recently cleaned or washed will produce a line of uniform thickness and intensity until all the diluted ink has been worked out; a substantial break-in period is necessary to achieve this.

Only the highest quality ink specifically recommended for reservoir pens should be used. The best inks are those designed for high-quality reservoir pens such as Staedtler Marsmatic 745 drawing ink or Koh-I-Noor 3080-F waterproof black drawing ink. Many other inks will clog and jam the pens and will not give as black a line owing to their natural inclination toward sedimentation; cheap ink also dries more slowly and smears more easily than high-quality waterproof ink. As inking is done for reproduction purposes, it must always be executed in black. The same quality ink is recommended for pen-holder nib pens.

FORMALINE TAPE. An important part of the finishing process for drawings involves the creation of borders which set off unrelated illustrations from each other or effectively delimit the graphic subject being drawn. Until recently, borders were drawn in ink with pen and straightedge, but a wide variety of Formaline tapes in different widths, colors, or designs now simplifies the process. A light line is scribed on the paper to indicate the alignment of the final border on each side of the drawing or page, and the tape is then laid down along it, overlapping perpendicular lines at right angles. Corners are made sharp and crisp by cutting through the apex of the triangle wherever lines meet rather than attempting to "square" them up with the X-acto knife. Tape width will be dictated by the eventual degree of reduction; a too-bold border detracts from the overall appearance of a drawing as much as one that is too light or indistinct.

ERASERS. As important as a good, sharp pencil is the proper eraser. Just as the standard grammar-school pencil is too hard for effective use in illustrating, the familiar pink rubber eraser is also unsuitable; both were designed with durability, instead of exactness of result, as the prime criterion. The best kind of illustration eraser should remove all pencil marks from any part of a drawing, be soft enough that the paper surface will not be damaged from repeated erasures, and yet be cohesive enough that it does not crumble. Finally, it should be retentive enough so that it does not shed or redeposit carbon on the drawing.

Erasers should be lightly rubbed over a clean piece of scratch paper after each use (to clean them), and should be used at an angle rather than bluntly in a vertical fashion. Rubbing the eraser vertically across the paper increases the danger of excess friction that can tear or crumple the sheet, while use at an angle maintains a beveled edge that can be more accurately used in removing small parts of a drawing without obliteration of other parts that must be left undisturbed. The best possible eraser for archaeological drafting is the bright white Mars-Plastic model 526-50, made by the German Staedtler Company. This tool is very good for ink erasing and does a superior job on penciled lines.

WHITE CORRECTION PAINT. White paint is as essential to successful inking as careful erasing is to penciling. The best kind to use is water-soluble titanium white acrylic tube paint. Commercial typewriter correction fluids should be avoided because they will eventually stain the paper, cannot be diluted or strengthened as precisely as acrylic paint, do not cover ink as well as white acrylic paint, and sometimes actually absorb the ink and turn gray or black. The white paint is applied with a very fine camel's hair brush which, when in use, is kept wet in a glass of water.

The brush simply is inserted into the end of the uncapped tube of paint and twirled until the required consistency is achieved; then the paint applied to the paper. Use as little as possible, for it can crack and flake off if laid on too thickly. Work away from the inked mistake to avoid endangering any preservable inked line, and remove all paint that is not absolutely necessary to cover the problem. If an entire inked line needs to be whited-out, slide the edge of a piece of scrap paper just up to the line and then remove the line with an application of paint. This keeps the seepage problem of the white color to a minimum, and the excess is removed when the scrap sheet is pulled up. Always be sure to wait until the paint is dry; test with a finger before inking over the correction. After each use, the excess paint should be removed from the brush by dilution in water, and the brush should be thoroughly dried before being put away.

LAYOUT MATERIALS

MOUNTING BOARDS. Drawings often need to be reduced to improve their overall appearance; this diminishes small mistakes or inequalities of line or just sizes them for reproduction. The usual means of submitting work for reduction is to mount camera-ready drawings on a semi-rigid board with a brilliant white background. The best kind of board to use is a smooth-finished hot-press mounting board, as it can easily be cut to size, and erased and/or white-painted if mistakes are made. Eventual page size and degree of reduction will determine the dimensions of the boards to be purchased. Using a nonphoto blue gridded mounting board can save a great deal of time in layout work, as very little effort is needed to center the various drawings, and few measurements need to be taken. Ready-made gridded boards are hard to find and expensive. An appropriate substitute can be created by spray-mounting sheets of Clearprint Fade-Out paper over hot-press boards.

CUTTING TOOLS. A very sharp cutting

tool is needed for making corrections on plastic sheeting after inking, for removing nonessential portions of the drawing page prior to mounting, and for cutting the mounting board to the proper size. In all circumstances calling for a straight cut, as well as in situations requiring fine cuts along curves, the only tool for the job is the #1 (thin handled) X-acto knife with #11 (fine pointed) blade. This small knife is very comfortable in the hand, and its point can be guided more accurately than any other cutting tool such as scissors or a lever-operated paper cutter. Its one disadvantage is that it becomes dull very rapidly; 90 percent of the cutting is done with the end point of the blade rather than its straightedge. Because a dull knife will rip and tear the drawing paper, the blade should either be resharpened on a fine-grit oilstone or replaced. As many as two new blades per day may be required during very heavy use.

For straight cuts, the blade should be guided along the edge of a metal cutting guide such as a T-square or ruler; plastic triangles and wooden architect's scales can easily be ruined if the blade accidentally nicks their working edges. All cuts should be made on a special cutting surface instead of directly on the tabletop; this keeps the blade from becoming dull too fast and also prevents damage to the drawing surface. A cutting surface may simply be a piece of hot-press mounting board or a linoleum tile; a stack of newspapers can also serve in a pinch, but tends to shred up rapidly and dulls the cutting edge. When not in use, protect the knife and your fingers by inserting the blade into a wine-bottle cork.

ADHESIVES. Two kinds of adhesives are used in archaeological illustrating; temporary and permanent. The first is used only to secure different parts of the drawing to each other, or the paper or plastic sheet to an anchored surface while work is in progress. The second is used to lock all parts of the mounted work together in exactly the same relationship as they will appear on the finished page. The best temporary adhesive to use is drafting tape. Some manuals or drawing guides suggest

pushpins or thumbtacks for securing the working drawing to the board or table, but this is not recommended as the tack heads can interfere with the free movement of tools across the paper surface. It is always better to tape the corners of the sheet to the drawing surface; besides allowing all tools to slide over the fixing points, tape actually provides a better anchor for the paper and inhibits ripping or tearing. Drafting tape (masking tape with a light tack) or black photographic tape is the only kind to use, for most others (such as transparent, magic, or electrician's tape) tend to "sweat" glue which remains on the paper, do not separate easily from the paper or cause tears or rips.

Permanent adhesive is used for affixing multiple drawings to a mounting board, for "corrective surgery" on drawings that need secondary overlays to cover poorly drawn portions of the original, and for dozens of other small but essential layout tasks. What is required is an adhesive medium that will not distort the surface of the drawing (white glue, for example, tends to make tracing paper "bubble up"), yet which will not fail under rough handling. The best medium for bonding all parts of the drawing to its base by even coverage of adhesive are spray glues such as Spray Mount Artist's Adhesive, marketed by Scotch 3M. No other adhesive (such as dry-mount tissue) is as easy to use or as productive of accurate results; practice in the use of aerosol glue, however, is necessary. The chief disadvantage of spray glues is that their application requires the use of a spray box and blow-by sheets to avoid covering the working area with small glue particles. Spraying downward into a large cardboard box with one corner or side cut down will contain most blow-by and keep it from the floor or other work in progress. Every drawing to be sprayed must have its own clean sheet underneath it which is discarded as soon as the glued drawing is removed from the box. If this is not done, wet glue from the previous spraying will adhere to the face of the next drawing and ruin it. A stack of newspaper squares can be cut to fit inside the box; after each spraying the uppermost sheet can be

Figure 1-2: A small collection of basic drafting tools for archaeological illustrating. Sliding calipers and flexible metric and English ruler at left, 360° protractor at bottom. From top: white eraser, hard and soft pencils, non-photo blue pencil, dip pen, crow-quill pen, two reservoir pens, and X-acto knife. At bottom right are X-acto knife blades and hone for sharpening.

discarded.

Many pasteup artists swear by rubber cement or hot wax as adhesives, as both allow for repeated repositioning. Rubber cement, however, is rather messy and must be used in tandem with a rubber cement pickup (an eraserlike item used to clean up excess cement around the edges of the pasted-up work) and solvent/thinner, which is used to thin the adhesive to a good working consistency and to loosen dried cement for repositioning. The archaeologist who must often hand-carry supplies into his field camp will obviously prefer taking just one container (of spray glue) over lugging the three necessary for rubber cement use. Hot wax is common today, as it is the cleanest of the three and has no odor. It is applied with either a hand-held waxing instrument (brand name Lectro Stik) or a considerably more expensive table model, through which the item to be waxed is fed.

Each adhesive system (spray glue, rubber cement, hot wax) has advantages and disadvantages, and it is up to the individual illustrator to determine which is best for his or her purposes. Spray glue does not permit much in the way of repositioning after the artwork has set, but then, on the other hand, drawings, captions, and other parts of the illustration do not come floating off the page as can happen when rubber cement or wax adhesives lose their grip. This is no minor point, as dozens of hours of work can be wasted if a finished drawing becomes separated from its page because of inferior adhesives and is lost. Of the three systems, hot wax may be the cleanest, but it is certainly the least suited to field applications. Rubber cement is as portable as spray glue, but bonds much more poorly and will eventually leak from or dry up in the bottle or jar.

FIXATIVE. Though not an adhesive, fixatives are used in similar fashion as spray glue, but only on the face of the drawing. Fixatives bond the surface of the drawing and prevent the smearing of soft lead or charcoal renderings. Fixatives should be used sparingly. An inked surface does not have to be protected in the same fashion, and a fixative sprayed over it can dull the reflectance of the white and black, make additions or corrections impossible, or texture the surface, all undesirable traits.

PHOTO-SAFE BLUE PENCIL. All mounting and layout alignments, any notes not intended for reproduction, and, most importantly, numbering of sketches during the mounting process should be made in photo-safe (or "non-photo") blue pencil. This is because light blue becomes invisible in xerographic and photographic processes. Photo-safe blue markers are also available in ballpoint and felt-tip pens; however, these leave a darker mark than the pencil, cannot be erased, and can produce a build-up of ink so thick that it becomes visible in a photo reproduction.

REDUCTION WHEEL OR COMPUTER. To determine the percentage of reduction or enlargement necessary to make a drawing of one size fit into a reserved space of different size, or to rapidly calculate the final size of a drawing after reduction, a reduction wheel is essential. This tool is most useful in layout work when oversize drawings must be made to conform to standard page or column widths, and when the amount of vertical room left in the column after insertion of the drawing must be calculated. Reduction wheels can be obtained for both metric and English systems; normally all layout in the United States is done in inches, so a metric computer is not necessary in this country. The wheel, essentially a circular slide rule, consists of two flat circles that revolve one atop the other, with one band marked off for the size of original and the other marked for the reduction size. A window on the body of the wheel shows what percentage of reduction is required for any correspondence between any two measurements; 4 inches on the "original" band, when aligned with 1 inch on the "reduction" band, for example, gives a reading of 25 percent.

ROLLER. For the final mounting of different drawings upon the board, a rubber-faced roller is essential. The roller fully bonds both surfaces together after gluing and firmly tacks the corners down. Care must be taken that the roller does not pick up glue from one part of a drawing and transfer it to another.

BURNISHER. When using wax adhesive, the burnisher should be used in lieu of the roller, as wax requires more pressure for a strong adhesion. A burnisher is really nothing more than a stick, wooden or plastic, with a flat, slightly rounded edge; they can be purchased or improvised.

SEQUENCE OF PRODUCTION

GENERAL PREPARATIONS AND PRECAUTIONS. Before beginning a drawing of any object, two preliminary steps should be taken which can save hours of later stages of production. The illustrator should first canvas the literature for similar attempts and plan out on paper the kind of goal to be achieved. He or she should try to locate drawings of objects of the same material and technique of manufacture in existing publications, and use successful attempts as models for his or her own work and for reference when specific problems develop. Secondly, a rough sketch quickly drawn to scale (but without any attention to detail) a few minutes before the serious work is started may prevent much time being wasted through poor planning.

This sketch should place all of the different views of the object being recorded in their proper relationships to one another, and must attempt to fit them onto the page in correct proportion. Depending upon the nature of the object, the conditions of its manufacture or use, and especially its degree of axial symmetry, a dorsal (back), ventral (front), lateral (side) and transverse (cross-section or profile) view should be made to give the best representation. All different views should be done on the same scale. If the object is concave, interior views may also be necessary.

Occasionally, many views can be combined in a single sketch, such as is conventional for the depiction of pottery vessels. In these, removal of a slice is implied: from left to right is the profile through the vessel wall, then the vessel interior on the near side of the centerline, then the vessel exterior on the far side of the centerline. The rough sketch will help the illustrator visualize the final arrangement of all parts of the finished drawing and help him to avoid oversights in spacing and sequence of production.

A completely clean surface is hard to maintain but is necessary for the production of a good drawing. The constant erasures that accompany penciling leave small particles over most of the table. These should periodically be blown away (rather than wiped) to avoid smearing. The ruler, triangle, and other tools in constant use should be wiped frequently with a dry cloth as they tend to pick up dirt, perspiration, pencil carbon, and ink, and can redistribute them over the rest of the drawing. The illustrator's hands should be clean and dry at all times; washing them every hour or so is recommended. The little finger and outer palm of the drawing hand will become quite dirty during penciling, as they are always in contact with the paper; just handling pencils, pens, and erasers will dirty the other fingers very quickly. Any ink accidentally left on the hand should be washed off immediately, as sweat may make dry ink flow again; a sweaty palm or thumb pressed across a recently penciled or inked line will smear it and can ruin hours of work.

If the illustrator is working away from himself, he will of necessity have to rest upon parts of the drawing already started or completed. It is advisable in this situation to cover the parts of the drawing not being immediately attended to with a protective sheet of clean paper. Some draftsmen prefer a "bridge" or wooden elevated support with low legs spaced wide enough so as to straddle the drawing in progress. All drawings not completed at the end of the working day should be protected, either by placing them in a folder or covering them with a large, weighted protective sheet. One must be sure to keep all food, drink, and smoking materials off the drawing table, and for obvious reasons, open ink bottles should never be placed on the same surface as that upon which the drawing rests.

Finally, no drawing in the process of completion should be left unattended for any length of time, for, as Murphy's law dictates, something bad is certain to happen to it. Disasters occurring to 90 percent completed drawings are too numerous to mention except in passing, and the contributors to this volume have probably in aggregate experienced every possible natural and human hazard to their artwork. We have had every liquid known to man spilled over our drawings, animals or insects eat, defecate on, or make nests in them, and have watched hours of work borne by the winds of fate into fires, swamps or neighboring countries. Drawings left out have been rained on, sat upon, used to light cooking fires by helpful students or laborers, stolen by the curious or the appreciative, become smudged, stained or smoke-blackened, and, if left out for long enough periods of time, have hosted new life forms such as mold and fungus. In fine then, if the draftsman is not prepared to protect his or her work during the process of completion and afterwards, the drawing should not even be attempted.

The motivation for producing an archaeological illustration is to facilitate the publication and dissemination of data in a graphic form. The end product must, therefore, be the most reproducible of all possible alternatives. The most reproducible illustration is that with only two colors: black and white. Tones of gray, to be effectively reproduced, require the production of half-tone plates and sometimes must be shot through a succession of screens. This adds to the production cost, and reproductions of gray tones usually are not true to the original shade. Thus, economy and accuracy argue in favor of the pen and ink drawing as the most suitable illustration medium for publication.

All camera-ready ink drawings are the end result of a systematic process. Successive steps in producing a usable drawing are:

(1) measuring and creation of a framework or context within which the drawing is to be placed;
(2) production of a preliminary pencil drawing;
(3) production of a finished pencil drawing;
(4) outline inking;
(5) finishing;
(6) layout;
(7) mounting;
(8) reduction;
(9) lettering.

THE FRAMEWORK AND MEASUREMENTS

The suggestions made in the chapter on ceramic illustration can be followed by the draftsman when attempting to reproduce allied kinds of archaeological objects with pen and ink. While it is not necessary to repeat those recommendations here, it is nevertheless important to stress that accurate measurements constantly must be taken of the object being drawn, be it a biface or a burial ground, and then transferred to the paper or plastic sheet. Freehand drawing, when done by a talented artist, may result in a most believable rendering but such attempts should be avoided by the beginning archaeological illustrator. Precision can be insured only by the laborious process of measurement and remeasurement.

Once the maximum height and width of the object to be drawn is known, these measurements should be noted on the upper right corner of the drawing page, along with any provenience information that might accrue to the object. If the drawing is to be reproduced at 100 percent of the original size (that is, the same size), then it is an easy matter to create a reference framework of lightly penciled lines on paper that will guide the drawing through its different stages.

This framework may be a box or rectangle that contains the object and exactly matches its length and width, or it may be two perpendicular centerlines that indicate the object's long and short axes and their respective lengths. When one is drawing bilaterally symmetrical objects, the centerline treatment is better than the "bounding rectangle" method. Here, the outline of only one side of the object need be drawn, for the other can be reproduced through folding the paper down the centerline and tracing the image of the first half drafted through the aid of a light box. Depending on the size of the object and how many re-drawings will be needed to create the finished product, the draftsman may elect to use graph paper (which already has innumerable bounding lines ready) or to create them himself. Just because an object "appears" symmetrical does not mean that all detail on both sides of its centerline exists as mirror images. Tracing is usually only acceptable for outlines; basic details must be drafted with constant reference to the specimen.

The only rule to be followed in the construction of the guiding framework is that it should be completely erasable. All framing lines must vanish once the drawing has been inked and is ready for publication. It is also unnecessary to write down each measurement on the drawing sheet, for these tend to multiply quite rapidly and needlessly clutter the page. It should be remembered that the less erasing done on any given effort, the cleaner the finished product will be.

PRELIMINARY PENCIL DRAWING

The first pencil drawing should establish the desired outlines and major features of the artifact in their correct proportions. The preliminary pencil drawing is in many ways a planning and familiarizing exercise. Rendering intricate details or elaborate shading is not necessary in the preliminary pencil drawing except as a "trial run" by the illustrator attempting to discover the best method of representation.

The first pencil drawing proceeds through a combination of ruled lines and freehand lines in order to give the closest approximation of the outlines and contours of the artifact. At all times the lines should be drawn very lightly; a light line can always be gone over and made darker if necessary, but a line drawn too darkly the first time will be almost impossible to erase. Some prefer to use a photo-safe blue pencil in the preliminary pencil drawing, for inking can be done directly over the blue lines without erasing and the concomitant danger of marring the paper's surface. Others, however, find that the blue pencil's point does not give a fine enough line for anything but drawing at the largest scale, and prefer a standard carbon point.

Curves pose special problems and in most cases must be drawn freehand. It is advisable to anchor the curve with beginning and ending points that are established through careful measurement, and then to experiment with a number of light freehand strokes that connect the end points. Once the correct line has been drawn, all prior attempts surrounding it can be erased and the next part of the drawing begun.

FINISHED PENCIL DRAWING

The finished pencil drawing now will serve as a tracing guide for the inking that follows. All detail on the completely finished drawing as it will be submitted for publication will be in ink only.

The final pencil drawing can often be made from the preliminary effort if the illustrator has managed to keep the first drawing clean and has not committed too many errors. If numerous erasures and dirt or carbon mar the surface of the preliminary drawing, these will show up on the final unless a new pencil drawing is made by tracing with the light box or the clean portion of the drawing is razored out and remounted. The final drawing, either done directly on the preliminary sheet or traced onto a new sheet, allows for no experimentation or freehand attempts at capturing any elusive lines, so the final pencil drawing should incorporate the minimum number of lines needed to accurately portray the subject. All lines penciled on the final drawing should be of the same value, that is, none should be darkened as would be the convention if the drawing were not to be inked.

OUTLINE INKING

The ink pen is now used for the first time in the process of drawing. The lightly rendered lines of the final pencil drawing are precisely traced with a controlled-flow pen. If the drawing is not to be reduced, it is advisable to use a very fine tip, but if reduction is planned a broader tip will be necessary so as to prevent the loss of line that sometimes results from excessive shrinkage. Obviously, if a pen point of specific diameter produces a drawing which "looks right" at 100 percent scale, that drawing may not appear as legible at 33 percent, and a point producing a line three times as broad may be necessary. Artifact outlines should always be drawn more boldly than interior details; this should be done with a broader-tipped pen than the one used in detailing. It is a mistake to darken an inked line by retracing it with a fine-tipped pen, for the consistency of the line can never be the same as that produced by a single pass with a broad tip (motor control notwithstanding).

Once the ink is completely dry, the entire surface of the drawing sheet may be erased to remove all traces of penciled lines. If the illustrator has been extremely careful during the preceding steps, no penciled lines should remain, (as they are now covered by the inked lines). The final erasure is done simply to remove any dirt that might have accidently gotten onto the drawing sheet.

If mistakes in inking are made, these should be corrected as they occur and should not be put aside for cumulative correction at the end of the drawing process. The illustrator must wait until the ink is completely dry, and then use the fine brush and white acrylic paint to cover the mistake. The paint is used sparingly and as much of the original inked line is preserved as possible. It is risky to re-ink a line over white paint because of the textural difference between the drawing sheet and the dried paint, and the illustrator should not presume that all oversights in inking can be easily and flawlessly corrected with just a stroke of the brush. In other words, by the time a drawing has progressed to the outline inking stage, it has passed the point of no return.

FINISHING

Finishing the drawing involves either making a two-dimensional rendering appear three-dimensional, or completing complicated details present on the original effort. Three dimensionality is usually indicated by shading. This can be accomplished either through inking (stipping, lining, or cross-hatchure) or through the use of Zipatone self-adhesive shading films.

It should be remembered during the finishing process that the goal of archaeological illustration is clarity in the expository sense. Excessive shading that obscures detail should be avoided. In some cases, the best result will be achieved by combining ink and shading film, that is, beginning with transfer screens and then inking over them to disguise their regularity or to increase the darkness of one portion over another. To accurately depict internal details, both processes can also be used in complementary fashion, as, for example, in standardized shading conventions used to indicate specific colors or shades.

The only tool needed when using Zipatone (or other) shading films is the X-acto knife. First, the size of the area to be covered is measured, usually through a quick overlay and nicking the transfer with the knife, then a slightly oversized piece of Zipatone is cut and placed over that section of the drawing. The drawing must be absolutely clean before the transfer is placed on it, for any dirt or eraser particles that are trapped beneath the film will show through it or even rip its surface. Once the oversized piece of shading film has been firmly secured by its own adhesive backing to the drawing, it is cut to the exact dimensions with the X-acto knife. Only a very sharp blade should be used, and only enough pressure should be exerted to cut the film. If the knife is used carelessly, the nearly completed drawing will be cut to shreds and a complicated gluing job will be necessary to salvage it.

To reproduce intricate details of

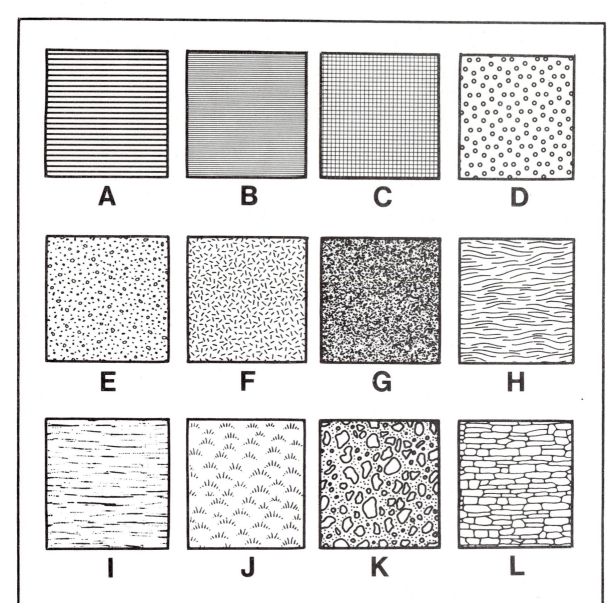

Figure 1–3: Shading films useful in archaeological illustrating. A–C are simple patterns for shading artifact drawings and may be rotated or overlaid so as to form more complex patterns; D–G are for use in stratigraphic profiles and can indicate different strata; H–L are specialty screens which can suggest leather or cloth, wood grain, marshy terrain, gravel and rubble fill, and bedrock in artifact drawings, architectural and stratigraphic profiles and maps. A: Zip-a-tone 231; B: Chartpak PT074; C: Chartpak PT075; D: Letratone LT129; E: Zip-a-tone 272; F: Zip-a-tone 285; G: Zip-a-tone 262; H: Formatt 7216; I: Zip-a-tone 695; J: Zip-a-tone 612; K: Letratone LT141; L: Zipatone 794. All screens reduced to 90% of original size for publication.

design or decoration, it is best to experiment in ink on a piece of high-quality scrap paper before actually beginning to ink the final drawing. If such attempts prove successful, it may then be best simply to cut the section of scrap paper with the inked design to fit the finished drawing and then to glue it. Conversely, if an attempt to ink a complicated design on the finished drawing fails, a new section of paper may be cut so as to cover the mistake and another attempt may be made without beginning the entire drawing anew.

LAYOUT

Before the process of layout (or mocking up a series of illustrations in their relationships to one another) can be done, the finished publication must be visualized in the form that it will appear to the reader. This involves not only planning the correct spatial relationships between graphic elements, but establishing the relationship with the accompanying captions and text as well. There are generally two options to choose between: illustrations added to the report on separate pages of their own, much as a kind of graphic appendix, or illustrations incorporated into the text. Different problems and solutions are dictated by either of the two alternatives, but generally speaking it is easier to do layout work if the illustrations are to appear on their own pages.

Once the format of the eventual publication or report is known, all finished illustrations are in hand ready for reduction and the archaeologist understands what kind of information is supposed to be conveyed, he is ready to begin work. In layout work, economy of distribution on the page should be the rule and entire pages should not be filled up with single artifact drawings if several can be grouped together. Small drawings should not "float" upon a sea of white in the middle of the page as this is wasteful of space; they should take up as little room as possible without overcrowding so that additional drawings, groups of drawings or text can be placed on that page and space (and, consequently, printing costs) can be saved. It may be necessary to make numerous

reductions early in the layout process in order to achieve this goal, but such tasks pay off during the final stages of work.

The first step in the layout process is to determine the degree of reduction for the drawings. Original drawings are often too large to be displayed economically at full size in many reports and must, therefore, be reduced. Reduction also has the positive effect of "cleaning up" drawings by lessening imperfections in them and by strengthening the overall composition.

Only a limited number of standard reduction percentages should be utilized: sometimes these will be dictated by the limits of the reduction machine. Once the standard reduction size has been established, variation should be kept to a minimum. The most logical percentages are those that can be evenly divided or multiplied to ensure compatability between a series of related drawings; for example, 100 percent, 66 percent, and 33 percent, and 100 percent, 75 percent, 50 percent, and 25 percent make much more sense than an unplanned succession such as 100 percent, 80 percent, 55 percent, and 30 percent.

With the reduction percentage selected and the page size of the final publication known, layout can begin through arranging the drawings on a mounting board. If the page size of the publication is to be 8.5 by 11 inches, and the reduction called for is 33 percent, the mounting board will then be three times the size of the publication page, or 25.5 by 33 inches. These dimensions, however, incorporate not only the drawing surface but the margin widths as well, and the draftsman that glues drawings right to the edges of a board of this size will find that a reduction smaller than 33 percent will be necessary to preserve any margins at all. Minimum margins on an 8.5 by 11-inch page of illustrations should be at least an inch on all sides, with an additional half-inch on the inside edge (the side that will be bound into the book); therefore, one would have to subtract at least a 3-inch margin from three sides of the 25.5 by 33.5-inch mounting board and a 4.5-inch margin from a fourth side, or simply cut the board to 21 by 30 inches and ignore the problem of margins.

A useful trick is to draw vertical and horizontal centerlines on the layout board with a photo-safe blue pencil so that different drawings can be arranged as symmetrically as possible. There is really no rule that governs the formal positioning of different illustrations on the mounting board, apart from the illustrator's own sense of balance and the need for the individual illustrations to approximate in sequential order the appearance of their descriptions in the text. While a harmonious balance of shape and mass between different drawings on a single page is desirable, such artistic concerns should never be allowed to interfere with the explanatory function of the drawings themselves. If different artifacts are related to one another in the text through formal typologies, drawings of such artifacts cannot be organized so that typological rules are violated. Obviously, the archaeologist is much better prepared to solve problems such as this than is the non-archaeological artist or layout person.

MOUNTING

Once the drawings have all been positioned on the board in their final locations, they must be securely attached to their backing. This should be done with each drawing on an individual basis. Each illustration is cut to fit, placed in the gluing box on its own gluing sheet, the spray-glue applied to it, and then positioned on the mounting board. It is then covered with a clean piece of paper and securely fastened to the board with the roller. While the illustration is being trimmed with the X-acto knife preparatory to gluing, the provenience information and vital statistics written in the upper right corner of the page are stapled to a provenience sheet in precisely the same positional relationship as the drawings on the mounting board. Once all the drawings have been glued to the board, the provenience sheet becomes the record identifying each illustration in its proper relation to all other drawings

and also preserves the vital information about the original object. Without such data for captions and text, the drawing is meaningless.

REDUCTION

When complete, the mounting board can be sent to the printers for reduction. It should be protected, however, before it leaves your hands. The best way of doing this is to tape a clean sheet of paper over the face of the board. This sheet should only be attached to one edge of the board so that when the drawings are photographed the technician need only turn the sheet aside. The cover sheet should also be the location for any written instructions to the printer, although some illustrators prefer to write their instructions directly on the board in non-photo blue pencil.

The reduction or enlargement of any drawing should be expressed as a percentage of the original. If you want the final product to be half size, write 50 percent; if you need it to be twice as large, write 200 percent. There can be no misinterpretation of a simple percentage of the original expressed in numerical form, especially since many photostat cameras have dials set to accept this kind of instruction automatically. It is very confusing for the technician to receive instructions such as "enlarge by a factor of two to five." Some people recommended marking reductions as follows: "Reduce to 6.5 inches wide" or "reduce to 3 inches high," but such instructions place the onus of accuracy on the printer. If the printer returns the piece to you and it is not the final size that you have marked, it is up to the printer to correct it free of charge. If, by contrast, you have marked the reduction as an incorrect percentage, you will have to pay to have it redone.

A graphic statement of the scale used (the amount of reduction or enlargement) is as important to a scientific drawing as the correct depiction of detail. For finished drawings, this should be expressed in the form of a scale bar, with divisions clearly marked and labeled. A

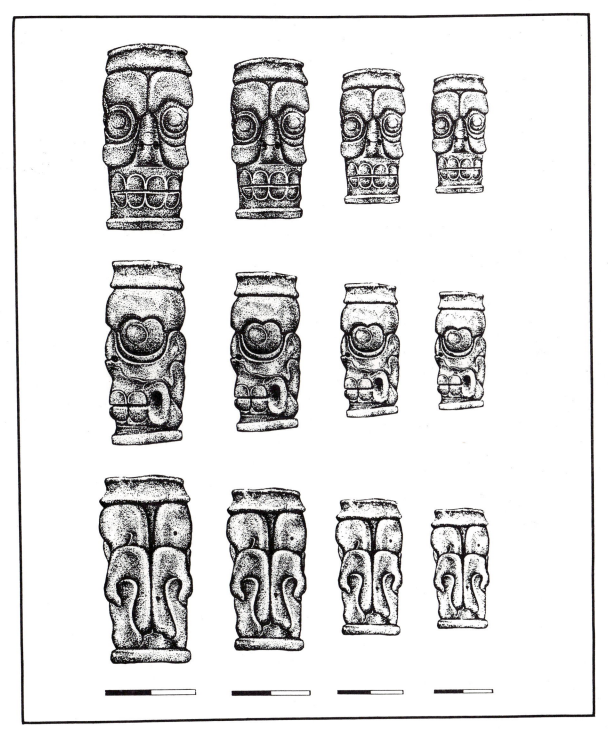

*Figure 1-4: Graduated reduction of the same artifact drawing. Note how no mat-
ter how large or small the final size of the drawing is, an accurate representation
of scale is provided by the 2 cm scale bar at bottom. Also note progressive light-
ening of highlight areas with increased reduction.*

written or percentage statement of scale on a drawing can be misleading, because once a drawing leaves the hands of its creator changes are often made to fit space requirements. If this is done, the original statement becomes incorrect. The scale bar, however, is reduced or enlarged in exactly the same proportion as the drawing it accompanies, and will always provide an accurate account of the drawing's true scale.

There are many reduction processes available, and this is not the place to describe them in detail. All work on the photographic principle, and most are quite rapid. The final product will be a modified kind of photographic print that can be considered "camera ready," or perfect for offset reproduction. The most common type is usually referred to as a "photostatic reproduction," and these tend also to be the most faithful to the original. Newer processes, such as PMT (photomechanical transfer), are also equally acceptable. When dealing with new or unfamiliar processes, such as are likely to develop in the future, the technician should be asked how similar the product will be to a photostat and if there will be any problems in reproducing it for publication.

Large printing houses and most universities now have xerographic reducing machines that can produce, in seconds, publication-quality reductions for a fraction of the cost of photostats. The price of a xerographic reduction is usually ten cents or less, while a PMT may run over seven dollars. The major drawbacks are that most xerographic machines can accommodate originals no larger than 11 x 17 inches, lines are less crisp than on a PMT, and a poorly-trained operator generally will not be able to produce acceptable results. Nevertheless, such machines should be used whenever possible so as to keep reduction costs down.

BORDERS

Illustrations of different kinds or in different locations must be separated from each other and from the accompanying text through the use of formal borders. Borders are best made with tape rather than inked, and if a large series of drawings are to be used at standard scales it may be appropriate to create a master sheet with perfect borders which is then xerographically or photostatically copied as many times as necessary. In general, drawings are fit to borders rather than vice versa. This is because the size of the border will be dictated by the size of the pages in the final publication, the width of text columns, and so forth. Borders of single black lines are best, and these shouldn't be overly bold. Excessively ornate, "busy" or dark borders distract the viewer from the drawings within them and defeat their very purpose.

LETTERING

Lettering is the final step in the illustration process before the page of drawings is sent to the publisher. Lettering is done on the final sheet (i.e., after all reduction has been completed) because otherwise, type will be reduced to different sizes and therefore will be inconsistent if used with drawings slated for different degrees of reduction.

Those archaeologists fortunate enough to be skilled in calligraphy need not bother with transfer lettering, Leroy sets, or other such aids for captions, keys or legends. Unfortunately, most of us write in execrable hands more worthy of glyphic decipherment than graphic reproduction.

An early attempt at standardizing lettering on maps and drawings was the Leroy system, by which alpha-numeric templates were used with the draftsman's own ink pen or a special Leroy pen. This produced acceptable results, but made lettering a maddeningly slow process. The ink, additionally, did not always bond to the reduced medium (some PMT and photographic papers would not take it), and the number and sizes of type faces was limited by the range of Leroy templates the illustrator could find or afford.

A more recent solution to the lettering problem was provided two decades ago by rub-on transfer lettering such as currently proffered by Letraset and other

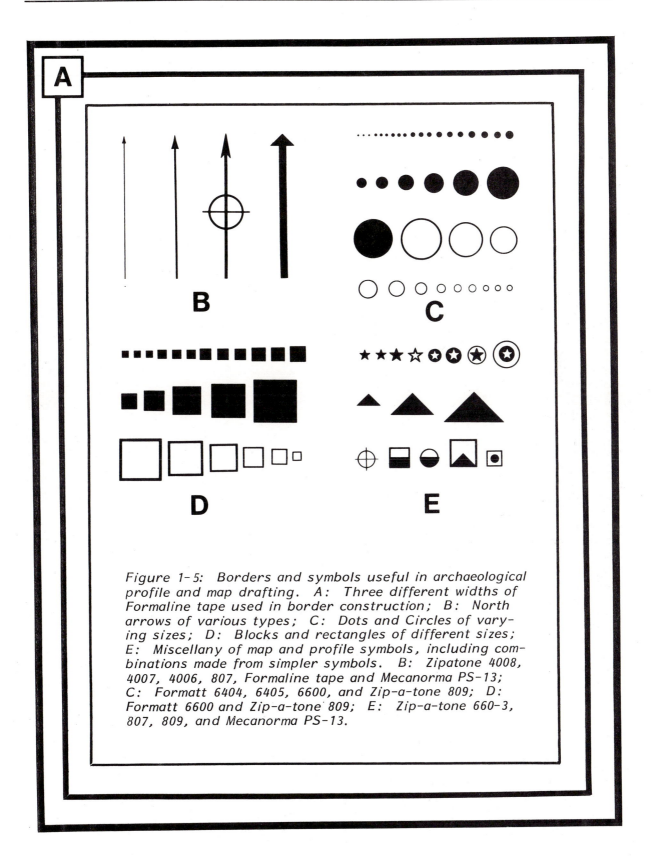

Figure 1-5: Borders and symbols useful in archaeological profile and map drafting. A: Three different widths of Formaline tape used in border construction; B: North arrows of various types; C: Dots and Circles of varying sizes; D: Blocks and rectangles of different sizes; E: Miscellany of map and profile symbols, including combinations made from simpler symbols. B: Zipatone 4008, 4007, 4006, 807, Formaline tape and Mecanorma PS-13; C: Formatt 6404, 6405, 6600, and Zip-a-tone 809; D: Formatt 6600 and Zip-a-tone 809; E: Zip-a-tone 660-3, 807, 809, and Mecanorma PS-13.

companies. An almost endless variety of type faces and sizes is now available on plastic sheets with pre-glued backings; all the draftsman has to do is align individual letters and rub them with a burnisher so as to bond them to the drawing surface. Letters on the sheets can be cut or modified with an X-acto knife, erased if misapplied, and take ink for correction if cracked or pitted. The only real disadvantage of rub-on lettering is its steadily escalating price; the sheet of transfer letters that cost two dollars in 1972 today costs over six dollars, and dozens of sheets are normally required for any complicated job.

The most recent and convenient lettering system for archaeological drafting is that produced by the Kroy lettering machine. These machines are very costly for individual purchase (their base price starts at around $600.00), but most institutions with publication programs either already have them or might be persuaded to buy them. The Kroy system produces perfectly aligned and evenly spaced letters, words, or sentences on a continuous strip of clear adhesive tape with a safety backing. The manufacturers offer a wide range of type styles and sizes, each one of which comes on a plastic rotating wheel that fits on the machine's central hub and impresses letters, numbers, and punctuation marks directly on the tape. By changing wheels one can change the type face or type size within an individual sentence or line of print in a matter of seconds. The Kroy machine eliminates that part of rub-on lettering which is the most time-consuming (alignment) and speeds up the job by at least 200 percent.

New wheels, however, are quite expensive, and should not be bought within a given type face just to obtain different sizes, for this can be achieved by setting the type at one size and then enlarging or reducing it with a reducing xerox copier. A few disadvantages exist with the Kroy system, the most important of which is that it is essentially laboratory-based and cannot be adapted to field use. The plastic type templates (or "letter wheels") are somewhat fragile, and if abused the quality of type produced will rapidly deteriorate. The tape that bears the lettering tends to have sticky or "gluey" edges, and these attract dirt and dust and form thin lines on captions unless whited out, and the text is highly erasable until stabilized with spray fixative. All things considered, however, the Kroy system remains the best lettering option for the archaeological illustrator who can obtain access to it.

Regardless of the lettering method used, the general rule is that radically different type faces should not be mixed on the same page and that lettering should not detract from the overall appearance of the drawing. Overlarge black block letters will dwarf small drawings of delicate artifacts, while excessively convoluted or baroque type faces either defy transcription or draw attention away from the illustration they are supposed to clarify. Sans-serif faces are preferable in most cases, such as the popular Folio or Helvetica styles, although some of the less elaborate serif faces can serve if a more decorative purpose is called for.

Rub-on transfers as well as Kroy tape should be burnished under a clean sheet of wax paper so as to ensure a firm bond with the drawing surface; Kroy tape will also usually require a spray fixative to prevent smearing or damage to the finished product. Transfer lettering can be erased or scraped away with the X-acto knife if major mistakes are made, and Kroy tape can be cut and repositioned if a word is misspelled instead of the entire word or sentence retyped. Still, it is always preferable to attempt a perfect job the first time around.

Nothing is more embarrassing than a beautifully drafted map or drawing legend that is misspelled; this can always be avoided by doing a pencil mock-up of the text first. Centering descending lines of text is best done by cutting the finished strips, measuring them, marking their centerpoints, and aligning and gluing them one atop the other on small sections of blue photo-safe graph paper. Attempting to count letters and estimate their cumulative widths backward and forward from the calculated centerpoint is frustrating at

A	**ARCHAEOLOGICAL**
B	**ARCHAEOLOGICAL**
C	**Archaeological**
D	ARCHAEOLOGICAL
E	ARCHAEOLOGICAL
F	*ARCHAEOLOGICAL*
G	ARCHAEOLOGICAL
H	ARCHAEOLOGICAL

Figure 1-6: Different type faces and printing techniques. A: Kabel Bold, commercially typeset; B: Helvetica Medium, hand set from Letraset sheet 727; C: Optima set on Kroy Lettering Machine; D-F: IBM Electronic Typewriter 50 print balls; D: Title; E: Arcadia; F: Essay italic; G-H: NEC Spinwriter 5510 printer driven by Zenith Z-150 PC word processer; G: Courier; H: Prestige Elite Legal. D-F typed with carbon film ribbon, G-H with cloth ribbon.

best and usually leads to poor results. A standard location for the text block should be selected and adhered to if a large series of drawings is to be produced, so as to avoid the appearance of clutter that can result from legends or legend fragments showing up in different areas of a succession of drawings without rhyme or reason.

Internal lettering within maps, profiles, or drawings should be large enough to be legible, but not so large that it draws attention away from the artwork itself. In no case should such kinds of lettering exceed the size of that used in the title block, nor should it be darker or bolder in density. Usually, italics are preferable in internal application, and if done with press-on sheets, words can be made to conform to the alignments of natural and cultural features such as coastlines, mountain ranges, roads or foundations. Finally, lettering should never be placed over or under toning screens, for blurring is the inevitable result. This problem can be avoided if the lettering is set outside the shaded area and connected to it with arrows or if small "windows" are cut in the shading so that the words appear against a light background.

For the internal lettering of drawing, diagram, or map parts, some modern typewriters with interchangeable type faces may be used. Sometimes, entire legends can be typed with electronic typewriters or letter-quality printers, then cut and inserted in the drawing. This process is made even more simple by typing the text on Avery (or similar) self adhesive label paper, which comes in all sizes including 8.5 by 11 inch sheets, and can be razored to any dimension. Electronic typewriters such as the IBM Electronic 50 or 85 feature interchangeable elements, allow the illustrator to make use of ten or twelve pitch elements, serif, sans-serif, and italic type, and have an automatic centering feature that makes alignment of different lines of text very easy. Other electronic typewriters with "daisy wheels," such as the Xerox Memorywriter, have even more versatility, but the quality of the type face is perhaps not as good. The final appearance of the text in this situation is what should be considered most carefully, and ease of production is no substitute for a less-than perfect result.

ILLUSTRATION EDITING

Illustrations, especially large groups of drawings made by different draftsmen, should be subjected to the same kind of editorial scrutiny as written text before they go to press. The illustration editor should take pains to let the contributing draftsmen know what the expected canons of representation should be. Common problems are diversity in drawing size, width of line, shading conventions, or type faces used in lettering between illustrations that are supposed to be similar in appearance. Quite often, especially in a field situation, many different students or draftsmen will produce unfinished pencil drawings or preliminary ink drawings to be completed by the archaeological project leader; if the same person finishes (or "edits") each drawing, uniformity is usually guaranteed.

The illustration editor's final task is to prepare each drawing for publication. To do this, he or she should be prepared to re-draw any portion of a drawing that is not likely to reproduce well in a given printing process, to reduce or enlarge drawings to fit space requirements standardized for different journals or report formats, to letter legends or type blocks with a standardized type face and size, to correct spelling in existing legends, to create borders around individual drawings, to remove ink blots, erase penciled lines that escaped the notice of the original draftsman, perform final checks on provenience data, and make certain that credit for individual drawings goes to the artists responsible. To do this successfully, the editor must have the cooperation of the various draftsmen he or she is working with, as well as their permission to make the necessary changes.

A final concern relates to the rights of illustrators, illustration editors and publishers. This is most succinctly stated as credit should be given where it is due. Legal aspects of this point differ considerably from what is ethically correct; it may be perfectly lawful to copy another draftsman's drawing and not credit its original creator if his or her name is unknown, but it is certainly unethical to assume credit for their work.

Most archaeological illustrators con-tributing drawings to publications do this on a voluntary (i.e., unpaid) basis. It is particularly irksome to find that their work is not only sometimes unappreciated but often goes uncredited to them. Even worse are cases in which credit for a drawing has been incorrectly attributed to some other person. When this happens it often is not the editor or publisher's fault, because literary efforts often incorporate many drawings by different illustrators frequently unmarked as to source. Illustrators who do not understand the layout or reduction process sometimes sign their work in areas that are later removed so as to make many drawings fit a single page, or even forget to sign their work entirely. Signatures can be names, initials or even "signs" or glyphic symbols, but they should not be obtrusive and should always be placed outside the drawing but close enough to it so that they are not razored away.

We now turn to the individual chapters that make up this book. Some of the tasks described call for very few of the tools and techniques discussed in this section; others require almost all of them. It may be well to repeat the caveat that opened the present discussion and remind the beginning archaeological illustrator that he will not produce a perfect drawing the first time around. Nor should he or she purchase hundreds of dollars worth of equipment or attempt an extremely difficult drawing at the outset. The best method for increasing one's confidence in the ability to accurately draw archaeological subjects, once again, is to start with the simple and work toward the complex. The result will be a gradually accumulating store of problem-solving knowledge, refined motor habits, and tools. The main thing is to begin drawing, and to keep at it.

CHAPTER 2: ARCHAEOLOGICAL MAP MAKING

Douglas V. Armstrong

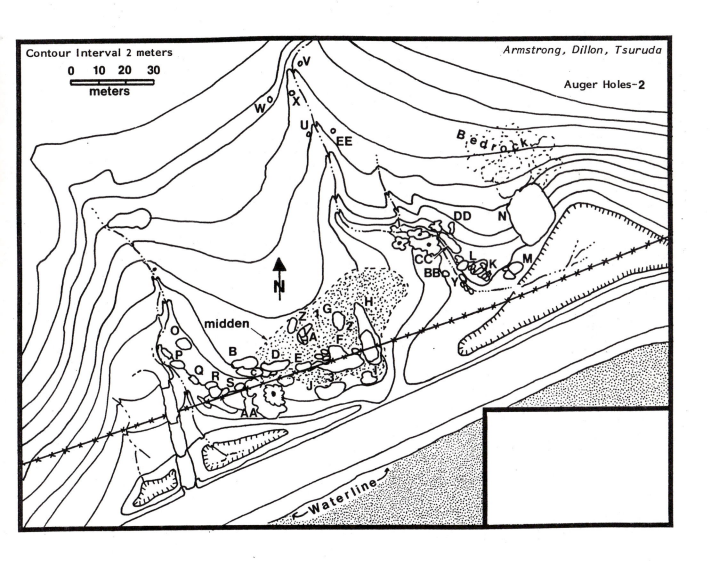

ARCHAEOLOGICAL MAP MAKING

Douglas V. Armstrong

In reducing the real world of a study area to the limited space allotted to a page of a report or journal, the archaeologist is usually confronted with more information than can be understood without modification. Cartographic principles may be employed to direct the meaningful presentation of such data. Cartography is the aspect of map making concerned primarily with the organization and presentation of spatial data simply and concisely (Robinson and Sale 1969; Raisz 1962; Hodgkiss 1970). Significant data is compiled, then generalized and simplified into a neat and comprehensible form; a process requiring careful planning.

This section aims to present a general outline of cartographic principles, operational procedures, and casual observations deemed useful for the creation of archaeological maps. Additionally, it serves as a guide to the literature relating to map making, but does not cover the essentials of field techniques in surveying and data collection. For archaeological perspectives on this subject, Hester, Heizer, and Graham (1975) and Napton (1975), as well as Aston and Rowley (1974) are basic references. Information on general surveying may be found in Detweiler (1948) and Raisz (1962).

While field methods for data collection are not explicitly dealt with here, it must be remembered that all archaeological maps begin in the field. Consequently, the accuracy and quality of the fin-

ished product is dependent on the care and precision exercised in the field. In the best of circumstances, well-made and complete field maps only need be "cleaned up" for reproduction in final form. The suggestions outlined below are predicated upon the assumption that the mapmaker can get the information from the ground and onto paper accurately and clearly.

The significant cartographic points made in this chapter are illustrated with examples from the archaeological excavations at Begho, Ghana, West Africa, and survey maps from St. Kitts Island, Lesser Antilles (Armstrong 1980), and Lake Isabella, California. These are not intended to be perfect models; rather, they represent practical solutions to actual problems encountered in the field and on the cartographic drawing board afterward.

COMPILATION

The first step in compiling a map is defining its objectives. As with other aspects of archaeological studies, data should be generated for a purpose and in a systematic fashion. Whether the archaeologist plans to draw his or her own maps or have them drawn, it is the researcher's responsibility to lay out all maps and line drawings (Dittert and Wendorf 1963:53). This is because he or she must have a firm idea of what the entire cartographic corpus of a project is likely to entail.

The types of maps included in a report are dependent on the kinds of infor-

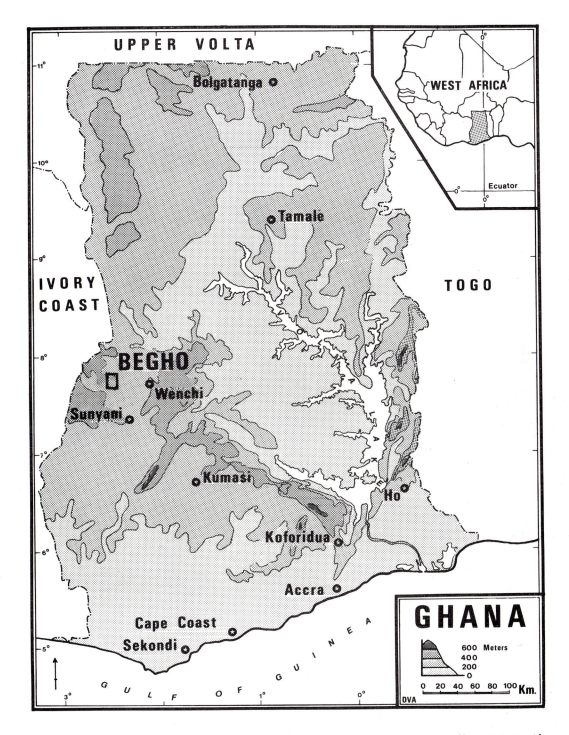

Figure 2-1: First in a series of locational maps which gradually narrow the geographic field and identify a site or region for an unfamiliar audience. Here, the Begho region is shown at center left within the modern country of Ghana. Smaller inset at upper right locates Ghana within West Africa. Note shading used to indicate elevations, lack of detail in neighboring countries.

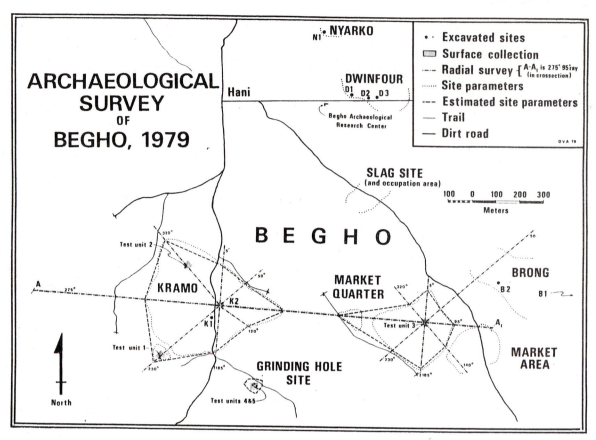

Figure 2-2: *Second map in the series, "stepping down" from large areas to progressively smaller ones. This map shows the immediate proximity of the archaeological site of Begho but does not precisely locate it for reasons of preservation.*

mation one wishes to convey. It is suggested that a "step down" series of maps be employed (ibid.:65), locating the study area beginning with a large regional area which can be easily identified by the reader then progressing through successively smaller spatial contexts. This approach is particularly important when the study area is poorly known or described in the literature, or the audience is generally unfamiliar with the territory. The archaeological site of Begho is a case in point; without a locational reference map (Figure 2-1), the Begho survey map (Figure 2-2) and the Kramo site map (Figure 2-4) give the reader little clue as to the actual location of these sites. The "step down" series of maps progressively directs the reader from the general location of the site, in this case West Africa, to the specific location of surveyed areas and/or

excavation units.

The manner in which data are compiled in the field, along with the availability of base maps upon which to plot this information, will have a direct bearing on the accuracy of the finished product. Small scale atlas maps are available for general topographic and spatial representations throughout the world. Maps such as United States Geological Survey topographic quads, British Ordnance maps, or those of any good national survey, along with aerial photographs, provide excellent bases on which to plot information. Major universities and research organizations usually maintain map libraries in which these different sources of information are assembled and organized for easy reference on most regions.

The maps illustrating the St. Kitts

Archaeological project, for example, make use of a topographic sheet prepared by the British Government Overseas Development Administration (Directorate of Overseas Surveys), and field data were simply plotted on this topographic map, and then simplified so as to emphasize the archaeological features (Figures 2-5, 2-6, and 2-7, respectively). No detailed topographic maps exist for the region in Ghana where Begho is located, consequently it was necessary to generate the base data (Figures 2-2 and 2-3). Most site maps require similar procedures because they are generally at a scale larger than standard base maps such as topographic sheets.

Because it is usually impossible to return to a location and pick up overlooked details, in the compilation stage one should gather as much information as possible. Extremely useful in the final construction is a sketch map made in the field, which simply locates major features in their general relationship to each other without precise scale or direction. A record should be kept that indicates how information was collected, and all sources should be checked for accuracy. Notes made directly in the margins of the map are more accessible than those taken down elsewhere.

A preliminary draft may be used to work out the rough spots in a map through actual trial and error. There is no absolute model of how a map should be arranged, and overall style and composition may change with the purposes to which the map is to be put. All maps, however, should be bounded by a margin or frame, and within this space several basic organizational devices are commonly applied for quick recognition of information, including title, key panel, scale, and north arrow. In the preliminary draft, the different elements should be moved around until the most satisfactory relationship has been achieved, for there is a tendency toward conservative positioning once the ink hits the map.

The compiler should take into con-

sideration the audience for which the map is intended, as well as how the map is to be used. An abundance of detail is warranted on a map to be presented in a research journal, but would do little more than distract the eye if rapidly flashed on a screen during a slide presentation. The influence of the audience also becomes an ethical problem when handling archaeological information (cf. R. H. Smith 1974); specifically, precise locations for sites and features sometimes should not be reproduced for general distribution. Such information in the wrong hands can serve as an invitation to vandalism or destruction.

Once all the diverse cartographic elements have been compiled, those data important for the specific purposes of the map are selected for presentation. Construction should begin with the line work, and then proceed to the cultural and physical information. Thus, locational information and boundaries are plotted and site locations, topography, drainage, etc. are fit within such parameters.

Normally a map is drawn at least twice the size of its expected final reproduction and subsequently reduced to fit the size dictated by the dimensions of the eventual publication. Reduction improves the visual appearance of any drawing or rendering by making minor errors relatively smaller, and a larger original is easier to work on than one drawn and reproduced at 100% size. In any reduction process, all parts of the map will be reduced proportionally, and important details or names should be emphasized with large and/or heavy line work and lettering so that they stand out after reduction.

The elements of cartography may be grouped into three categories: simplification, classification, and symbolization (Robinson and Sale 1969). The mixture of these interrelated processes should combine to form a clear and informative map. A map cannot effectively show every detail; rather, each study is generalized in order to communicate key bits of information, and some features are emphasized while others are omitted.

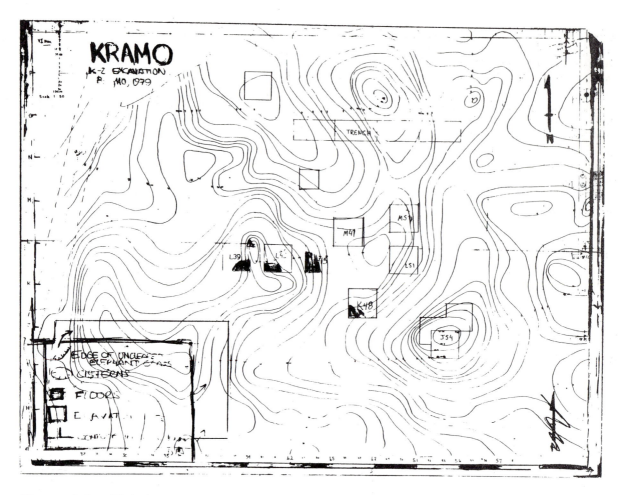

Figure 2-3: Third map in the "step-down" series is of a section of Begho that was carefully mapped and excavated. This is how most finished field maps (or draft maps) appear prior to final drafting in the laboratory. While rough, all proportions and measurements are nevertheless accurate.

SIMPLIFICATION

The basic guide for simplification is that all that is unnecessary for the purposes of the map should be omitted, while all helpful features should be shown without being crowded or unclear (Raisz 1962:34). By means of analogy, a photograph can capture all the details of an area from one perspective, yet tell one little or nothing of archaeological significance unless the extraneous information is eliminated. In other words, simplification is a process of subjective reasoning and selection.

If the purpose of a given map is to show the spatial arrangement of excavation units with respect to mounds, then the map will emphasize the architectural topography and precise placements of pits dug rather than, for example, vegetational patterns over the site (Figure 2-4). Surface elevations may be systematically recorded and these simplified into contour lines which reflect surface features but do not clutter up the map. At Begho, surface elevations were recorded at 1.5 meter intervals throughout the area of the Kramo 2 excavation, and these were then simplified in a field map which had a contour interval of 10 cm. In sketching out the site map and accounting for eventual

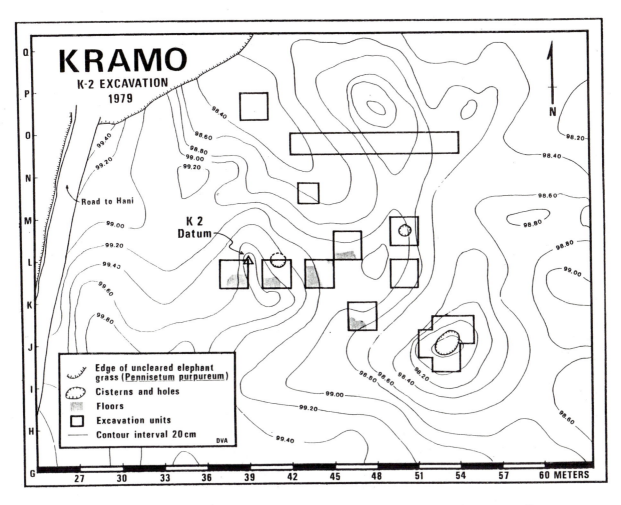

Figure 2-4: Final or publication version of the Kramo excavation map after secondary tracing and general cleanup in the laboratory. Note how contour intervals have been simplified and standard cartographic symbols substituted for written notes.

reduction, the 10 cm interval was found to be too cluttered, so for clarity the interval was increased to 20 cm. The difference between these two contour intervals is visible in Figures 2-3 and 2-4.

CLASSIFICATION

As described by Robinson and Sale (1969:57-59), classification is the process by which data are sorted into mutually exclusive categories. This sorting occurs in several ways, the most important being nominal and ordinal scaling. Simply distinguishing between such classes of observable features as roads, rivers, oceans and

so forth is nominal scaling (scale here means degree of generalization). Ordinal scaling on the other hand makes relative distinctions between such things as large sites and small sites by rank within a nominal class. The use of such classification systems enables much information to be condensed into a few symbolic marks on a map.

SYMBOLIZATION

All graphic notations on a map are symbols. From dots representing archaeological sites to lines representing roads, symbols allow the cartographer to generalize a

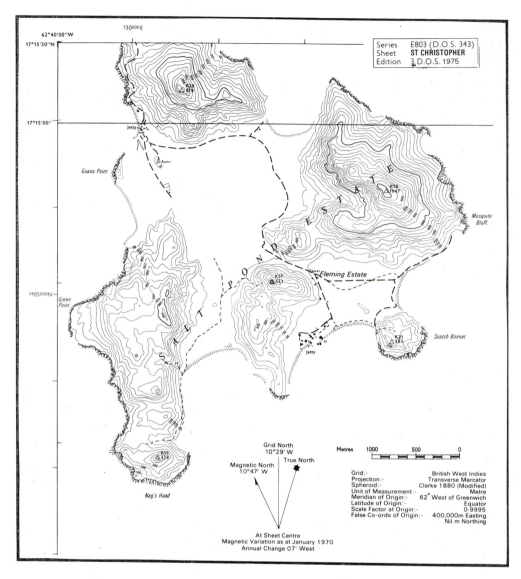

Figure 2-5: First step in converting existing cartographic renderings for specific archaeological purposes. This is a copy of the unaltered survey map used in field research. Normally a clean copy is kept in the lab while a field copy is annotated as exploration, surface collecting, or excavation progresses.

series of specific archaeological and distributional data. Symbolization is not restricted to marks representing discrete features of small size, but also involves depicting essential elements of large scale. An example is the generalization of the coastline on the peninsula of St. Kitts (Figures 2-5 and 2-6). The shoreline here is represented by a simplified line which gives the general shape of the coast. In reality, the shape is much more complex

and inconsistent, for it varies with changes in the tide. When further reduced, as in the inset in Figure 2-7, these features are generalized further to symbolically depict the shape of the island.

The general rule of symbolization is that "a symbol should be simple yet distinctive; small and easy to draw" (Raisz 1962:34). The USGS has devised a set of standard symbols for most topographical

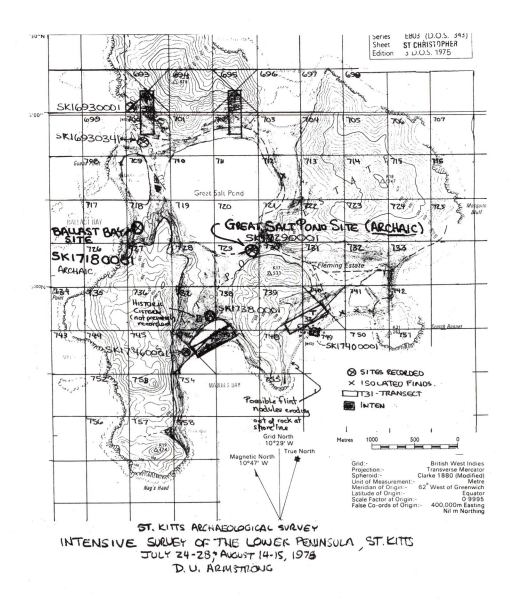

Figure 2-6: Second step in converting a standard cartographic rendering into an archaeological area map. This is a copy of the laboratory map upon which has been entered all data derived from successive field days. Note the grid overlay which simplifies cartographic localization of field discoveries and survey accounting of lands prospected.

and cultural features, and these can be found in Lahee (1961) or in a number of publications issued by the USGS itself. At present, there are no standardized symbols for archaeological sites, and people working in different areas tend to adhere to different local traditions of graphic expression. When devising a set of symbols to depict archaeological features, consistency should be the goal, and symbols should be unambiguous. The best are those which give the viewer a visual impression of the phenomena they represent, rather than appearing as simple abstract designs (Bryant and Holz 1965:281). Reduction factors must be taken into consideration particularly if line and dot patterns are to be included.

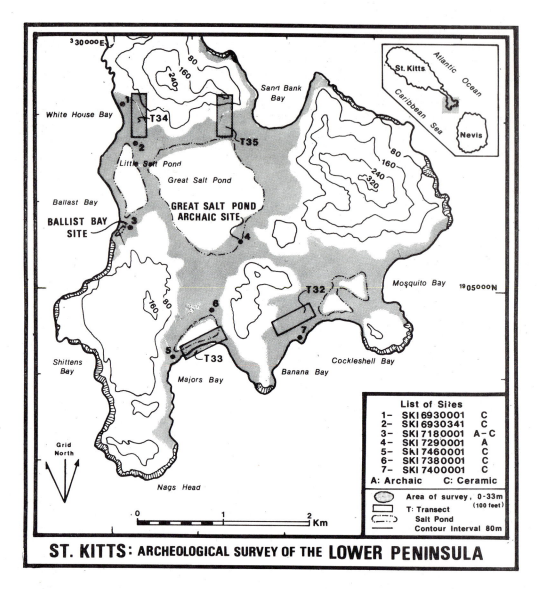

Figure 2-7: Final version of archaeological survey map. Note how all inessential detail has been deleted from both the original government map, shading indicates both elevations likely to have been inhabited and the actual land areas surveyed.

INTERNAL FEATURES

Maps attempt to interpret what is seen on or in the ground by several methods, usually the superpositioning of explanatory features over a representation of existing topography. These features can be discussed separately as there is great diversity in their appearance and intended function.

MARGINS. As stated above, all maps should be bordered with a margin or frame in order to define and delimit the study area. Borders should be simple, single or double lines, and heavier or darker than all other lines on the map. Ornate scrolls or designs should be eschewed for these tend to detract from the formal purpose of the map (Monkhouse and Wilkinson 1971:22-23).

The various maps accompanying this paper contain different margin forms.

NORTH ARROW. An orientation or compass heading should be indicated on all maps by means of a north arrow. The usual convention in large area maps is to orient the side margins so as to parallel the north arrow, but this does not always hold true with maps of smaller areas. In general, north is at the top of the page, no matter the precise orientation, and the north arrow should be long enough to allow additional alignment measurements. The north arrow should be identified as representing either true, magnetic, or quadrangular (grid) north, and the date of measurement should be included somewhere on the map if magnetic north is used in order to compensate for declination changes.

SCALES. A bar scale is the most useful and versatile means of presenting the relative size of all elements on the map as they relate to each other and to the standard of measurement being used. Unlike verbal scales or representative fractions, bar scales retain their true proportions relative to map details regardless of the amount of reduction or enlargement.

KEY PANELS. All symbols used on any map should be identified and/or explained in the key panel. Care should be taken to ensure succinct description and an overall balanced appearance. If shading is used it should be keyed out in rectangular blocks within a line border, and when this indicates topographic changes, place the darkest shading (conventionally the highest land) at the top of the series (Monkhouse and Wilkinson 1971:23).

LEGENDS. The legend or caption states the source of information, such as reference to a base map, and the participants in the ground survey. Credit should always be given where it is due and the work of others should be acknowledged. If copyright laws are unclear, request permission to reproduce another's map in writing, and do not go to press until permission is received.

LETTERING. In order to assist in the quick recognition of pertinent features on a map, lettering should be easily readable and well placed. The position of locational names affects the clarity of presentation, and conventionally these are placed above and to the right of the points in question and generally within the area being represented. Robinson and Sale (1969:290) outline seven specific rules of lettering, including such obvious suggestions as not lettering upside-down, as well as often-ignored points such as when a conflict between shading and lettering occurs, shading should be interrupted.

The significance of map features may be indicated either by increased use of capital lettering, or by the relative size of the lettering. In general, capital letters are used for map titles and place names that command attention, while lower case letters describe the more routine data. Differences in type size should not be so great that the largest overshadows the next smaller size; what is desired here is a gradual diminution. Obviously, the same type style should be used for all normal purposes, a change (such as italic, cursive, or different fonts) being reserved only for peculiar or irregular features. The fewer the number of type styles used on a single map the better, for needless distractions to the eye result from too great a diversity. Regarding the weighted significance of letters (i.e., size and intensity or capitalization), the following order of importance is suggested by Dittert and Wendorf (1963:65): 1) region or state; 2) research unit (site, excavation, etc.); 3) town or other modern feature; 4) drainage or other modern natural feature.

CONCLUSION

The suggestions presented in this paper are, of course, subject to modification and expansion, for the process of cartographic representation is as variable as are features on the ground. Local traditions in archaeological mapping necessitate that the archaeological cartographer be familiar with what has gone before. For ease of comparison, each new map for a previously studied region should be as similar in style as possible to earlier ones. While the final rendering of any map is necessarily governed by the quantity and accuracy of field data available, final production is crucial in its own right. Without a carefully thought out and legible graphic representation, the basic archaeological data can end up being suppressed or eliminated.

The archaeologist who excavates a site or explores a region is the best qualified person to understand what is important about it. Ultimately, it is his or her responsibility to make sure that the archaeological information characteristic of the study area is translated into cartographic form.

CHAPTER 3: ARCHITECTURAL FLOOR PLANS

Timothy P. Seymour

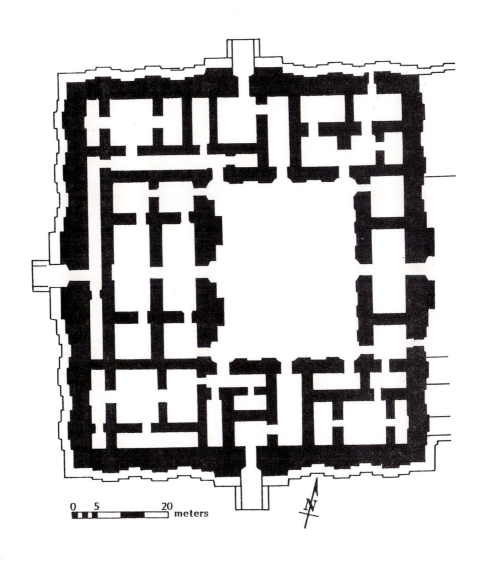

0 5 20 meters

ARCHITECTURAL FLOOR PLANS

Timothy P. Seymour

Architectural floorplans are basic, often much simplified, pictorial representations of the configurations of walls, floors, and other architectural features as depicted from above. In other words, they are schematic planviews of archaeological sites which concentrate on architectural remains. Recognizing such remains and properly interpretating them is one of the most demanding and problematic aspects of field archaeology. This is particularly true in the Mesopotamian area, from which my major experience and the following examples derive.

We may happily leave aside the thorny problem of recognizing architectural features as they emerge from the ground, for this is the responsibility of the excavator. Once the architectural remains have been carefully exposed, their proper stratigraphic relationships must be determined. This stratigraphic analysis places the remnants of ancient construction into a sequential framework and associates it with the surrounding archaeological features.

Such analysis often is quite involved, particularly in urban tells where habitation and deposition were continuous over thousands of years. Periodic rebuildings in the same general location create artificial mounds of great size. While these are best known from the ancient Near East, examples are plentiful in North, Middle and South America and can be found on almost every continent.

The constant human activity at such sites produced new deposits while at the same time disrupted earlier levels, thus greatly confusing matters for latter day investigators. The tells grew as old mud-brick houses collapsed or were knocked down. This rubble, often along with the stubs of walls or foundations of earlier buildings, became the foundations for later houses. It was also not uncommon for the foundations of new buildings to be excavated down into older deposits; these often cut into the buried walls of older buildings. When we add to this the frequent intrusions of ancient and modern pits and the independent variable of site erosion, we obtain an intellectual unraveling job of major proportions. Even though such problems may not involve the illustrator directly, he must be aware of them if he is to correctly interpret the field notes and successfully render the final conclusions into a coherent drawing or series of drawings.

Frankfort, Lloyd and Jacobsen (1940), Frankfort (1970), and Plommer (1961), to mention but a few references, offer very good examples of archaeological floorplans from a variety of Near Eastern sites and can give the reader a wider exposure to styles and formats of presentation now in use.

ARCHITECT'S PLANS

Most large excavation projects, especially those likely to run for many successive seasons, will have a staff architect whose primary job is to make accurate drawings of architectural features as these emerge at the dig. Most such experts are trained architects first and archaeologist second, and in effect are doing the job they were trained to do backwards.

The main source of architectural data for the finished or "publication" drawings is not to be found in the field, but in the architect's notes and drawings, once these have been finalized. The finished notes and drawings contain the precisely measured locations of all features and excavation units recorded at the site. Figure 3-1 is a portion of such a plan from a Mesopotamian site. All exposed architecture, as well as modern (in this case Islamic) pits and excavation boundaries, is shown. In this example several distinct overlapping phases, or rebuildings, of a structure (in this case a temple) are depicted. An architectural floorplan of this excavation would be a schematic simplification of complex data with reconstruction if necessary where architectural features are cut through or obscured by other building phases or features, or are poorly known through a lack of excavation.

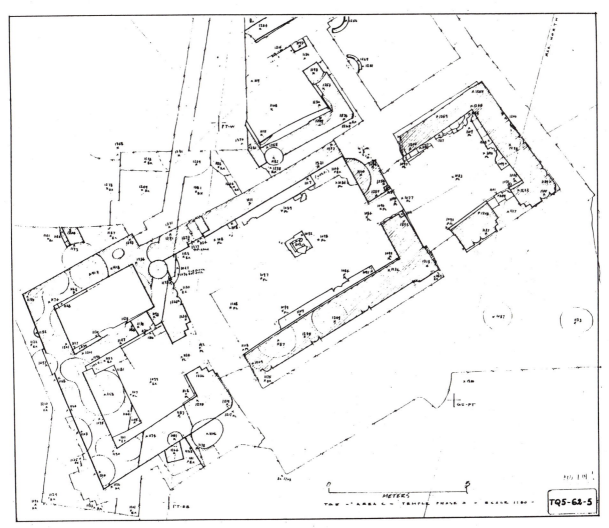

Figure 3-1: Portion of an architect's plan originally done in pencil at a scale of 1:50.

PRELIMINARY OR INTERMEDIATE FLOORPLANS

Depending on the intended use of the artwork, a variety of floorplans and related archaeological features may be represented graphically. Figure 3-2 illustrates a drawing intermediate between the field architect's site plans and the finished floor plan. Commonly used in preliminary pub-

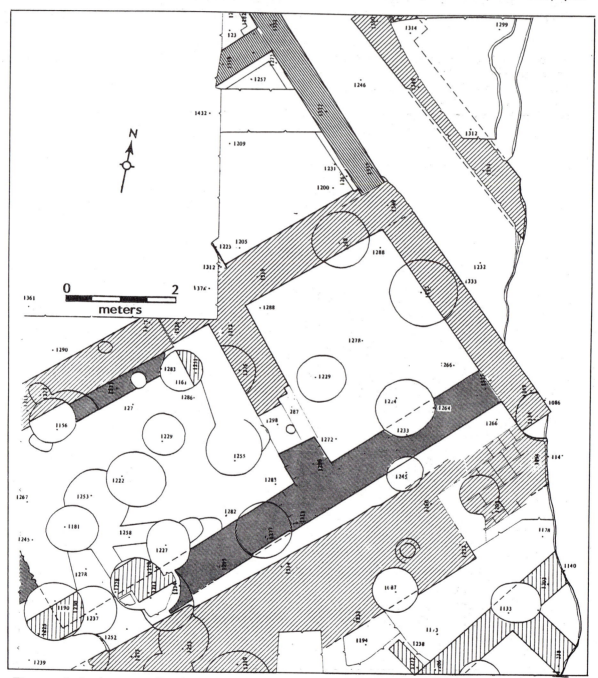

Figure 3-2: Intermediate floor plan showing basic archaeological features such as intrusive pits, erosion, and exposed architecture.

lications, such drawings give both the architectural features and some selected archaeological elements such as intrusive pits, indications of erosion, and elevations above datum. Also shown are the limits of the excavation symbolized by a line with "tick marks" pointing in the direction of the unexcavated area. The differential shading here is a preliminary indication of the stratigraphic relationships of the walls. Similarly shaded walls thus are contemporary with each other and pertain to the same building phase. It should be noted that solid lines separate all elements of apparently the same phase. Such lines indicate the nature of the wall juncture at the points where they occur. Where the walls conjoin and are bonded together into a single unit, no lines should appear. Where they are poorly bonded or merely abut each other, individual lines should show the separation.

SUPERIMPOSED PHASES

Once the successive construction phases have been clearly identified, another stan-

dard way of illustrating architecture is to draw floorplans of two or (rarely) more phases superimposed on a single drawing. An example of this is Figure 3-3. As in the previous example, construction phases are distinguished by differential shading. Such drawings concentrate on the superimposed buildings and usually omit all extraneous (or post-constructional) features such as pits and erosion. As with all the examples discussed herein, the intended use of the illustration and its purpose will dictate which pictorial data are included or deleted; in this case all numerical data, excavation boundaries, and pitting have been omitted. Only the fully reconstructed walls are shown accompanied by a shading key, north arrow, and meter scale. Note that the key need not be labeled "key" as its function is obvious. North arrows, scales, and keys usually are required and their form and placement can vary widely. For some suggestions concerning these important elements see the "Symbols" section below. The actual building phases as shown on the drawing nearly always require some reconstruction (see Figure 3-3). Reconstructions of partially destroyed wall sections may be inferred and usually are restored with a solid line. Whole portions of buildings which are surmised to have existed are often drawn in dotted or phantom lines.

INDIVIDUAL BUILDING PHASES

Final publication drawings of architectural features most often present the individual building phases separately. A sequence of drawings is extracted from the superimposed phases and each building floorplan is shown as it existed at a specific point in time. Shown sequentially, they illustrate the changing plan of the structure as it was rebuilt over the centuries (Figure 3-4a and 3-4b). For such drawings the walls may be shaded or unshaded depending upon the illustrator's preference or to achieve consistency with previous publications. Often it may be desirable to distinguish a particular building from surrounding architecture, such as a temple from surrounding private houses. In this case, light shading of the temple walls will produce the desired effect.

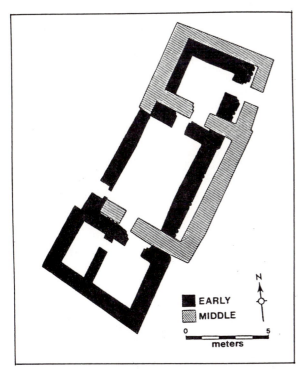

EARLY
MIDDLE

0   5
meters

Figure 3-3: Much simplified floor plan showing superimposed phases.

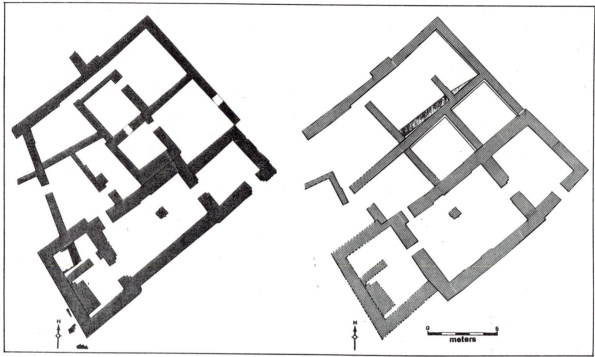

Figure 3-4: Individual floorplans representing successive rebuildings and enlargement of the original structure.

Also frequently appearing on such drawings are installations within walls such as bins, hearths, platforms, etc. Whether or not the walls are shaded, these features usually are drawn in outline without shading. It will often be necessary to identify particular rooms or structures on the face of the drawing. This may be done with numbers, letters, or the field designation for such features. Occasionally, keyed shading may be employed for this purpose. The main concern here should be in keeping all such coding consistent.

indicate where specific activities (cultic or domestic) are thought to have taken place within the complex. The possibilities for such codings are limited only by the illustrator's imagination and the complexity of the excavated material itself. Perhaps the only constraint on such artwork is that it must be done in proportion to the format of the projection system. If it is to be photographed onto a 35mm slide, for example, the ratio of the artwork height to width must be 2:3.

OTHER FORMATS: COLOR SLIDES

All of the observations presented above, although offered here for black-and-white renderings, may be applied to colored artwork for slides or other means of projection. Inked floorplan outlines on vellum or Mylar may be shaded with a variety of color screens so as to accent any features under discussion. Figure 3-5 (reproduced here in black and white) shows a floorplan distinguishing a variety of details. Blue and green shading on the floor areas here

SCALE

Since all the illustrations under discussion begin ultimately as tracings from the excavation project's architectural site plans, or an intermediate copy of that plan, the scale the architect chooses will frequently be the scale of the resulting artwork. This tends to produce rather large drawings at a common scale of, say 1:50. Reducing them down to a more usable size is no problem if the illustrator has access to photoreduction facilities.

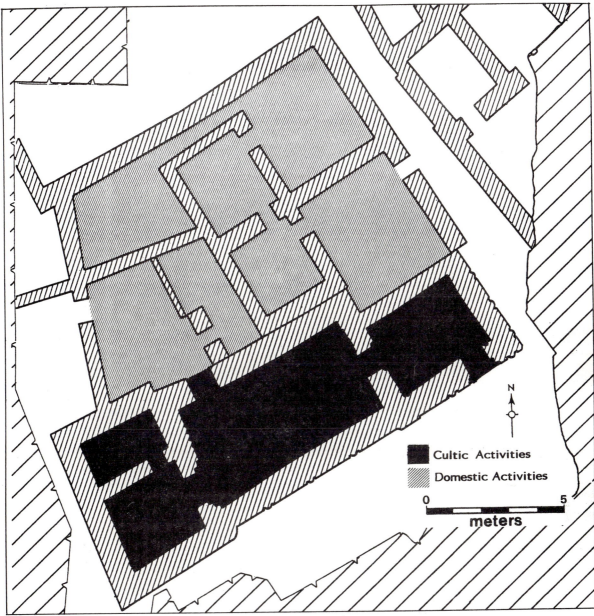

Figure 3-5: Black and white example of differential shading such as is often em-ployed for color slides. Here different colors would indicate distinct functional areas of the building complex.

Indeed, as noted elsewhere in this volume, it is always a good idea to do inked artwork oversize and then reduce it, for the line quality and overall appearance of the drawing is greatly enhanced. In the field, however, it is another story. Although publication quality drawings are unlikely to be done while still in the field, other types of floorplan drawings (often merely sketches) frequently are done during excavations. Lacking photostatic reproduction facilities, reductions must be made by redrawing to the desired scale. Here a good drafting machine and proportional dividers are essential. One way to avoid some of these production difficulties is to acquire a set of photostatic reductions of the architecture excavated during the previous season to take into the field; these may be traced from if the need arises.

MATERIALS AND TECHNIQUES

Most architectural floorplan illustrations employ conservative Sans Serif letter styles such as Caslon, Helvetica, or Mecanorma. The point size depends on the degree of reduction the artwork will undergo or on the image size of a projected slide. A common rule of thumb for determining point size in the latter is to choose a letter size which will be clearly readable on the unprojected slide.

SCREENS

Screens for shading or toning come in all manner of black and white patterns, shades of gray and colors and are quite easy to use; however, some precautions should be observed. Most importantly, while sketching and inking, one should avoid hand contact with the surface of the drawing. Minute amounts of oil or perspiration will prevent the screens from adhering properly and will result in their invariably peeling up overnight. Finally, screens will sometimes peel up when the artwork is stored rolled in a tube. The prudent illustrator of archaeological architecture will store such materials flat in a drawer or portfolio.

SYMBOLS

On most drawings a north arrow, meter scale, and occasionally a symbol key need to be placed. Although there is no set rule for their positioning (and little standardization in the various literatures), some constraints should be borne in mind. These elements should generally be grouped together so that the eye is not distracted by having to move from place to place on the drawing so as to obtain basic information. Frequently they are located near the title block (if there is one) and/or near the right or left bottom edge of the drawing. Sometimes, however, the layout of the illustration will dictate other positioning. The illustrator must then locate them on practical as well as aesthetic grounds. In any case, it is important to maintain as consistent a placement as possible on all drawings of a series.

CONCLUSION

Architectural floorplans can be created in a diversity of forms which vary depending on the type of information the drawing is meant to convey. The examples and techniques cited are typical of the illustrations appearing in the archaeological literature. However, the examples given here are not exclusive; the student illustrator undoubtedly will have to borrow or invent techniques here and there to solve the particular problems at hand.

CHAPTER 4: ARCHITECTURAL RECONSTRUCTION DRAWINGS

Mark C. Johnson

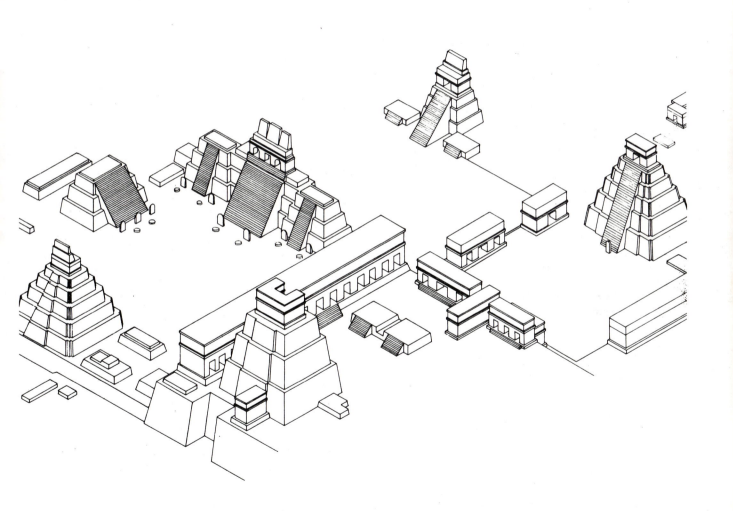

ARCHITECTURAL RECONSTRUCTION DRAWINGS

Mark C. Johnson

When describing architectural remains it is often quite instructive not only to visualize but to attempt a pictorial image of the architectural feature, structure, or site as it probably appeared at the time of its construction or during its active use. A line drawing is the most effective means by which this goal may be accomplished and can provide a more complete understanding of architectural remains than any other medium. Through illustration, the various bits and pieces of architectural data collected and recorded during archaeological investigations may be pulled together, and discernible architectural elements arranged to recreate the structures and sites of which they originally formed a part.

In this manner, visual images of the past can be conveyed that photographs or other recording methods can never hope to capture. Such illustrations usually are referred to as reconstruction drawings, and one might consider them to be pictorial syntheses of architectural data. They are, however, also projections or interpretations, for they attempt to rebuild decayed or eroded portions of structures; consequently they create an image of what the archaeologist feels the original architect had in mind.

While some so-called "reconstruction" drawings illustrate only those portions of a structure that are preserved, most true reconstructions restore the damaged or missing parts of architectural units as accurately as possible. This ac-curacy is dependent upon the quantity and quality of data available; the more specific and the greater the number of measurements employed in a drawing the more likely the depiction will resemble the original construction. Archaeological maps, plans, and profiles usually supply this data for preserved structural features; however, the dimensions of eroded or destroyed portions of a structure may often be reconstructed solely by close study of remaining parts. For instance, where bilateral symmetry of a feature is indicated, only half of it is necessary to recreate the whole.

Frequently, however, the greater portion of a structure is completely destroyed, and no trace is left of its original dimensions or appearance. This is particularly true when the construction materials were of a perishable nature (e.g., wood or thatch). In such cases, reconstruction requires the fabrication of the missing portions. Such a recreation of destroyed elements can be greatly aided by searching for clues in preserved structures or recorded information that can be associated directly or indirectly with the damaged construction. For example, a site or an entire area might place within a particular architectural style, in which case the general guidelines for reconstruction would be set by the stylistic canons seen to govern all other constructions of that style.

Reconstructions are sometimes possible for structures for which only functional information (and no preserved por-

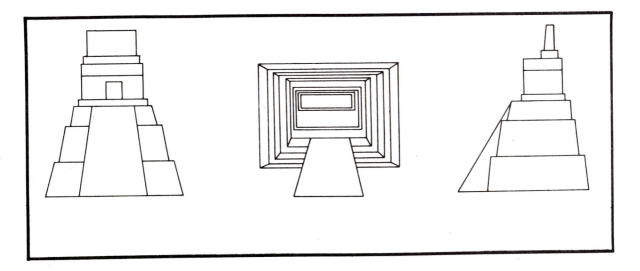

Figure 4-1: Multi-view projection of a simple architectural structure. Note the flattened, two-dimensional aspect of front, top, and side views.

tion) can be determined or presumed through association with standard architectural designs. Ethnographic and ethnohistoric data might be reviewed to obtain insights into the construction techniques that are and have been employed in the study area. Through the process of analogy ancient architecture may be reconstructed along the lines of more contempory structures with a comparatively accurate rendering. This aid to reconstruction is viable only when the contemporary structures are built of locally obtainable materials that would have been available in the past, and modern techniques of construction can be considered "traditional".

Occasionally, reconstruction drawings may be "replicative experiments" promoting completely hypothetical ideas about ancient architectural designs. This is particularly true in situations where surface features of a construction are so badly eroded that no concrete traces of their original configuration are evident. This is also necessary when little or no excavation has taken place so that no internal, subsurface clues to the construction design have been obtained. Reconstructions in these cases may nevertheless

be attempted by projecting the original configuration of a structure or feature based on the observable prominent topographical features of the architectural remnant. Here again, preserved structures can be compared to the topographical landmarks of the remnant, however roughly, and provide a basis for reconstruction of the structure. This point will be discussed in greater detail during the description of Figures 4-5 and 4-6. It should here be emphasized, however, that reconstruction drawings of this type should be offered only with disclaimers regarding their accuracy. The absence of concrete constructional data (e.g., foundation dimensions) leaves reconstruction open to subjective interpretation; the result may be a drawing of something which is far from the original design.

MULTI-VIEW PROJECTIONS

The simplest kind of reconstruction drawing is that called a multi-view projection (Figure 4-I), which is composed of at least three separate renderings of a single construction, each from a radically different viewing angle. Each view is two-dimensional and presents a flattened aspect of architectural features. Multi-view drawings are made directly from the plans and profiles produced through careful mapping and excavation, and great attention should be paid to detail and accuracy when undertaking these drawings for they often provide the basis for drawings of greater complexity.

The presentation of flattened, straight-on views in multi-view projections enables a maximum amount of information to be conveyed about architectural features. It also facilitates the rebuilding of "missing" features in permitting the treatment of each face of the construction individually. Each side of an architectural feature may be reconstructed as completely as possible in this manner; the reconstructed side views contribute significantly to the quality of more complex drawings which frequently draw directly from such views to create more elaborate structural renderings. The individual treatment of each view also helps to restructure badly damaged architecture, assisting in the parallel interpretation of the curvilinear topographic lines that are often the only kinds of topographic representation discernable from the original remnants of angular, geometric elements. Figure 4-5 illustrates this conversion of topograpic into architectural lines.

It is highly recommended that one begin with multi-view projections before attempting reconstruction drawings of greater complexity. To be effective, multi-view drawings must be identical in scale (particularly when juxtaposed on a single sheet of paper). After selecting a desired scale, one should begin the drawing by illustrating the prominent lines of all remaining structural features for which there are field measurements. It is best to start from the structural foundation and work upward. All features recorded through field measurements must be drawn even if they are only partially intact, for every bit of existing architectural information is valuable for the recreation of destroyed architectural elements.

Once all remnant features of a construction are drawn, the illustrator's job is to rebuild the missing parts. This may be done in a variety of ways. The most obvious step in the restructuring is carrying out incomplete lines. Lines drawn for partially intact features may be followed out to their union with lines of similarly intact features. Where the union of structural lines is not made apparent through the projection of existing lines, one must rely on the identification of symmetry or balance in the construction and draw in the missing structural lines necessary to maintain that symmetry. As pointed out above, when there are no such clues to a structure's original configuration, the basis for reconstruction must follow analogy using architectural data from contemporary and/or ancient structures as comparative material.

ISOMETRIC PROJECTIONS

The method most commonly used in reconstruction illustration is the isometric projection, as seen in Figure 4-2. An isometric drawing is one of the easiest ways to convert the flattened, single plane views derived from field measurements into composite three-sided, multiple plane views of a structure. A construction's three-dimensionality is conveyed in this way and a sense of depth is emphasized. Architectural features in these types of projections are always viewed from a common corner, that is, the corner which forms the line of union of the contiguous sides of the object that are to be illustrated.

In addition to the advantage of making a construction "come alive," isometric drawings are relatively simple to produce. All principal lines in the drawing are parallel to each other within the same plane, and thus the laborious process of calculating the angle of each line that attends perspective renderings is avoided. Additionally, these lines may be measured directly instead of being intentionally foreshortened; the dimensions of the structure, once converted to the scale of the drawing, can be applied directly without alteration to compensate for perspective.

Isometric drawings are begun by selecting the scale and determining the

Figure 4-3: Dimetric projection. Note similarities with isometric projection of the same building (Figure 4-2) but subtle changes introduced by alteration of the basic guiding angle.

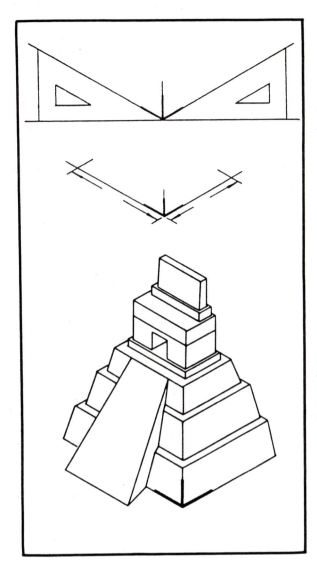

Figure 4-2: Isometric projection of the same architectural construction. Note how guiding lines are established simply through use of triangles and used for establishing the "false perspective" of parallel lines. Note also the three-dimensional volume absent in multi-view drawings.

faces of the architectural structures or features that are to be presented. As the overall projection always will be a view from a corner, three contiguous sides always will be portrayed in the rendering. The illustrator must take into consideration the sides of the object that he or she

wants to emphasize. For instance, the illustrator may decide that a reconstruction view should contain a frontal view of the object. The front of the object, therefore, would be set as one of the illustration planes and the illustrator would then choose two others from those which are contiguous to that plane. As in Figure 4-2 the choice was the structure's right side and its top.

Isometric projections are built up on a skeleton of three lines representing the basal and corner edges of the object illustrated. These three lines form what are called the isometric axis; angles created by these lines must be equal and total 120 degrees. The basal axes, therefore, will always be drawn with the 30 degree triangle while the corner axis will be a vertical line (see Fig. 4-2). The principal lines of each side of the illustrated object will be drawn parallel to the axis representing that side. Structural measurements are made directly on the axis lines after converting them to the scale of the drawing.

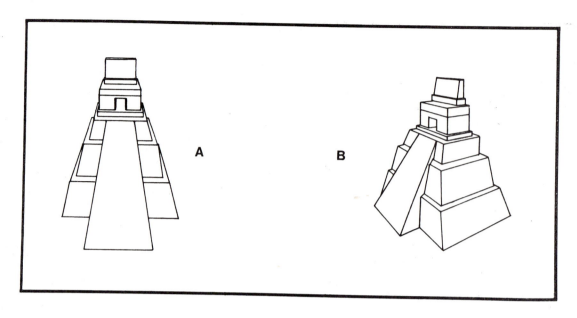

Figure 4-4: *Perspective drawings incorporating lines drawn to a vanishing point. In all such views, portions of the subject which are closer to the observer are drawn larger than those farther away. A: One-point perspective, with vanishing point at top; B: Two-point perspective, with vanishing points to either side.*

DIMETRIC PROJECTIONS

A dimetric projection (Figure 4-3) is created through a process similar to, and is close in appearance to, an isometric projection. While the principal lines are again measured directly and are drawn parallel to three established axes, the axes are oriented differently and the perspective is changed slightly. More specifically, in an isometric drawing three axes make equal angles with the picture plane whereas in a dimetric drawing only two do so. In dimetric projections, the basal axes are not oriented at the same angle of 30 degrees above the horizontal as they are in an isometric projection, rather each will have an independent orientation. The illustrator selects the axes' orientations based on the change in the viewing angle that he or she desires to effect. For example, one axis may be oriented at 25 degrees above the horizontal while the other is oriented at 15 degrees. The result is a much lower perspective of the object, giving the illusion, in the case of architectural drawings, that one is viewing the object from much closer to the ground.

Neither form of drawing is a true perspective drawing method; neither method pictures a construction as it would actually appear to the eye. Both isometric and dimetric drawings fail to accurately represent depth and distance and the distortions in line that these factors create. Nevertheless, they do provide a very simple and effective means of illustrating an object so that it may be visualized in its entirety.

PERSPECTIVE DRAWINGS

Perspective drawings are the most effective way to depict an architectural construction for they recreate an image exactly as it is seen through a viewer's eye. While great accuracy can be achieved, perspective drawings are usually fairly complicated undertakings. Accurate perspective drawings derived from structural plans and profiles can require a great deal of calculation. It is easier to draw perspectives in the presence of the object being recorded, as the angles and lengths of the object's lines (each of which is different due to the distortion created by the perspective) may be transferred to paper by observation rather than calculation.

It is possible, however, to project lines directly from equally scaled, multiview plan and profile drawings to create a perspective view. One and two point perspective drawings (Figure 4-4) differ from each other in that the former makes use of a single vanishing point, usually at the top of the page or directly behind the object drawn, and the latter makes use of two vanishing points, usually at opposite sides of the page. These two methods reflect different relationships between the viewer and the object being viewed, for each minor variation in the angle of observation will result in proportional shifts in the drawing.

PRODUCTION TECHNIQUE

Once a structure or site has been drawn, the reconstruction can be enhanced by shading to establish a greater visual contrast and to increase the illusion of three-dimensionality. The structural environs can be filled in with vegetation and human figures or other elements of the natural and cultural environments that can serve to establish a scale for the drawing and give a fullness to the overall composition. At the same time, this eliminates distracting empty space and creates a sense of depth.

Both freehand sketching and the use of mechanical guides may be employed in reconstruction drawing. While the drafting paper should be sturdy enough to absorb ink without seepage and resist constant erasure, it is preferable if it is slightly transparent. The production of freehand sketches may benefit from the use of lightly lined graph paper, and there is a paper available that is ruled in isometric lines that can greatly facilitate the freehand drawing of isometrics. In drawing reconstructions for publication, it should be remembered that a reduction in the size of the original usually is required

to conform to space restrictions, and that standardizing the scale of reduction with line width should be a primary consideration.

DIFFERENTIAL INTERPRETATIONS

While reference has been made to the importance of the use of analogy in architectural reconstruction, especially in reference to those situations in which accurate measurements for one reason or another are not available, great caution must be taken to avoid overly manipulating the result in the direction of more familiar appearance. In order to illustrate this point, a single famous example should suffice; that of Complex C at the Olmec site of La Venta in Tabasco, Mexico (Graham and Johnson 1980).

At the time of the original publication of the site report (Drucker, Heizer, and Squier 1959), Complex C, the largest structure at La Venta, was presumed to exist in the form of a truncated, four-sided pyramid. This reconstruction resulted from a lack of both adequate clearing and measuring of the mound. A later field season at the site witnessed the clearing of the mound and the production of an accurate topographical contour map (Figure 4-5a) which showed the structure to have fairly regular depressions or flutes up its sides, making obsolete the previous reconstruction (Heizer, Graham, and Napton 1968). Based on the contour lines of the topographical map a new interpretive drawing of Complex C (Figure 4-5b) was offered which changed the general shape of the mound to a fluted cone with a truncated top. This gave rise to speculation in some directions about the direct architectural imitation of volcanoes and mountain worship as the original stimulus for the construction of the form.

Recently, an entirely new interpretation has been put forward, expressed graphically in Figure 4-6, with only minor variation between constructions A and B. In these drawings the hypothetical fluted cone has been represented as a rectangular, step-sided pyramid in which the ridges and depressions of the cone's flutes

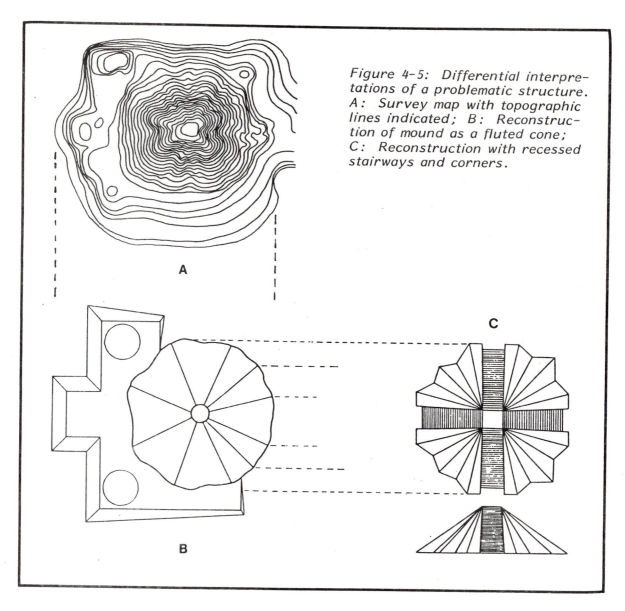

Figure 4-5: Differential interpretations of a problematic structure. A: Survey map with topographic lines indicated; B: Reconstruction of mound as a fluted cone; C: Reconstruction with recessed stairways and corners.

have been reconstructed as angular architectural features. While the accuracy of these renderings may be somewhat speculative, the attempt to project the angular architectural style of the period on the structural remnants of Complex C may be the best approximation of the structure's original configuration that can be made. The point being made in this discussion is that each of the above reconstructions of Complex C seemed plausible at the time of illustration, and each is directly reflective of the amount of evidence about the pre-erosional external appearance of the mound available at the time.

CONCLUSION

Reconstruction drawings can be a valuable means of presenting visions into the past. This short review of techniques and applications by no means exhausts the available information on this subject, and for more detailed information, any of the better manuals on architectural and mechanical drafting should be consulted (see French and Svenson 1957; Patten and Rogness

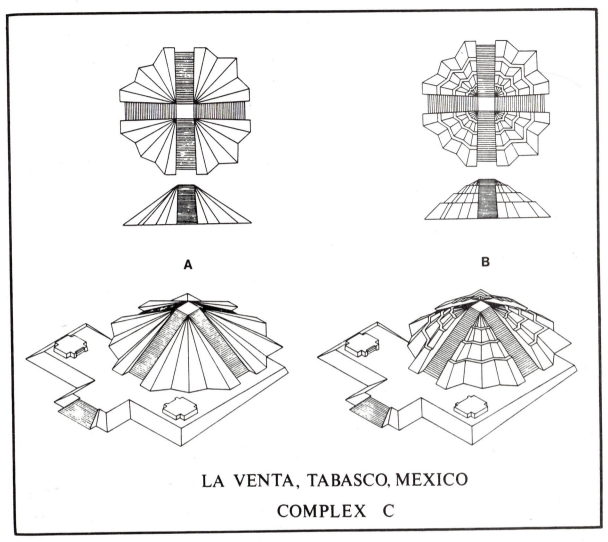

A

B

LA VENTA, TABASCO, MEXICO

COMPLEX C

Figure 4-6: Final interpretive reconstructions of the problematic mound using multi-view projections (at top) and dimetric projections (at bottom). Note how interpretation A differs from B only in the addition of steps between stairways.

1962). A familiarity with the archaeological literature will provide the student with a grounding in the existing architectural data available for his or her area and cannot help but result in greater accuracy and ease of execution. After an understanding of the basic processes involved has been obtained, reconstruction drawings of any architectural remains may be undertaken with confidence.

CHAPTER 5: STRATIGRAPHIC SECTIONS

Giorgio Buccellati

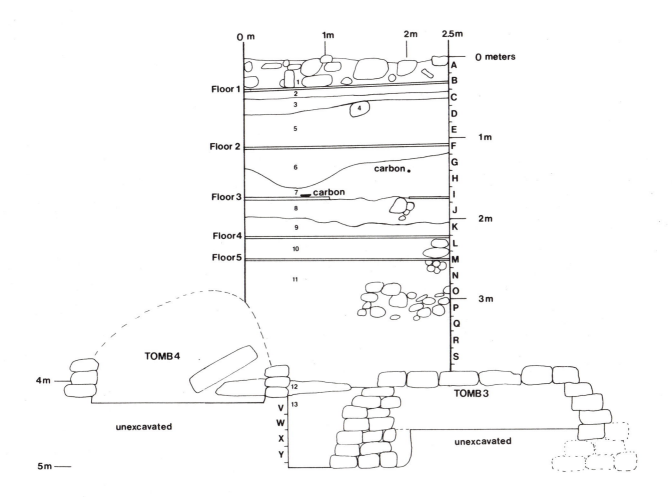

STRATIGRAPHIC SECTIONS

Giorgio Buccellati

The primary goal of archaeological excavations is to establish and record the stratigraphic sequence of the remains of cultural deposition. One of the main components of the stratigraphic record is the section (or profile), i.e., a graphic rendering of a plane which cuts through deposition at chosen junctures. A few words must first be said about the concept of section and its underlying presuppositions before we describe the technical procedures for its recording.

A section is by definition the rendering of a plane. Specifically, it must be stressed, a plane that cuts through a volume. It is easy to misconceive of a section as only a flat and linear surface; however, it must be understood in relation to volume and mass. A section cannot be viewed as an end in itself, graphically or conceptually; rather, it must be viewed as one of two or more axes that cut through a solid volume for the purpose of correlating the spatial components found within the block itself. In archaeology, such volumes are the stratified result of cultural deposition over time. Thus "stratification" refers to the concrete build-up affected by the two concurrent processes of accumulation and emplacement, while "stratigraphy" refers to the conceptualization of stratification. The recording of this conceptualization can be expressed either in analytical or analogical form: the former includes verbalization, digitation and diagramming, while the latter includes photography. Stratigraphic sections are a part of the analytical record.

THE SECTION

In order to better understand the concept of section, and to respond to some objections raised against its use, we may visualize a simple conceptual model to represent the underlying concept of stratification. Commonly, the analogy is made between an archaeological site and a layer cake. More aptly, however, a site should be compared to a machine in which the parts all fit together. As indicated in the exploded view (Figure 5-1), to remove any one part one must follow an order inverse to the assembly sequence. Of course, the assembly of a machine responds to a single purpose and is essentially a one-time event, whereas cultural deposition has an almost unbounded time depth and responds to many purposes when it is not wholly accidental. But, by referring to an assembly chart, the point may be more easily grasped that the most suitable graphic recording is the one which best represents the spatio-temporal relationships of volumes.

Note the qualification "spatio-temporal": what matters is not only the reciprocal location (in space) of the parts, but also the combinatory process (in time or relative sequential order) whereby they came to be where they are at the time of discovery. From this point of view, a section is a convenient graphic device for a concentric and layered type of deposition; it is suitable, precisely for a layer cake, but less so for a machine or—an archaeological site. Obviously, a section

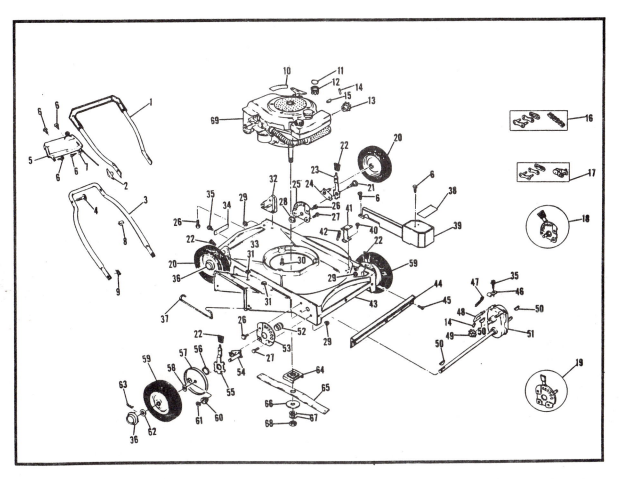

Figure 5-1: A popular analogy for stratigraphic layering in archaeological sites is that of the layer cake. Most archaeological deposits, however, are much more complicated, and a better analogy would be that of a machine which must be assembled or disassembled according to a specific sequence. Identifying each meaningful stratigraphic unit in an archaeological deposit can therefore be compared to an exploded assembly view such as that above.

cut through the lawnmower represented in Figure 5-1 would be much less transparent and much less revealing of the component parts and their relationship than the corresponding exploded view. What, then, are we to do for archaeological sites, which are all, in fact, stratigraphically more complex than a layer cake? Is there a better graphic device than the section, some kind of archaeological equivalent of the machine assembly chart?

The answer is mixed. Short of utilizing complex and costly computer graphics procedures, the section will remain a useful and necessary tool for stratigraphic

recording. Yet, it should be conceived of as serving at the same time both a documentary and an indexing function. It is documentary in that it gives a true depiction of stratigraphic relationships as seen at selected junctures; but, it is also an index in that it refers to volumes which are beyond the juncture plane and thus are not registered in it. The section is a window into the larger spaces through which it is cut, not a full account of the third dimension. An exhaustive recording of the data in their three-dimensional form will have to focus on the individual items in their stratigraphic context. One procedure to this effect has been suggested in a jointly

Figure 5-2: Different cross-sections of the same sidewall showing different interpretations and methods of depiction.

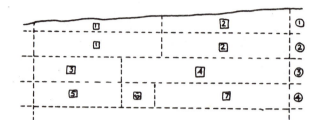

A: Section through a stratigraphic unit showing volumetric elements.

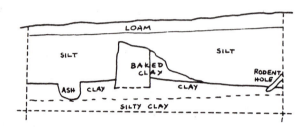

B: Section through a stratigraphic unit showing natural elements.

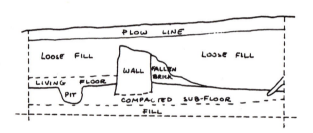

C: Section through a stratigraphic unit showing cultural elements.

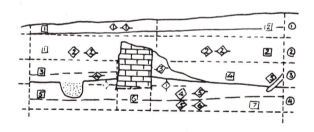

D: Section through a stratigraphic unit showing a combination of volumetric, natural, and cultural elements.

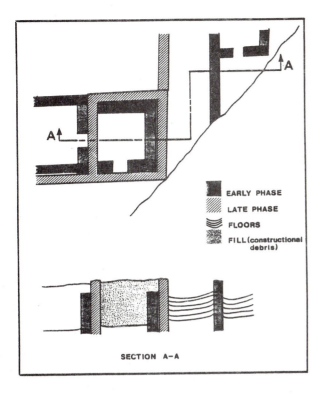

EARLY PHASE
LATE PHASE
FLOORS
FILL(constructional debris)

SECTION A-A

Figure 5-3: Cross-sections do not always cut along a single alignment. A typical stratigraphic profile (below) may in fact reveal deposition encountered along two parallel planes (above), more than two planes, or non-parallel planes.

authored manual (Buccellati and Kelly-Buccellati 1978): here stationary units and movable items are all recorded individually and are indexed according to strata which identify a slot in the stratigraphic sequence. Similarly, Harris (1979:73-80) has proposed a recording procedure based on a single-layer plan, indexed according to a "matrix" which embodies the stratigraphic sequence (ibid.:86-89). In this chapter, however, we are concerned exclusively with the section proper. Having now outlined its theoretical import and characteristics, we may proceed with the descriptive portions of our paper.

TYPES OF SECTION

A section may be physical or graphic: the

former is one which is left standing in the ground after the excavation has cut through the deposit (a baulk), while the latter is the graphic rendering of the former (except in the case of a projective section, for which see below).

A section may further be diagnostic or documentary. The former is used as a heuristic procedure during excavation, to provide clues that may help in "reading" the deposit; the latter serves as a visual record of a given sequence after exposure has been attained. Note that a documentary section need not be drawn graphically simply because it has been left standing and has been used for diagnostic purposes: that decision will depend on explicit recording policies.

The orientation and geometrical configuration of the section are in principle indifferent; in practice, however, sections are only vertical or horizontal, and they are always straight. Oblique or curved sections would require excessive computation for easy correlation among sections and floor plans, whereas right angle and straight sections can be readily correlated through a normal triangulation system. Note that a horizontal section is different from a floor plan. A floor plan (Seymour, this volume) is not a geometrical plane but a rendering of cultural features disposed along a surface that is generally flat, but not necessarily straight or perfectly horizontal.

A horizontal section, on the other hand, is a geometrical cut through the deposition, which ignores the solid contours of cultural features. It is used primarily for diagnostic purposes, when excavating in an area where the solid configuration of the cultural deposit is still unknown; graphic documentation of horizontal sections is not as useful because it reveals more in terms of planimetric than stratigraphic relationships, and the former are better accounted for by means of floor plans than horizontal sections.

The following three-way classification may be used to clarify the difference between objective and subjective aspects of a section:

culture-free {volumetric elements=arbitrary
             {physical elements   }
culture-bound=cultural elements {natural

A volumetric section has the limited function of marking the "arbitrary" parameters of the triangulation system, by reference to such volumetric entities as levels (often symbolized by numbers within squares). A physical section shows natural boundaries and describes the component parts in terms of their physical properties, especially the nature of the soil or of modified deposits such as ash or baked clay. A cultural section also shows natural boundaries, thus it generally overlaps with a physical section; the component parts, however, are described by their cultural properties, so that a given layer of soil, for example, will be designated a floor because of compaction and association with other items such as walls. In practice, sections are normally drawn only once, combining into a composite the major items from each category. Figure 5-2 (Buccellati and Kelly-Buccellati 1978:12f) gives a schematic rendering of the various types of sections just described.

Finally, a section may be viewed in terms of the procedure followed in recording it. Thus we have an integral, an incremental, or a projective section (see Harris 1979:53-55), where these three types are defined as "standing," "cumulative," and "incidental"). An integral section is one which is recorded when all the component parts are still standing. This is the standard approach, and presupposes that baulks are physically maintained throughout the excavation. An incremental section is one recorded in increments, with the corresponding physical components being removed in the measure in which each increment is recorded. A projective section, recorded without the benefit of full visual inspection of a physical cut is extrapolated from an existent volume or mass that is left physically standing in the excavation but is not cut through. This applies, for instance, to masses of masonry when they are not physically cut through along the line of

the pertinent section. A "birds-eye-view" of the course of such sections shows not a completely straight line but one with projections from it: hence the name.

Sections are especially common in two circumstances: either along the sides of an excavation unit that corresponds to a site grid, or along the axes of structures or features. The first, or grid section, is independent of the contours of cultural deposition and responds only to a volumetric design imposed a priori over the site. The second, or structural section, presupposes recognition of patterns of cultural deposition and aims at documenting the deposition itself from the best available vantage points. In this type, especially, it is often counterproductive to leave the baulks standing as in an integral section, since within a structure or feature it is more desirable to expose floors and other features to their full extent. Thus it is that structural sections are best recorded following an incremental procedure.

THE PHYSICAL RECORD

Just as artifacts are cleaned before being drawn and photographed, so a section too must be prepared before a graphic recording is possible. While a section refers to a volume and mass, as emphasized above, it is in fact, in and of itself, a plane: hence the record shows only lines and surfaces. It may be said that the first task in an excavation is to identify cleavage lines. These lines may be the result of compaction, cutting, juxtaposition, and so on, but they are in any case visible to the eye as the alignment of homogeneous elements; as such, they stand out because of such factors as discolorations or texture variations on either side of the line. The lines, in other words, are not so much separate items as they are boundaries between heterogeneous bands, i.e., they represent the interface between discrete features (on this see the excellent remarks by Harris 1979: 43-48).

From such observations derives the principle that section lines ought to be scored with a sharp point draw through the face of the section. This procedure has given rise to objections, primarily on two grounds: first, that scoring may obliterate the record itself, and second, that it introduces an undesirable degree of subjective interpretation. One may, however, respond to the first objection that since the line is a boundary between features rather than a feature itself, nothing is in fact obliterated; and to the second that if sufficient attention is paid to measurable criteria such as color and texture, there is an adequate control on objectivity. It need hardly be pointed out, finally, that the very identification of such lines is often subjective, and scribing them is no more or less so.

Cleavage lines are boundaries between volumes, and volumes are concrete masses which do not disappear into thin air at one end. It follows that, just as topographic contour lines must always close upon themselves, section lines cannot stop suddenly without some degree of resolution. This means that either they meet another line, or else they exhibit a progressive loss of markedness. In the first instance, the juncture of two lines corresponds to the juxtaposition of two discrete volumes, while in the second the disappearance of a line corresponds to the gradual merging of two volumes which are discrete at one end and fused into a homogeneous whole at the other. Such a merging boundary must be carefully assessed in terms not so much of the line itself but of the bands (i.e., volumes) that surround it.

Reading a physical section is difficult if one pays attention to minute details and not only to the broad outline. It is important, therefore, to correlate it as closely and as often as possible to the corresponding known volumes exposed by the excavation, and it is also important to read the section while it is still fresh. Protracted exposure to air, sun, and dust obscures the face of a section. As partial remedies, one can shave back the face and spray it with water, but the best solution remains that of reading the section, scoring it, and ideally, drawing it while it is still fresh.

THE GRAPHIC RECORD

As stressed above, a section can only be understood in relation to a floor plan. In the case of a grid section, i.e., a baulk which corresponds to the side of a volumetric excavation unit (a "square"), it is sufficient to qualify the section as being, for instance, the western baulk of the unit, facing west. But whenever a section is cut at a different juncture, i.e., in what we have called structural sections, the trajectory will have to be indicated on the floor plan, where it is marked by a solid line with arrows pointing in the direction toward which one looks in drawing the section. The line may be segmented, in order to accommodate given peculiarities of a given floor plan; for example, in Figure 5-3, the section as drawn shows the stratigraphic relationship of three rooms, part of which have been eroded away.

The details of the physical and cultural components of a section must be indicated as fully and objectively as possible. This implies the use of standards that either are in common use (such as the Munsell color chart) or are made explicit for a given excavation (e.g., the soil record chart form given here as Figure 5-4, adapted from Buccellati and Kelly-Buccellati 1978: 44). There are no uniform conventions used in the coding of such details in sections. A somewhat complex, but flexible and transparent, system has been proposed by the writer in the context of a site report, and is reproduced here in Figure 5-5 (adapted from Buccellati 1979: Fig. 10). Here there is an alternation between two coding registers, one graphic and the other one alpha-numeric. The alpha-numeric register is characterized by notes, signaled by a rhomboid. The notes indicated here in Figure 5-5 are of the recurrent type, and are marked by letters; additional non-recurrent remarks may be similarly signaled by a rhomboid followed by a number. The various categories are kept rigorously discrete according to the standards noted above.

The interplay between physical and

IIMAS
1978-FF36

Chapter 36, p. _____
Master p. _____

SOIL RECORD

Initials _____   Date _____   Square _____   Stratigraphy _____

Color (Munsell): dry _____   wet _____

Texture Matrix

- ▰ present
- ▨ partly present
- ▱ absent

Column headers (vertical):
grains detectable by hand & eye / leaves color on fingers / surface can be made to shine / when moist coheres into pellets / if dry, pellets break up & fall apart / pellets dry out hard / pellets can be molded into shapes / silty feel apparent / silty feel dominant / when dry, rubs off as loose fine powder / when dry, blows away easily

Rows:
clay
sandy clay
sandy clay loam
sandy loam
loamy sand
sand
sandy silt loam
clay loam
silty clay
silty clay loam
silt loam

Structure

For individual peds:

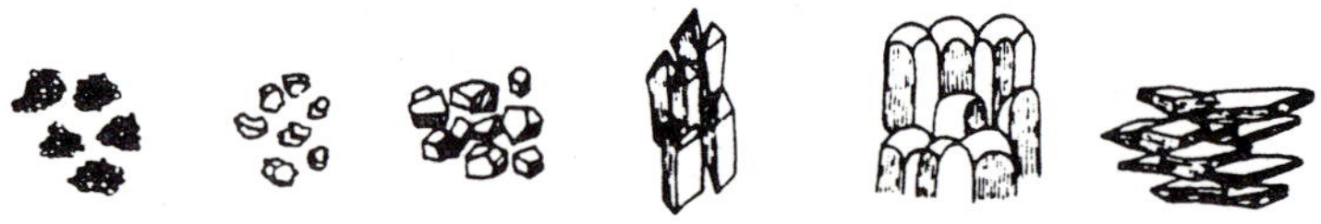

	crumb	granular	blocky	prismatic	columnar	platy
fine	☐ < 2mm	☐ < 2mm	☐ < 1cm	☐ < 2cm	☐ < 2cm	☐ < 2mm (thin)
medium	☐ 2-5mm	☐ 2-5mm	☐ 1-2cm	☐ 2-5cm	☐ 2-5cm	☐ 2-5mm
coarse	☐ > 5mm	☐ > 5mm	☐ > 2cm	☐ > 5cm	☐ > 5cm	☐ > 5mm (thick)

For cluster of peds, when peds cannot be identified:
☐ massive: holds together as a coherent mass
☐ single grain: is incoherent and disintegrates into separate particles when disturbed

Consistence

dry: ☐ hard (difficult to crush)   ☐ soft (easy to crush)
wet: ☐ sticky (sticks to fingers if pressed)   ☐ plastic (can be rolled into "worms")

Boundaries

	merging/sharp		smooth/wavy/irregular		
upper	☐	☐	☐	☐	☐
lower	☐	☐	☐	☐	☐

Figure 5-4: Before a stratigraphic profile can be drawn, or a series of profiles at a given site made to conform to each other in systematic depiction of similar deposits, a standard of reference must be created for interpreting, identifying, and classifying different kinds of strata. An objective "checklist" form such as the above can help to eliminate confusion and increase standardization.

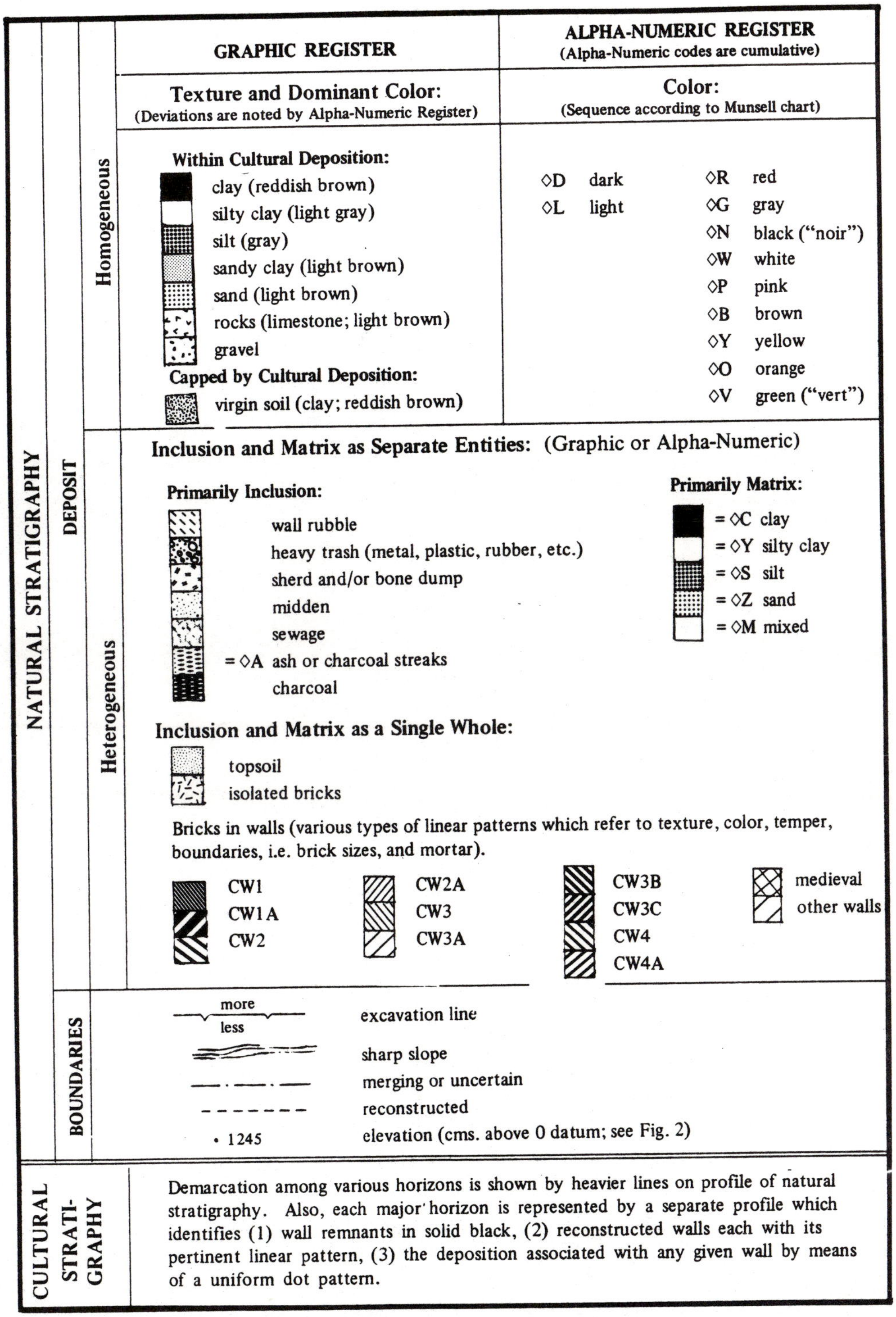

	GRAPHIC REGISTER	**ALPHA-NUMERIC REGISTER** (Alpha-Numeric codes are cumulative)

NATURAL STRATIGRAPHY

DEPOSIT

Homogeneous

Texture and Dominant Color: (Deviations are noted by Alpha-Numeric Register)	**Color:** (Sequence according to Munsell chart)

Within Cultural Deposition:

- clay (reddish brown)
- silty clay (light gray)
- silt (gray)
- sandy clay (light brown)
- sand (light brown)
- rocks (limestone; light brown)
- gravel

Capped by Cultural Deposition:

- virgin soil (clay; reddish brown)

◊D dark
◊L light

◊R red
◊G gray
◊N black ("noir")
◊W white
◊P pink
◊B brown
◊Y yellow
◊O orange
◊V green ("vert")

Heterogeneous

Inclusion and Matrix as Separate Entities: (Graphic or Alpha-Numeric)

Primarily Inclusion:

- wall rubble
- heavy trash (metal, plastic, rubber, etc.)
- sherd and/or bone dump
- midden
- sewage
- = ◊A ash or charcoal streaks
- charcoal

Primarily Matrix:

- = ◊C clay
- = ◊Y silty clay
- = ◊S silt
- = ◊Z sand
- = ◊M mixed

Inclusion and Matrix as a Single Whole:

- topsoil
- isolated bricks

Bricks in walls (various types of linear patterns which refer to texture, color, temper, boundaries, i.e. brick sizes, and mortar).

CW1	CW2A	CW3B	medieval
CW1A	CW3	CW3C	other walls
CW2	CW3A	CW4	
		CW4A	

BOUNDARIES

- more / less — excavation line
- sharp slope
- merging or uncertain
- reconstructed
- • 1245 elevation (cms. above 0 datum; see Fig. 2)

CULTURAL STRATIGRAPHY

Demarcation among various horizons is shown by heavier lines on profile of natural stratigraphy. Also, each major horizon is represented by a separate profile which identifies (1) wall remnants in solid black, (2) reconstructed walls each with its pertinent linear pattern, (3) the deposition associated with any given wall by means of a uniform dot pattern.

Figure 5-5: Once strata have been differentiated from one another through use of an objective standard of reference (Figure 5-4) a shading key that incorporates all possible stratigraphic variables must be developed. Use of such as key (above) obviates duplication and mislabelling.

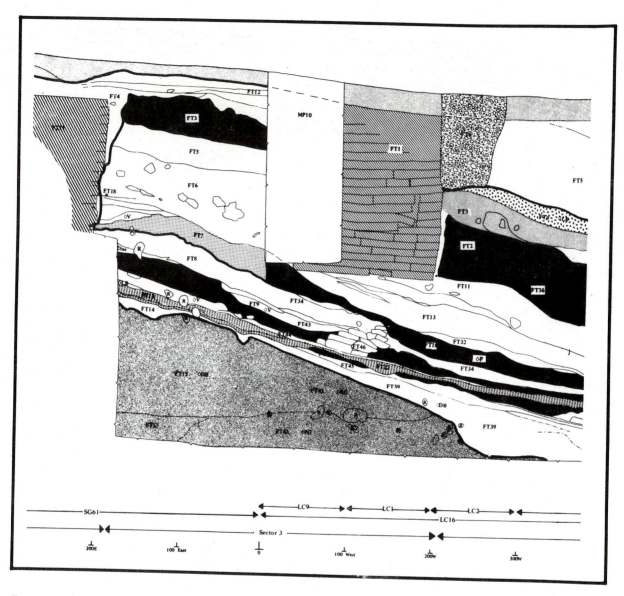

Figure 5-6: An overall stratigraphic profile of a vertical section which depicts as many significant depositional units as possible. The sequence of deposition must be inferred from the stratigraphic relationships and subjective labelling.

cultural elements may become too complex to be shown effectively in the same drawing. In this case, two different and complementary renderings may be given, as illustrated here in Figures 5-6 and 5-7 (adapted from Buccellati 1979: Fig. 12). These are sections cut through a city wall and its moat, with four major phases represented for the construction of the city wall. Figure 5-7 gives a schematized rendering of the various phases, with each phase corresponding to the one shown in bold in the detailed physical section.

CONCLUSION

The preceding discussion underlines the notion of complexity in interpreting and graphically representing stratigraphy in archaeological sites. Certainly the exam-

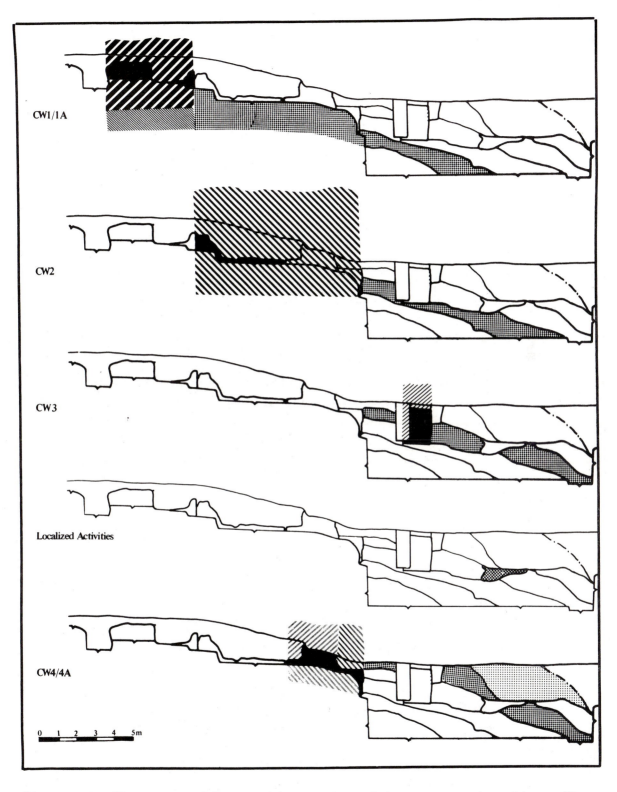

CW1/1A

CW2

CW3

Localized Activities

CW4/4A

0 1 2 3 4 5m

Figure 5-7: Five sequential, repetitive versions of the same stratigraphic profile, each highlighting a different constructional or depositional phase.

ples were selected from a part of the world offering some of the most challenging archaeological deposits that any field researcher could excavate. Most situations will be somewhat simpler; these can range from the almost "invisible stratigraphy" of hunter-gatherer sites, where depositional differences can only be detected through chemical testing, to more involved deposits incorporating refuse, architectural units, and later intrusive pits.

Correspondingly, the more complicated the archaeological excavation, the greater the demands placed upon the person doing the stratigraphic section drawings. It is best to begin with the simple, as with all illustration learning exercises, and work gradually towards the complex. Even those researchers accustomed to recording only simple excavations without much visible natural stratigraphy can benefit from the study of more complicated stratigraphic situations, for this exposure can lead to new thinking about the nature of deposition, and even on occasion, to new discoveries.

CHAPTER 6: RELIEF MONUMENTS

James B. Porter

RELIEF MONUMENTS

James B. Porter

The objective of monument illustration is to record as much as possible of what the original artist intended to convey. Ancient sculptures are often in a poor state of preservation, and this presents various complications and frustrations to the illustrator who may sometimes be tempted to represent more than actually exists. Accuracy of recording must always be the primary consideration; every possible detail that can be extracted from the monument must be rendered as precisely as possible, and all interpretations on the part of the illustrator must either be rigorously suppressed or clearly indicated as supposition instead of evidence. If the original monument is lost, stolen, damaged or effaced subsequent to its recording, an illustration may provide the only record of its features. This fact, coupled with the rapidly increasing rate of damage or theft of important pieces, especially in the New World, argues for as precise an illustration as possible.

Sculptural illustration, unfortunately, cannot be reduced to a formula or set of standard rules, for each new monument presents the recorder with a different set of problems. While rubbing and photography are the preferred methods for recording stone monuments in the field, the results of both processes are difficult to "read" for iconographic or epigraphic content and sometimes are visually confusing. Rubbings record only the frontal or forward planes of a sculptured surface, and many of the forms in the composition may be defined only by incised lines in these forward planes.

Since the rubbing technique emphasizes not the incised line itself but the edges of the planes on each side, there is a tendency for a single line of the monument to be interpreted as a double line when a drawing is made from the rubbing. Rubbings are also the least successful of all methods by which three-dimensional aspects of sculpture can be reproduced. Photographs, on the other hand, record a considerable amount of irrelevant detail and can distort or under-emphasize features on planes not parallel to that of the negative at the time of exposure.

While rubbings and photographs constitute the most basic study aids for sculptural research, line drawings can present all the elements of the composition at once, without visually distracting erosion or defacement. Compare the facsimile of the original wax rubbing of the two glyphic elements in Figure 6-1 with the line drawing of the same two elements below, and note the immediate increase in clarity of the drawing over the rubbing. This is also true for photography, as a comparison of the photograph with the line drawing in Figure 6-10, will show.

Translating sculpted monuments into line drawings is a three-step process requiring: 1) original recording of the piece through a rubbing or photographic technique, 2) enlarging or reducing these original recordings to a manageable size, and 3) producing and inking the final illustration.

Figure 6-1: A wax rubbing (top) of eroded glyphs and the line drawing at same scale made from them (below) through direct tracing. Note the clarity of the drawing and the difficulty of making out glyphic features from the rubbing.

WAX RUBBINGS

In recording an inscription or design which is lightly incised upon a planar surface, a wax rubbing is probably the fastest and easiest method by which successful results can be obtained. This is no less true for certain kinds of ceramic illustration (Olin and Dillon, this volume) than it is for sculpture in stone. For rubbings the following equipment is needed: black heelball wax, a soft scrub brush, drafting tape and lightweight white paper. Before making a rubbing of a monument clean its surface and allow it to dry. Then tape the paper to the stone, covering the area to be recorded and leaving a fairly large margin.

Begin the work by gently rubbing the paper with the broadest surface of the wax until a light impression of the design

appears as white lines upon a black ground. At this point use the tip of the crayon to exert more pressure on a smaller portion of the wax and increase the contrast between the lines on the ground. Continue rubbing the paper with the tip of the crayon until all incised lines are clear. The resulting image is a negative version of the original, and can be rendered as a positive image by a direct tracing over a light table (as was done to produce the line drawing in Figure 6-1).

INK RUBBINGS

The ink rubbing technique, as a means of recording Maya sculpture, is best known through the work of Merle Greene (Greene 1966; Greene, Rands, and Graham 1972; Greene and Thompson 1967). Her application of the technique has met with great success and has resulted in a number of iconographic and epigraphic discoveries on monuments previously recorded only by photography.

The main advantage of this technique is that design elements on the stone surface which may be too eroded to photograph well are rendered visible. Required for this process are: strong, absorbent fine-grained rice paper, a natural sponge, a soft scrub brush, clean water, liquid Sumi ink, a spritzer with adjustable nozzle, a comfortable seat and a pad for applying ink. The ink applicator can be made from a piece of cloth rolled into a ball which is then wrapped in water-proof plastic and covered with a final layer of any absorbent cloth.

The rubbing technique is essentially a two step process, first the rice paper is molded to the stone, then the ink is applied to the paper. Before making a rubbing of a monument, clean the surface and allow it to dry. When this has been done, tape a sheet of rice paper to the uppermost portion of the sculpture. Saturate the sheet of rice paper with water to make it soft and flexible by spraying the water onto it with a spritzer. Once the paper is saturated, press it against the stone with a wet sponge. Working from the center

Figure 6-2: Rubbing made of low-relief sculpture. Note how two separate sheets of paper have been joined at midpoint to create the whole.

Figure 6-3: Reversal or negative image of the same rubbing; this puts light and shadow in their normal relationships.

outward repeat this process until the entire sheet is molded to the surface of the monument. The elements of the design will then stand out in relief and the high points of the composition can be inked when the paper is sufficiently dry. Repeat this process until the entire sculpted surface is covered by rice paper.

Allow the paper to dry until it is only slightly damp before inking. This will prevent the water-soluble Sumi ink from staining the stone or blurring the rubbing. While the paper is drying squeeze small amounts of ink onto the stamp pad until it is saturated. If there is any excess ink it may be removed by blotting the applicator on a cloth. Watch the color and transparency of the paper closely while it is drying. It will grow lighter and more opaque as it dries. To check the dryness of the paper daub a dot of ink from the stamp pad onto the paper with your finger. If the ink runs the paper is too wet. If the ink does not run it is time to ink the rubbing.

Inking begins by pressing the applicator lightly against the rice paper where it covers the raised portions of the composition. Working from the top down and the center outward, repeat this process until all of the high points of the composition have been inked and the details are clear.

Timing is all important in the inking process, for if the paper is too dry it will stick to the applicator and pull free of the stone, yet if it is too wet the ink will run and ruin the rubbing. The only real solutions to this dilemma are patience, and to practice at home before going into the field.

Ink rubbings are valuable tools for on-site analysis of eroded monuments and as the first step towards the production of line drawings. Rubbings, however, do not truly illustrate the volume of a composition or its actual depth of relief, and should be used in concert with photographs, fieldnotes and field sketches to produce a finished line drawing. The kinds of errors in a final drawing which can result from an overreliance upon rubbings are discussed later in the context of Figure 6-10. Since a black rubbing on white paper is essentially the opposite of what the eye is accustomed to seeing, reversing the fields will usually render the recording easier to "read" and study; compare Figure 6-2 with Figure 6-3.

PHOTOGRAPHS

The best time to photograph monuments is at night when a constant source of artificial light can be manipulated to sidelight the surface being recorded and shadows will not vary with the passage of the hours as is the case during daylight. Experiments with different lighting angles and elevations should be made with constant exposures being taken with different colored filters, and with and without fill-in flash. Figure 6-4 provides a hypothetical lighting situation with different portions of a single monument sidelit. The lights should be stationary and placed at angles between 10 and 40 degrees to the plane of the surface to be photographed. These angles are only approximations, and much experimenting must be done in order to bring out maximum detail, as has been successfully done in Figure 6-5.

Flat light (perpendicular to the plane being photographed), either natural or artificial, should be avoided, for it obliterates many traces of sculptural detail. If night photography is unfeasible, the monument should be studied for the entire daylight period of one day, and exposures taken at regular intervals in order to derive maximum benefit from the changing light conditions. Generally, early morning light is best for natural light sculptural photography.

FRAGMENTARY MONUMENTS

The different portions of a broken monument almost always must be recorded through combining separate photographs taken from different angles or positions. As should be the case in all sculptural photography, the plane of the negative must be as parallel as possible to the plane of the sculptured surface. In recon-

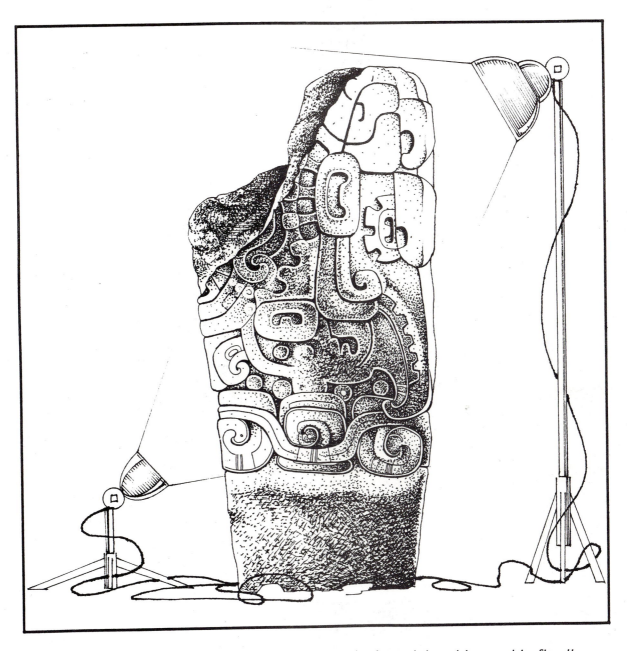

Figure 6-4: Relief sculpture is best photographed at night with movable floodlamps so that light and shadow can be completely controlled. Multiple exposures and experimentation with lighting angles will be necessary for recording all detail.

structing fragmentary monuments from multiple prints, the second important consideration is that the scale of each photograph be absolutely identical. This can be accomplished in the darkroom during printing by selection of a single design element that would be continuous if the piece were not broken, measuring its width on one print, then reducing or enlarging the other print until its opposite side is identical in dimension (see Figure 6-5).

If the pieces of a monument do not fit together, a common scale can still be

Figure 6-5: Unlike "ideal" situations of perfect or near-perfect preservation, many stone sculptures will be encountered in fragmentary condition. This example was discovered in two major sections (left) which were photographed separately. The combined photographs (right) form the first reconstruction.

Figure 6-6: The first step in making an accurate drawing from slide or opaque projection is light pencil tracing. This is a facsimile of a typical first effort with pencilled lines shown darker than they would normally be.

established by measuring the outer dimensions of both pieces. If the outer dimensions are not apparent, establish a common scale based on the size or "modular width" of the scrolls, fretwork, human figures, and other elements of the composition.

LINE DRAWINGS FROM PHOTOGRAPHS AND RUBBINGS

Freehand drawings, whether made from the monument itself or from photographs or rubbings of the monument, are undesirable for the purpose of scientific study. Any drawing not directly traced from a two dimensional image of the monument will probably incorporate inaccuracies sufficient to render it unfit for publication. Therefore the serious monument illustrator

will require clear photographs or photographic slides of the monument or the rubbing of the monument. A good slide projector or opaque projector will be necessary for producing line drawings from these materials.

Using the slide projector or opaque projector, a large two dimensional image of the monument is projected onto a standard 14 x 28 sheet of drawing paper. At this stage align the image on the paper to approximate the original alignment of the monument in the field. Once this has been done, the lines of the composition can be traced directly onto the drawing paper with a soft graphite pencil. This pencil drawing is then secured to the drawing board and any errors or omissions of detail are corrected (see Figure 6-6). through careful comparison with slides, prints, rubbings, and, preferably, field-checking against the original monument.

At the very least throughout this process constant reference must be made to a series of prints showing the monument under varied lighting conditions. Thus, when there is confusion about the contour of some element of the composition, one of the prints in this series will frequently resolve the issue.

After the corrections are completed, the pencil drawing is covered with a sheet of clear acetate and the main lines of the composition are traced with the #1 pen, as in Figure 6-7a. Then the fine incised lines are traced with the #0 pen, as in Figure 6-7b, and the relief is emphasized by creating a regular system of cast shadows with the #3 tip pen as in Figure 6-7c. Finally, a sheet of 'gravel' or 'sand' transfer shading should be cut to fit the background plane of the monument (as in Figure 6-8): this will set off the carved portions through contrast.

Sometimes photographs of exceptional clarity can be directly traced over so as to obtain a preliminary sketch. This is done by anchoring the photograph to a solid drawing surface and then making the sketch in photo-safe blue pencil upon a clear acetate sheet. This will, of course,

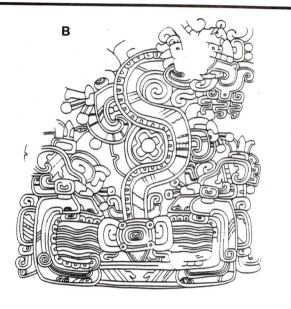

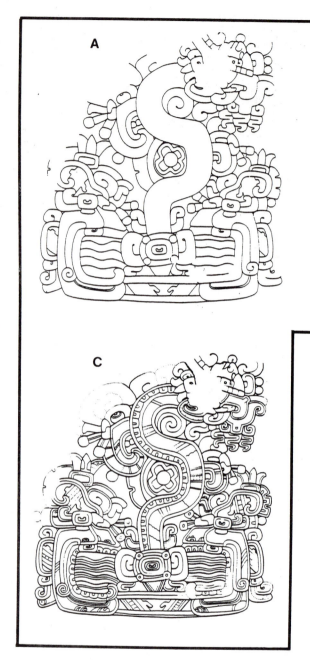

Figure 6-7: Successive stages in production of a drawing from a projected slide. A: The main lines of the composition are first traced, then; B: finer details are then traced within the existing framework; C: a system of shading selected lines through thickening them is the penultimate step.

the clearest print exhibiting the most detail should be selected as the master copy. The print should be positioned on the drawing table so that the monument is in a true approximation of its original alignment in the field, and then taped securely to the table surface.

In order to transfer the proportionate scale of a small photograph to a drawing many times larger, a common frame of reference must be introduced by the superimposition of a grid system over both mediums, different in size but equal in proportion. The grid should be laid out with the aid of a T-square or parallel rules so as to ensure that the vertical and horizontal lines are truly and invariably perpendicular to each other, and the lines on the drawing paper are best delineated with photo-safe blue pencil. To avoid obscur-

produce a drawing only as large as the positive photographic print, and additional steps must be taken in order to enlarge a drawing from a small original photograph. First of all, a series of prints showing many different views of the monument should be assembled for ready reference as specific problems in recording arise, and

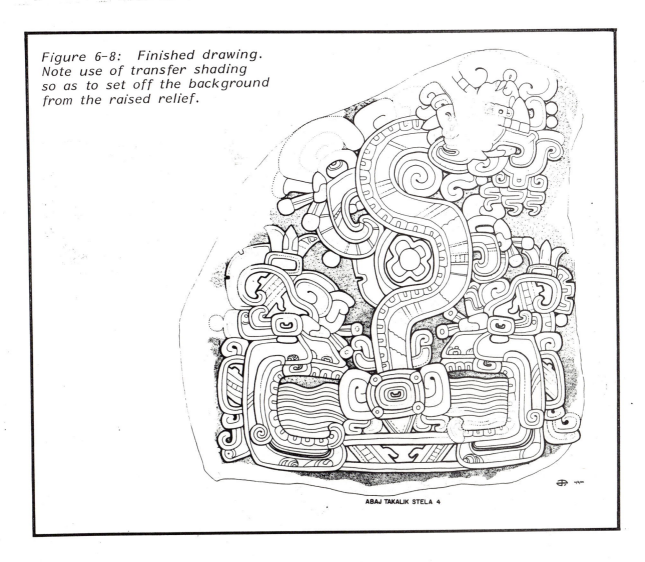

Figure 6-8: Finished drawing. Note use of transfer shading so as to set off the background from the raised relief.

ABAJ TAKALIK STELA 4

ing detail on the master photographic paper, a better system is to plot guide-dots around the print on the drawing board. These then form a base for the grid which can be made through aligning fine black thread with these dots so as to cover the print (Figure 6-9).

If a drawing is to be five times the size of the original photographic print which has one-centimeter grid system superimposed over it, the drawing paper will be covered by a series of five cm. squares. Design elements that show up within specific squares on the original photograph are measured in from the bounding lines, and tranferred after the measurement has been multiplied five times to the corres-

ponding square on the drawing sheet, using the scaled rule. The reverse of this process is utilized when a rubbing of 100% size is to be reduced to smaller drawing.

All preliminary sketching should be done in photo-safe blue pencil, and the finished pencil sketch should be completed in graphite pencil with a very fine line. During this preliminary drawing stage, reconstructions can be attempted in pencil and erased until the most likely version has been decided upon.

For inking and reproduction a number of conventions must be followed that admit little variation, for each is a graphic representation of a specific statement

*Figure 6-9:
Scaled reductions
or enlargements
in drawings made
from photographs
can be simplified
by superimposing
a grid over a pos-
itive print. Note
inked alignment
dots, tape holding
black thread.*

of evidence.   These conventions are:

Solid Lines are only used to indicate lines which are clearly present on the original monument.

Thickened Lines are selected and executed by the illustrator to indicate shadows created by oblique lighting. These define differences beween sculptural planes.

Broken Lines are used to indicate doubtful lines on the original.

Dotted Lines are used to indicate reconstructions provided by the illustrator.

Stippling is used to represent the flat surface of the background plane.

White is used to indicate areas which have been effaced.

As these graphic conventions are generally agreed upon, any features which cannot be rendered by any of these methods should be reserved for commentary in

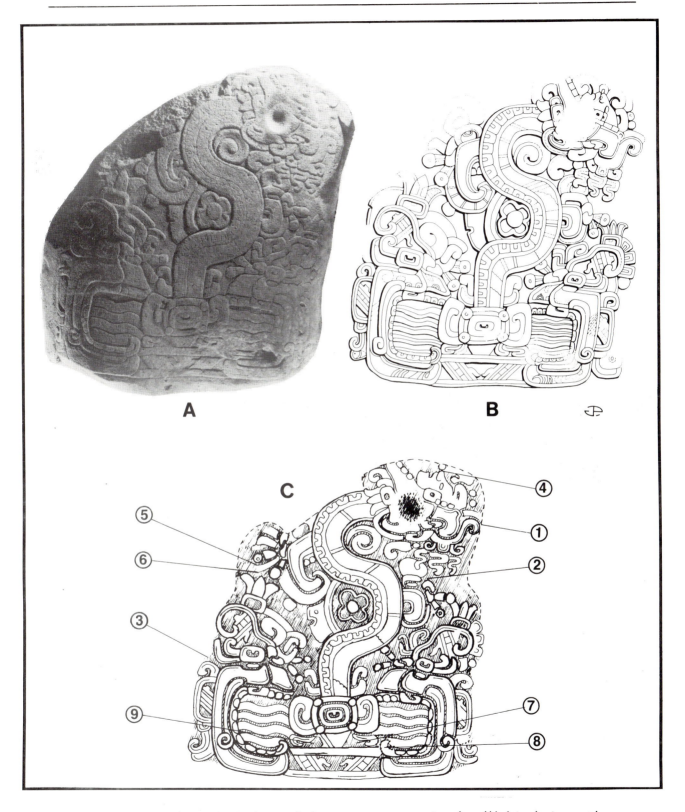

Figure 6-10: Three depictions of the same monument. A: Night photograph; B: Drawing from photographs, rubbings and field measurements; C: Earlier drawing made solely from rubbings, 1-9 are specific errors which have been corrected in B.

Figure 6-11: Original field photographs of an irregular-shaped stone monument. Views are from four different directions, prints selected from many exposures made with natural and artificial light.

the written text.

When the design continues around the sides of a monument, the clearest method of presentation is to represent the whole composition in "rollout" fashion as if it were done on a flat surface. This presentation eliminates the distortions caused by perspective and the single viewpoint of the camera. In such cases the unbroken outline of the frontal face of the monument is represented by a solid line, except where the design overlaps the sides (see Figure 6-10).

The importance of obtaining as many parallel lines of evidence as possible about each sculpture is underlined by the different results obtained by two different illustrators of the same monument, as demonstrated in Figure 6-10. Here are shown three reproductions of the same monument; Figure 6-10c is the original published drawing (Parsons 1972), 6-10a is a photograph taken five years after first publication of this drawing, and 6-10b is my own line drawing of the monument, made from photographs, rubbings, and field measurements. The errors visible in Figure 6-10c are of two classes; those typically resulting from the use of a rubbing as the only model, and those of observational oversights and mistakes in line reading.

Figure 6-10c has been analyzed as a concrete example of specific errors in monument illustration, and each problem area isolated and identified. In making a drawing from a rubbing, the following conventions are to be avoided: 1) using double lines to indicate a single incised line; 2) separating elements which in reality press against each other (this can result in expansion of the "ground" at the expense of the "subject" or "figure"); 3) indicating the "ground" or rearmost plane with parallel hatching (this gives an overly "busy" and confusing appearance to the overall composition); 4) altering the features of any human figure; 5) drawing in cracks, damage or erosion as part of the composition, for this confuses the eye by distracting it from the depiction of intentional design; 6) indicating lines that do not exist on the original; 7) omitting elements that are clearly indicated on the original; 8) improperly indicating reconstructions; and, 9) failing to indicate all broken and flaked areas occurring within the composition.

SCULPTURE IN THE ROUND

Sculpture in the round presents the illustrator with challenges distinctly different from those found in illustrating reliefs. While the goal remains to record as much as possible of what the original artist intended to convey, the flowing surfaces of sculpture in the round are not amenable to linear reproduction, nor are night photography and ink rubbings necessarily the definitive methods for recording sculpture in the round in situ. Here, only focused photographs can supply the illustrator with information about the tone changes, interrelationships and volumes of the forms as they would appear to an observer standing before the monument itself.

As with relief sculpture, photographs by themselves present a visually confusing impression of sculpture in the round. The advantages of black and white drawings over photographs are many; drawings are easier to reproduce, drawings give sharper definition of the features of a monument, drawings can lighten or eliminate obscuring shadows and drawings show

the true nature of cracks or chips, which might otherwise be read as elements of the composition.

Another challenging aspect of recording sculpture in the round is the necessity for multiple viewpoints of the same monument. Usually these views are four: front, back, right, and left. Occasionally a monument will require top, bottom, and oblique views as well. Usually however, the four primary views of a monument will show each of the carved surfaces with a minimum of distortion (see Figure 6-11).

SCULPTURE IN THE ROUND DRAWN FROM SCALED PHOTOGRAPHS

Working from pre-scaled photographs will save much time and expense that would otherwise go into enlarging or reducing the various finished drawings (Christensen, this volume, provides alternatives to the methods described below). Also, working from scaled photographs will ensure uniformity of line width and tone depth in all the completed drawings of a single monument (as in Figure 6-14).

Here the task of the illustrator is to create a faithful reproduction of the on-site photograph through the use of stippling. This is done by making print of the monument at a convenient size, such as 8 1/2 x 11, which is secured to the drawing board and covered with a sheet of clear acetate. The outline of the stone is then traced onto the acetate using a #0 pen and the outlines of the major features of the design are then picked out using the same pen (as in Figure 6-12).

The shadows defining the surface of the monument are represented by a regular field of dots. These should be applied more densely where the surface is closer to the observer and less densely where the surface slopes away from the observer. This procedure is applied to all meaningful variations in the surface of the monument and care must be taken to identify and accurately define these variations (see Figure 6-13).

This initial stippling is done very

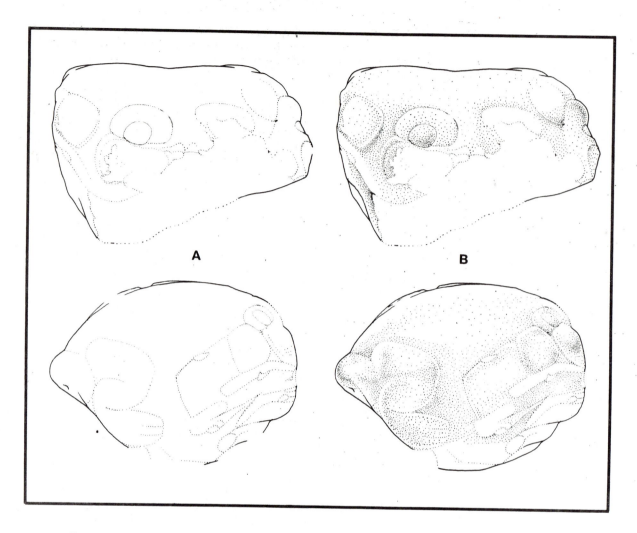

Figure 6-12: Drawing begins on two views of the monument. A: Outlines are inked and internal design areas are dotted in. B: Dot stippling is begun so as to isolate shadowed and highlit areas.

sparsely so that errors can be corrected easily. Thus, if an area is too light it can be darkened by placing a second application of dots between the existing ones, and if an area is too dark it can be 'lightened' by darkening the rest of the surface in the same manner.

Once the major features of the design and the significant tone variations on the surface of the monument have been indicated through stippling, the areas of deep incision and high relief must be defined. This is done by cutting sections of a sheet of 'sand' or 'gravel' transfer to fit

those areas where dark shadows define such features (as in Figure 6-13).

Where these areas of dark shadow fade gradually into neighboring areas of lighter tone, this transition must be created by carefully inked dots of decreasing density. Here the pen size used must blend well with the stippled dots on the commercial transfer sheet (as in Figure 6-14).

Once this has been done, a transfer sheet is placed over the entire surface of the monument drawing and the portions

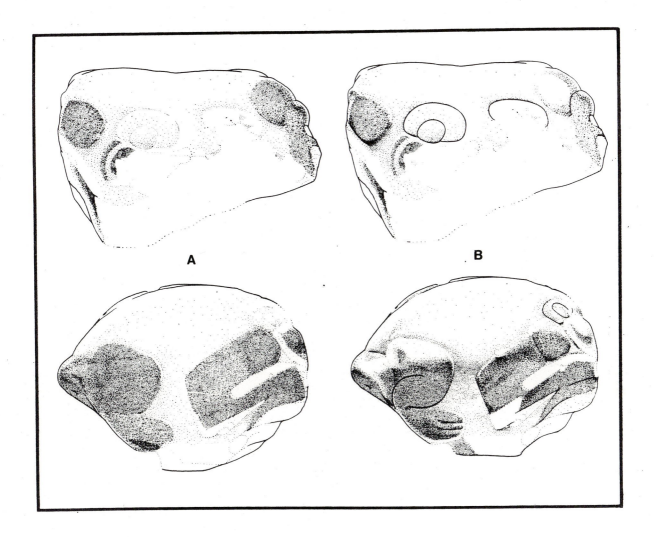

Figure 6-13: Shading continues through stippling and the addition of transfer film (A); areas in relief are then outlined in ink (B).

extending beyond the outline of the stone are cut away. Finally, cracks, chips, and other damage to the surface of the monument are indicated by an application of white to those areas where the final sculpted surface no longer exists (as in Figure 6-14).

Just as in relief illustration, there is a series of conventions that permit little variation, for each is a graphic representation of a specific statement of evidence. These conventions are:

Solid Lines are used to represent the abrupt intersection of distinct planes of sculpture, as well as grooves and incising.

Stippling is used to represent the final sculpted surface.

White is used to represent areas where the final sculpted surface no longer exists.

HIGH RELIEF AND HALF-ROUND SCULPTURE

Due to its position half way between relief sculpture and full round sculpture, half-round and high-relief sculp-

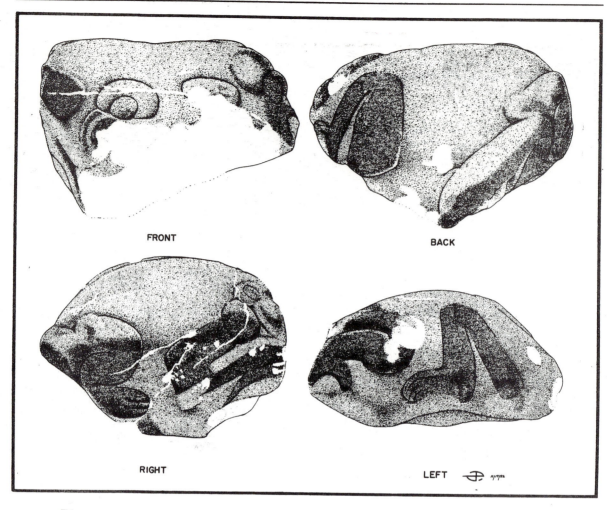

FRONT

BACK

RIGHT

LEFT

Figure 6-14:   The finished drawings of the monument now convey a much more three-dimensional quality than the flatter, two-dimensional photographs in 6-11.   Cracks, damage indicated in white.

ture must be drawn with techniques taken from both sculptural extremes. The frontispiece to this chapter shows an example of the treatment of a high-relief sculpture which borders on the half-round. The lines of the figure were first traced as described in the section on drawing relief monuments, then the flowing surfaces were built up with stippling and commercial half tones as described in the section on drawing sculpture in the round.

CONCLUSION

Each new monument presents a different set of challenges to the archaeological illustrator, and no two may even require the same kinds of techniques for accurate recording. Nevertheless, if the student of ancient monumental sculpture is able to

precisely render pieces with the aid of rubbings, tracings, positive prints and slides, he or she will be on the path towards understanding the artistic and technical problems faced by the ancient sculptor. Perhaps more importantly, he or she will be in a better position than any other modern student to interpret the degree of success achieved. By identifying and drawing every detail of a sculptural design, these can be retained more easily in the memory of the recorder and identified in different contexts. This ability to remember and recognize a wide variety of sculptural elements in different contexts is the basis of all epigraphic and iconographic research. This skill is also necessary in discerning cultural and stylistic relationships between different monuments.

CHAPTER 7: CERAMICS

Joyce Olin & Brian D. Dillon

CERAMICS

Joyce Olin & Brian D. Dillon

Just as the technological hallmark of hunting and gathering groups is often the stone tool, that of sedentary peoples, agriculturalists and of civilization most commonly is pottery. Ceramics numerically constitute the overwhelming majority of artifacts recovered at most urban or semi-urban sites in both the Old World and the New. The student who learns to carefully render pottery, consequently, is usually guaranteed a place on nearly any kind of excavation project. As an added bonus, the techniques learned in ceramic illustration can easily be applied to renderings of certain kinds of stone, metal and basketry containers.

This chapter presents a variety of elementary as well as advanced methods, techniques and "tricks" by which a diverse range of recording problems can be solved. Processes by which comparatively simple ceramic artifacts are measured and illustrated should be, in most cases, also applicable to more complex examples. Even the most sophisticated drafting techniques tend to build upon the rules learned through experimentation with simpler pottery objects. Ceramic illustration therefore is best understood to be a cumulative learning process.

In general terms, two kinds of ceramic evidence exists to be recorded: complete vessels and sherds. Complete vessels are assumed to be fairly close in appearance to their original state, and sherds (far more commonly encountered in archaeological contexts are simply fragments of previously complete vessels. Different drawing methods are used in rendering sherds as opposed to vessels; these are described separately below.

STYLISTIC UNIFORMITY

While one of the goals of the technical description of ceramics (Shepard 1976) is terminological uniformity, it is surprising to note how little stylistic uniformity exists between graphic representations of sherds and vessels appearing in different reports. Drawings of new discoveries which conform to the stylistic canons which are generally accepted from depictions of previous finds in any given area allow for easy comparison and lessens the need for interpretation by the viewer. Situations in which stylistic uniformity was not considered important have sometimes produced a divergence in illustration quality between different reports on the same archaeological site or area (compare Kidder, Jennings and Shook 1946, with Wetherington 1978).

All of the illustrations in this chapter are of ceramics from the Maya site of Salinas de los Nueve Cerros (Dillon 1977: n.d.). Therefore our drawings of the Nueve Cerros materials must be comparable to those of sherds and vessels from sites where the ceramic sequences are better known and to the accepted style of drafting in use at those sites. In most instances our artistic conventions conform

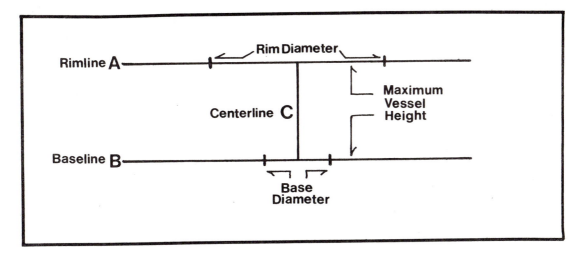

Figure 7-1: Guidelines forming a bounding framework for drawing a complete vessel. This is made from direct measurement of the vessel and no part of the finished drawing will exceed these parameters.

to the stylistic tradition pioneered by the Carnegie Institution of Washington (R. E. Smith 1955) and subsequently perpetuated by the Peabody Museum of Harvard University (Adams 1971; Sabloff 1975). This tradition in its graphic expression was the creation of such brilliant artists as Antonio Tejeda and Antonio Oliveros, of the Museo Nacional de Arqueologia y Etnologia de Guatemala. If we were to use Persian, Inca, or Shang ceramics as examples, our illustration style would have to change so as to conform to the traditions of depiction current in each other area of research.

MEASURING AND DRAWING COMPLETE VESSELS

The first step in ceramic illustrating is careful measurement. Measurements are taken of the vessel's height and rim diameter and these are noted in pencil on the upper-right corner of the paper just underneath the provenience information. Calipers are then used to measure the thickness of the rim, and if possible, the thickness of the wall slightly below the rim where thinning is often evident. These values are then noted in pencil along with the height and rim diameter measurements so that they can be referred

to as the drawing progresses; they also provide a means for quick tabulation after the drawing is completed.

The next step is the creation of a bounding framework of guidelines within which to place the vessel. One edge of the large plastic triangle is aligned with the left side of the drawing paper, allowing perpendicular (or horizontal) lines to be lightly drawn in pencil. The first line should be near the bottom of the page as it will serve as the baseline delineating the lowermost extent of the vessel being drawn.

Next, the height measurement taken earlier is transferred directly to the page, starting from the baseline just drawn. A second light pencil line is now drawn with the aid of the triangle and left side of the paper at the point indicated as the maximum upper extent of the vessel: this is the rimline. The drawing page now contains a pair of parallel, horizontal lines, spaced as far apart as the vessel is high. Figure 7-1 illustrates and labels the various sections of framing and guiding lines that must be drawn before the vessel can be rendered, with "A" representing the rim line, and "B" representing the baseline.

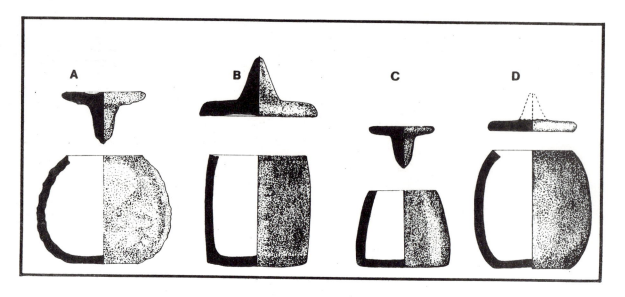

Figure 7-2: Variations on a theme: simple, unslipped vessels showing a standard convention of presentation. In each example the profile (or cross-section through vessel wall) is at left and half of the exterior is at right. The varying positions of the lids reflect individual contexts of discovery. Note how each vessel incorporates a partial bounding framework as in Figure 7-1, but with irrelevant line sections erased.

Next, the vessel's rim diameter is plotted along the upper, or rim line, with its center at page center. The exact center of this rim diameter is located and marked on the rim line, and a vertical line ("C" in Figure 7-1) is lightly penciled from this point perpendicular to and intersecting both rim line and baseline. This vertical line is referred to as the centerline; as most ceramic vessels are bilaterally symmetrical, the centerline is assumed to exactly bisect the vessel being drawn. The diameter of the vessel's base is then measured and transferred to the baseline in correct relationship to the vertical centerline, and the guiding framework for the drawing is complete.

It is important to carefully study each vessel before the next step is attempted and to rehearse the procedures mentally before additional drawing is done. After a number of vessels have been successfully drawn, it should become easy to visualize the final sketch in the mind's eye before the actual drawing commences. At this point it might be useful to examine a series of completed vessel drawings; figures 7-2a through d, for example, show four different versions of a simple ceramic idea.

As should be immediately apparent, each vessel's right half as drawn is quite different from its left half. This is the result of a standard convention employed to convey specific kinds of information to the viewer. The importance of the "centerline" previously discussed now becomes obvious, for it serves to divide the vessel into different sections displaying different information, and allows one drawing to do the work of several. To the right of the centerline in each example is illustrated the exterior surface of the vessel and its corresponding lid; this surface is heavily stippled so as to show curvature and texture as well as to indicate the absence of slip. To the immediate left of the centerline the interior surface of the vessel is rendered. This is also stippled, but more lightly, and at the extreme left is found the actual profile or "cross-section" through the vessel's wall which is always indicated in solid black. Stippling here has been done with a combination of 00 and 000 point reservoir pens, while the profiles have been filled in with a dip pen and broad, flat tip.

The vessel lids are drawn using the same techniques as were applied to the vessels themselves. The dotted lines in the area of the handle of figure 7-2d shows a presumed reconstruction of a missing portion, and the lids of a and c were found reversed in situ and have therefore been illustrated as such. Additional differences between the four examples are noticeable; in A and D, the lip is bevelled in at an angle to the rim line, while B has a slight dip or groove in its lip, and C has a flat lip. Note also that the exterior surfaces of A are rough and uneven whereas those of the other three vessels have been intentionally smoothed.

Now that a number of finished examples have been studied, let us return to the step-by-step procedures for drawing. The sides of the vessel must now be drawn in correct relationship to the guidelines already plotted on the page. This is done by directly transferring measurements taken from the vessel (with the ruler and triangle) to the sheet in the form of light pencil dots. The vessel is placed upon its base on a completely flat surface, such as a table, and the plane of this surface (for measuring purposes) will correspond to the baseline (Figure 7-3a) already established on paper.

One of the short sides of the 90 degree triangle is now placed against the flat surface upon which the vessel rests; thus the other short side of the triangle now is perpendicular to the vessel's baseline and parallel to its centerline. The triangle is advanced towards the left side of the vessel until its vertical edge just touches the outermost point of the vessel. This is the point of contact and is noted on the page by a dot after two measurements are taken, the first being the horizontal distance from the rim exterior to the edge of the triangle (Figure 7-3c), and the second being the vertical distance from the table top/baseline to the point of

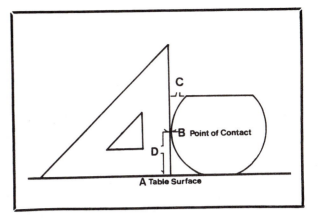

Figure 7-3: Measuring technique for complete vessels, with table surface (A) identical to baseline previously drawn in the bounding framework.

contact (Figure 7-3d).

Next, points along the vessel wall above and below the point of contact are plotted with dots on the page after a vertical measurement up from the table and horizontal measurements have been made in from the triangle's vertical edge. An additional reference line is necessary for this procedure, and it is drawn to represent the triangle's edge intersecting the point of contact and perpendicular to both the baseline and rim line.

Using a light freehand pencil technique, as the locating points are connected, the left exterior profile of the vessel will begin to take shape. After this line has been penciled in and any errors corrected, inking can proceed. The portion of the rim line contained within the rim diameter points (the actual extent of the vessel's orifice) is inked with reservoir pen and straightedge, and the penciled lines on either side of it are now erased. Next, the centerline, exterior left profile just completed, and the base are inked, and after these lines are dry, all remaining penciled guidelines are erased.

So far, we have the top, bottom, and left side of the vessel completed, and

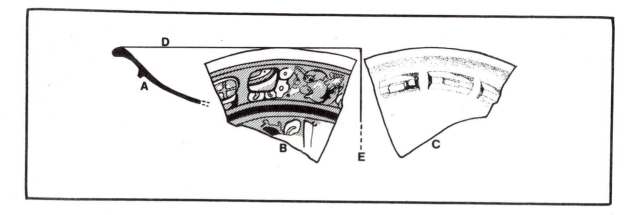

Figure 7-4: Conventional presentation of a decorated rim sherd. Profile (A) at left, interior view (B) to right, exterior (C) at far right. Note also rimline (D) and centerline (E), sherd rotation so as to reveal decoration.

if we can prove bilateral symmetry for the vessel being illustrated, the right side can be drawn without taking any additional measurements. The drawing sheet is folded along the centerline just inked, with care taken not to break the paper surface at the fold. The inked centerline will disguise the permanent crease for later reproduction, but the crease above and below the drawing may have to be painted or razored out later. The folded drawing is placed over a light box with the inked profile against the box and underneath the right half of the sheet. The left (inked) profile should show through the paper as a reversed image and should be lightly traced in pencil and then inked so as to produce the outline of the right side. After the tracing has been done, unfold the paper to its original condition, and apply pressure with the roller to flatten the folded area.

As the right half of the drawing is to portray the vessel exterior, the interior surface of the vessel need only be represented on the left side, and the methods by which the profile is drawn are described in the section on rim sherds. At this point, the drawing should appear similar to the outline sketch on the right side of Figure 7-3. The treatment given to the vessel exterior and interior will vary depending upon the kind of decoration present, specific examples of which will be presented later.

ILLUSTRATING RIM SHERDS

Rim sherds, if drawn carefully, can provide a great amount of information about the vessels from which they originated. The experienced eye, for example, can usually discern the original form of the vessel from a glance at the sherd drawing. If the sherd is from a vessel that was unelaborated, or if erosion has removed all traces of decoration, a profile (cross-section) is often all that is possible for complete graphic recording of the piece. If the sides of the sherd are decorated, a profile by itself is inadequate for recording purposes, and a convention of depiction similar to that employed for complete vessels must be used.

Figure 7-4 illustrates a sherd with elaborate decoration represented under the rules of this convention, with the profile (a) to the left, the interior surface of the sherd (b) shown to the right of the profile, and the exterior surface (c) shown to the far right. The rim line (d) is shown in correct relationship to the angle of the rim on the profile, and extends to the right until it intersects with the vertical line E which represents the centerline of the vessel or midpoint of the rim diameter (as determined by use of a circle chart).

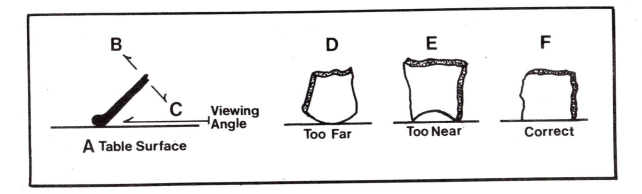

Figure 7-5: Determining the rim diameter of a sherd with a circle (diameter) chart. The chart is placed face up on the table surface (A) and the sherd positioned over the closest curvature while being rocked forwards (B) and backwards (C) until its rim plane is rediscovered from the correct viewing angle (C). Once the rim plane is flush with the table surface (which is also identical to the rimline drawn in the bounding framework), exact checking against the circle chart is possible.

Lines D and E therefore not only locate the profile in space, but immediately tell us how large a vessel the sherd originated from. The broken end of line E indicates that since the lower portion of the sherd is missing, no precise information is available on the overall vessel height, and the dotted lines shown on the profile (a) show where missing sections are presumed to have extended. In the interests of clarity of depiction, the inner and outer surfaces of the sherd (b and c) are not in the same relationship to the rim line (d) as the profile is; if they were, the curvature of their rims would be represented as a straight line and would be indistinguishable from line D and its logical extention to the right.

The steps involved in measuring and drawing rim sherds generally follow those already described for complete vessels, but two specific problems have not yet been discussed: determining the rim diameter with the use of a circle chart, and determining the angle of the sherd wall relative to the rim line. Whereas the diameter of a complete vessel can be measured simply by placing a ruler across its orifice, a rim sherd represents only a small part of the total orifice (and, consequently, the diameter) of its original vessel. The entire rim diameter of the ceramic vessel from which the sherd is derived can be reconstructed with the aid of a circle (or diameter) chart very simply and with surprising accuracy.

Hold the sherd rim-side down against a circle chart which has been placed on a flat surface (Figure 7-5), so that the curvature of the rim runs in the same direction as the diameters on the chart. Position yourself so that your line of vision is level with the surface upon which the sherd rests; now you can determine the proper angle at which to hold the sherd so that all points along its rim are touching the flat surface of the circle chart. If the sherd is tilted too far away from the viewer (Figure 7-5d), only one point at the center of the rim will be touching the chart, but if it is tilted too near the viewer (Figure 7-5e) only the two outermost points of the rim will be in contact with the chart.

Neither position will result in an accurate diameter reading. When the entire rim is flush with the table surface, it will appear similar to the example depicted in Figure 7-5, and the sherd will be in the correct angle relative to its original rim line. Maintaining this angle, move the sherd horizontally across the central axis of the circle chart until the outer curvature of its rim matches that of one of the circles on the chart. The written diameter of that circle on the chart then gives the diameter of the vessel's orifice.

Since sherds are often uneven and orifices are seldom perfectly circular, precise determinations of rim diameters are sometimes unavailable. When such situations arise, it is usual to indicate the maximum possible range in writing on the drawing. Several attemps may be necessary for each reading and some repetition is unavoidable the first few times this process is undertaken.

The sherd profile is drawn relative to a rimline penciled on the page which represents the surface of the drawing table against which the sherd is held at its correct angle. With the rim flush against the table, advance the 90 degree triangle towards the broken edge of the sherd until a point of contact is established. Then take measurements horizontally from the edge of the triangle to the outermost edge of the sherd's rim, and vertically from the table surface to the highest point on the sherd. Once again, the sherd must be positioned at its correct angle for these measurements to be accurate.

Bounding lines can now be drawn, making use of the measurements just taken, to indicate the maximum horizontal and vertical extent of the sherd. Again using triangle and ruler, take a series of horizontal and vertical measurements

along the sherd exterior, and plot these points in pencil. Once the exterior side has been sketched in, measure the thickness of the sherd's wall at regular intervals with the calipers and transfer these measurements directly to the page by laying the jaws of the calipers against the drawing and dotting in pencil where necessary. The rim and lip section of the sherd is the most crucial part of the drawing, as well as the hardest to draw. A close visual inspection and repeated sketchings in light pencil are usually necessary before successful results are achieved.

ILLUSTRATING BODY SHERDS

Body sherds (those with no portion of the vessel rim or base connected) are usually not drawn unless they contain some unusual form of decoration, represent the only examples of a certain kind or type of pottery, or can be related in the same drawing to rim or base sherds from the same original vessel. Figure 7-6 illustrates three body sherds that were drawn because of design elements present upon their outer surfaces.

To the left of each sherd's exterior is positioned the profile that corresponds to it. Note that the flanges that have been modified with impressed designs are on the same horizontal plane between each profile and exterior. Interiors are not shown since in each case they are not decorated. As nothing exists to relate the body sherd to a reconstructed horizontal rim or baseline, the alignment of the profile is entirely conjectural but the angle attempts to approximate that of the sherd's presumed position in the vessel wall. The exterior sides of the sherds are rendered through a combination of measuring and tracing around their outlines so as to obtain the outermost edges; the profiles are drawn with the aid of calipers. The dotted lines extending above and below each profile indicate that the piece is a body sherd and suggest the curvature of the vessel wall as it continues to meet the rim and base.

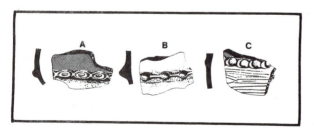

Figure 7-6: Body sherds drawn without reference to rim or base. Each sherd is depicted in its "best guess" position relative to the presumed curvature of the vessel wall.

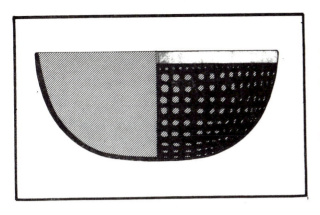

Figure 7-7: Curvature of vessel wall indicated through compaction of simple, repetitive geometric design elements.

CURVED SURFACES; PROBLEMS OF PERSPECTIVE AND THE USE OF OVERLAYS

The overwhelming majority of ceramic vessels have forms that are variations upon a basic theme; the curve. Completely flat or planar surfaces usually exist only as panels or occasionally as part of the vessel base. Unslipped or monochrome vessels are easily drawn so as to demonstrate curvature for variations in intensities of shading do not interfere with design motifs. Many technical problems exist, however, in transferring a three-dimensionally curved surface with design elements to the two-dimensional medium of the drawing sheet, and there are a variety of solutions (see also Becker, this volume). The usual means by which curved surfaces are represented is through the use of roll-outs of one kind or another, usually in company with a standard two-dimensional view of the vessel produced along the same lines as described earlier. The designs reproduced on this kind of drawing must be conventionalized so as to appear as they would to the eye of a viewer looking directly at the centerline of the vessel, and thus two-point perspective must be utilized.

Figure 7-7, a drawing of a bowl with exterior decoration of resist-painted circles of a standard size, illustrates this principle. Although all dots on the surface of the vessel are in reality the same size and roughly the same shape, in the drawing they appear not only as circles, but as ovals, and range in size from large to quite small. As the side of this vessel curves under at the base, and around at the right edge, the rows of circles are drawn as ovoid, and the spacing is compressed so as to create the illusion of curvature as it appears to the eye.

Figure 7-7 illustrates a simple, repetitive geometric design which can be understood in its entirety from that one drawing. Vessels with more complicated decoration call for more sophisticated recording methods so as to transfer designs from the curve to the flat surface. Figure 7-8a and b presents two separate views of a rounded bowl with a complex gouged and incised or plano-relief exterior decoration, and neither view is as informative by itself as it is in combination with its companion. Figure 7-8 shows the standard sectional view with profile to the left, the black-slipped interior wall to its right (separated from the blacked-in wall profile by a white line), and the elaborately decorated exterior to the right of the centerline. Figure 7-8b is a roll-out drawing created through a series of tracings from a rubbing of the vessel exterior. Thus, while the roll-out does not appear the same way the eye would see the vessel exterior, it nonetheless preserves the exact spatial relationships of all design elements to one another.

Figure 7-8a's exterior (right) side was adapted from the direct rubbing that Figure 7-8 began as, in the following way: the paper containing the section view of the vessel with a blank right side was placed over the rubbing atop the light box, and a section of the rubbing was traced directly onto the upper sheet, preserving proportions exactly at the intersection of the exterior with the centerline, but compressing them along the right edge through freehand correction so as to create per-

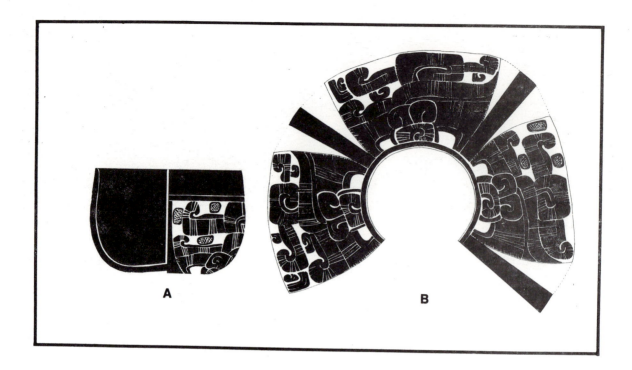

Figure 7-8: Rollout drawing of the three panels that make up the total exterior decoration of an elaborate vessel. This "orange peel" convention is similar to that used in mercator projections.

spective and to more nearly approximate what the eye would see. Roll-out views can only be made accurately if one of the two forms of overlay recording, i.e., direct tracing or rubbing, is utilized.

Rubbings are successful only when design motifs are executed by some process of excision that will show up as a micro-elevational irregularity on the vessel surface through the rubbing sheet. In all other cases, such as with most painted vessels, a direct tracing through plastic medium must be made.

Figure 7-9 represents a vessel with accompanying lid decorated through fine-line incision on its exterior and freehand modeling on the lid handle. As in Figure 7-8, the section views of the vessel and its lid to the left side of the page have been drawn through adaptations of the direct roll-outs to the exterior (right) sides. As the exterior decoration of the vessel exists

in a series of horizontal design bands disconnected from each other, each was found to be more easily and accurately drawn as a separate unit. The two design bands (c and d) of the lid (a) and the three design bands (e, f, and g) of the vessel body (b) are shown in the drawing in correct vertical relation to each other. Only panels c and g in the roll-out are depicted as the eye would normally see them, the former from a "bird's eye" and the latter from a "worm's eye" view; also note that basal panel g is not visible at all in the standard two-dimensional section drawing, b.

In order to create Figure 7-9, a series of rubbings and tracings had to be made. For each panel of the bowl and its lid, pieces of very thin paper (such as newsprint, or onion-skin typing paper) were taped against the surface and rubbed over very gently with a hard pencil. Because of the vessel's curvature, no single sheet

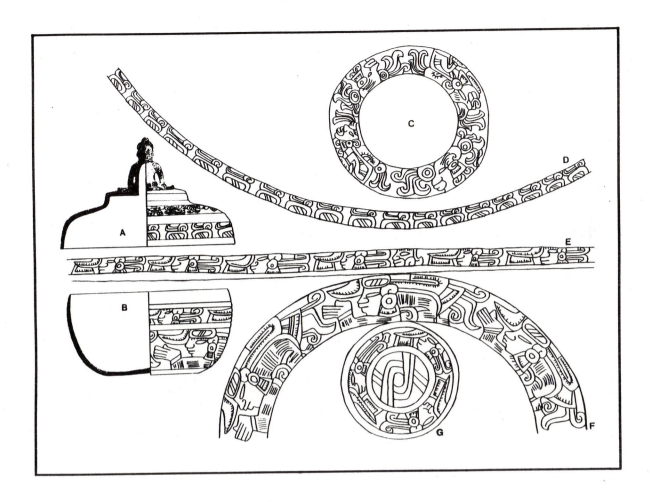

Figure 7-9: Method of rendering six separate design bands in their entirety on a vessel with fine-line incision. Design band on most vertical portion of vessel (E) can be drawn as an almost straight strip, while those on upper surface of lid (C) and on base (G) can be rendered as disks.

of paper could accommodate an entire design panel without distortion; consequently, it was found most effective to do the rubbing in very small sections on separate pieces of paper.

This produced very accurate results at the center of each rubbing, with accuracy diminishing towards the outer margins. Obviously, the greater the number of narrow sheets involved in the rubbing, the greater the potential accuracy of recording, but accompanying this is the greater chance of mis-alignment when matching up the various sections through comparisons of the overlapping outer margins. This problem is hardly unique to pottery. Once all the rubbings of a design band had been taken, they were fitted together and locked into position with spray adhesive. Some techniques of specialized ceramic illustration owe as much to methods of sculptural recording (Porter, this volume) or direct tracing (Christensen, this volume) as they do to traditional pottery rendering.

The paste-up sheet containing the different rubbings was then placed over the light box, and a mylar outline tracing made of the underlying designs in light pencil. Once the mylar tracing was completed, it was checked directly against the vessel and lid exterior by placing it against the design bands and rotating the vessel and lid as the sheet is pulled against the direction of rotation. Once all corrections were made to the penciled mylar drawing, it was inked. The final step in the process was to trace the inked mylar drawing onto finishing paper with the use of the light box. The intermediary use of mylar is necessary because the pasted-up rubbing sheet is usually so thick as to prevent penetration of light from the light box. Direct tracings of design motifs on curved surfaces where rubbings are not required can usually be accomplished by piecing together small sections of mylar in a manner similar to the process described above. Becker (this volume) describes this process in expanded detail.

Figure 7-10: Use of the cartouche method for illustrating discontinuous design panels. Identical panel on reverse not shown because a text reference is all that is needed for adequate representation.

When designs on curved surfaces are contained within bounded panels or "cartouches", as in Figure 7-10b, a roll-out drawing may not be necessary. Here, a simple conventionalization of the curved (three-dimensional) panel into two-dimensions (flattening it) can be produced without overly distorting the design elements. Figure 7-10 demonstrates an example of such a procedure, and also exhibits the convention used in drawing vessels that are all black: incised or gouged lines show

Figure 7-11: A fragmentary polychrome vase shown as reconstructed (left) and as it exists in sherd form (right). Although painted design in missing portion may repeat that of preserved area, it is best not to assume that this was the case.

up reversed as white lines.

ILLUSTRATING POLYCHROME CERAMICS

Polychrome ceramics present special problems in recording because they tend to be occasionally quite eroded. Reconstruction of overall design and eventual iconographic or epigraphic interpretations therefore often must proceed from very small fragments. Figure 7-11 illustrates a polychrome vase in section (a) and roll-out view (b); this vessel was recovered in fragments, and was eroded, incomplete, and very fragile. In order to copy the design, a piece of mylar was cut to the size of each fragment (with a slight excess margin) and was then carefully taped to the broken edges so as not to inadvertently remove any slipped sections on the sherd interiors or exteriors. The designs were then traced onto the surface of the mylar with a soft pencil, the mylar was removed, inked, the different pieces of mylar assembled in their appropriate positions relative to each other, and then an overall tracing was made with the light box. As the glyphs were eroded and, in some cases, unclear, they were checked for accuracy with epigraphic comparative material before they were inked. Sections that could not be exactly rendered were left blank if sherds were missing, or lightly stippled if effaced. In Figure 7-11b, a dis-articulated section to the upper left of the main body of the roll-out is related to the rest of the design in its probable location through the use of dotted lines.

Different shading techniques have been used to indicate different colors, and in most parts of the world, tradition dictates one form of cross-hatching or stippling over another to indicate the desired color tone; throughout this article all illustrations adhere to the color conventions set out for the Maya area by Smith, 1955.

ILLUSTRATING MODELED CERAMICS AND USE OF A CONTOUR GAUGE

Figure 7-12 represents a black-slipped bowl with exterior design in high relief created through careful modeling of clay elements then appliqued to the original vessel surface. The design motifs include a row of modeled Spider Monkey (*Ateles* spp.) faces directly beneath the impressed rim flutes on the upper part of the vessel, and full-figured monkeys modeled on the lower portions. The left profile was drawn by the standard method of measuring in from the point of contact with ruler and triangle, but in addition a contour gauge was found to be a useful aid to accuracy. This was of the sliding rod type, and the vertical clamp was held parallel to the centerline of the vessel while the rods were pushed out so as to make contact with the left side of the bowl and conform to the modeled relief. Care was taken that the rods did not scratch the surface of the vessel while a correct negative impression was being made, and once this had been accomplished, the gauge was placed against the profile drawing and a rough tracing made.

This tracing was checked at numerous points by direct measurement and was constantly corrected through freehand sketching. In the completed profile, note the hollow section containing a ceramic bead forming the interior of the mouth of monkey head.

Modeled designs require some measuring, especially of the linear elements, but depend primarily upon freehand drawing with attention to perspective and curvature. Quite often, shading indicating tone or color must be deleted from drawings of modeled vessels so as not to interfere with accurate depiction of relief. For vessels with modeling finished in monochrome, stippling is the most effective way to represent the differences in overall relief, as was done on the right side of Figure 7-12. Heavy stippling is used to show the outlines of raised areas and areas of shadow, and highlights are rendered either white or lightly stippled.

ILLUSTRATING COMPOSITE VESSELS

Composite vessels are those in which more than one basic decorative technique has been utilized. These ceramics therefore

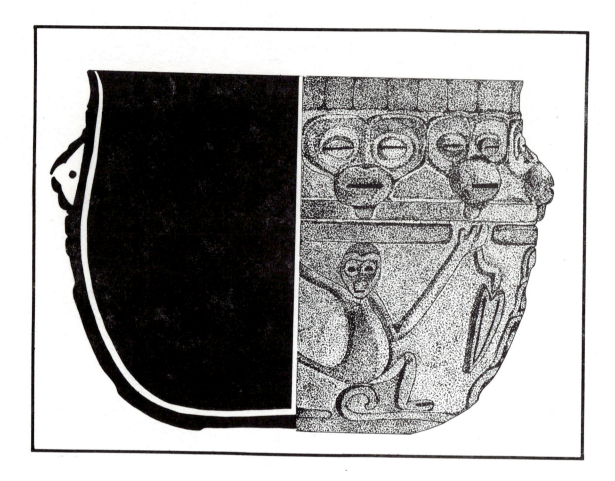

Figure 7-12: Rendering of a ceramic vessel with complicated modelling. Exact measurements were taken with a sliding-rod contour gauge and transferred to paper in order to draw the wall profile. Drafting technique used on exterior owes much to similar methods employed for relief sculpture.

present the illustrator with several drawing problems in basic representation. In most cases, for the sake of visual uniformity, a single method of depiction is selected through a process of compromise. Figure 7-13 depicts an unusual vessel exhibiting decoration through gouging-and-incising, resist painting, and stamping.

Since the exterior of the vessel was only slightly hyperbolic, it proved possible to make a rubbing of the gouged and incised feathered serpent panel (b) on a single sheet of paper, and to make a tracing of the resist-painted panel (c) on only one piece of mylar. An intermediate mylar tracing was then made of both panels, compared to the vessel exterior, and then transferred to the finishing paper as a single roll-out. The stamped design on the central tripod foot (a) was picked up through tracing after a rubbing had been made. Note the three views of the tripod legs; left shows the cross-section of the hollow leg and indicates both the perforations in front and back as well as the bead rattle inside.

CONCLUSION

The archaeologist who works with a simple pottery-producing culture or one in which

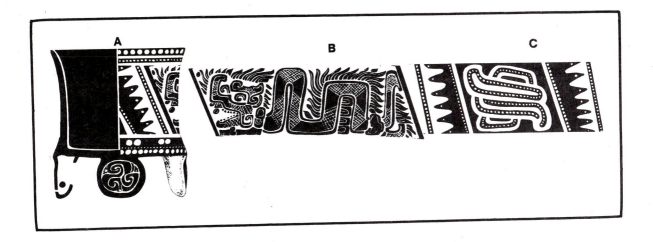

Figure 7-13: A composite vessel illustrated through use of a variety of drafting conventions. Reconstructed vessel (A) is shown in standard "cutaway" form; note hollow feet with bead rattle, stamped medallion. Frontal panel (B) of feathered serpent was executed in gouging incising, was drawn with the aid of a rubbing. Rear panel (C) was resist-painted, was drawn through direct tracing.

little experimentation or variation exists will find that he or she can master just about all of the recording techniques necessary for the production of accurate illustration in only a few days. Conversely, those ancient cultures that used pottery as a primary vehicle for artistic expression present the archaeological draftsman with a much more complex set of recording imperatives.

In many cases, as we can attest, rendering only one polychrome vessel can absorb weeks of work. Sometimes as many recording tricks as innovations developed by the original creator of the piece have to be invented by the archaeological draftsman in order to render it. This being as it may, few other kinds of illustration activities teach the student as much about forms of technological and artistic expression. And, after the first few dozen sherd drawings, it is likely that the student illustrator's visual "vocabulary" will be substantially broadened.

CHAPTER 8: SPECIAL PROBLEMS IN CERAMIC ILLUSTRATION

Jane Becker

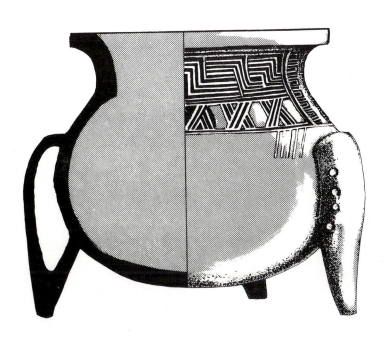

SPECIAL PROBLEMS IN CERAMIC ILLUSTRATION

Jane Becker

The fundamental recording techniques for ceramic illustrating have been described in the preceding chapter, and these are used as a point of departure for the present discussion. The archaeologist illustrating ceramic artifacts is constantly faced with new or unique pieces that challenge his or her skill and scientific recording ability; often, no pre-existing examples of illustrations exist for use as guides and new recording efforts must be devised on the spot. Such problems are somewhat simplified by attempting to understand the underlying goals and stylistic canons of the original artist.

If this is done, a true "re-creation" of the ceramic artifact is achieved that is usually much more accurate than would be the case if a too-rigid set of recording procedures were followed. Regardless of how unusual vessel shape is, or whether indentations, angles, smooth or rough textures or very elaborate painting makes up part of the surface decoration, all can be translated into two dimensional form on paper through the use of familiar symbols and conventions. These, in the hands of a skilled illustrator, can always be combined in a pleasing, artistically honest fashion for illustrations are, after all, diagrams communicating information which must not only be seen but understood by the viewer.

CUTWARE RENDERINGS

Examples of unique form are to be found in Harrapan cutware pottery from Mohenjo-Daro. One problem presented by these artifacts is found in transferring three-dimensional shapes with their delicate, tiny cuts, to the two-dimensional surface of paper. At the same time, control of optical illusion must be maintained. The cuts in these artifacts must be obvious in the drawing so that they appear as sharp indentation and not the reverse, that is, tiny ridges or mountains protruding from the surface.

The best solution seems to be one that is applied to flake scars in flint projectile points (see Rosen and Corsiglia, this volume). Using line as opposed to stipple clarifies the direction of the cut. Figure 8-1b exposes tiny angular cuts into the surface of the artifact. The central deep terminating line of these cuts would be a blurred gradation of inked dots if the stippling technique were used. Although line can have the capacity to cause an optical popping in and out, stippling seems to have an even more ambiguous effect. The reason for stability of line may in part be the fact that adjacent areas are either stippled or wide open spaces. This is enough to set off the line used to describe direction of cuts. The stippling process is kept to a bare minimum, which suggests a slight curvature over the entire object's surface. Broken edges are stippled to indicate their roughness and irregularity. The open hole regions are represented by an absence of inking and then bordered with an inked line. This helps to establish the adjacent line work as deep cuts. An example of the procedure is found in Figures 8-1a-e. Straight angular

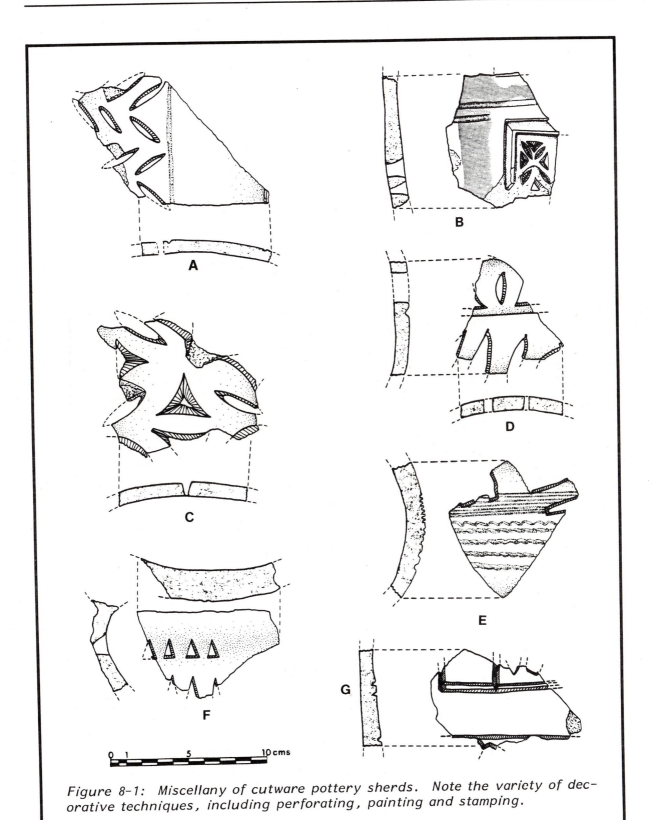

Figure 8-1: Miscellany of cutware pottery sherds. Note the variety of decorative techniques, including perforating, painting and stamping.

triangles of Figure 8-1f harbor line work to delineate cuts. Overall curvature to the object is indicated with stipple work immediately adjacent to the outlines, terminating the clay with open space to indicate a hole.

Figure 8-1g requires an emphasis on unusual multiple cuts and open spaces. Therefore, surface area is left unstippled and emphasis is drawn to the unusual running angular cuts. Rope patterning is represented with repetitious stippled forms in Figure 8-1e. Traces of surface paint are indicated with overall texturing in Figure 8-1b. Implications of shape to missing cuts are indicated with broken line as seen especially in Figures 8-1a, c, and d. The portion of the vessel missing in Figure 8-1e is difficult to project. Therefore, it would seem better not to make a conjectural reconstruction.

Taking the time to first study the artifact and then drawing a couple of sample versions in stippling, hatched lines or combinations of these will help the draftsman decide which method best represents the object. When confronted with unusual shapes, locating elements that occur in more familiar artifacts may provide clues as to how problematic pieces can best be illustrated.

Rules that were followed with the Harrapan cutware illustration that could be applied to similar problems of diagramming:

1. Stipple work demonstrates overall form.

2. Line work diagrams angle and direction of cut.

3. Adjacent symbols set up certain optical solutions.

4. Stippling adjacent to a line signifies the overall surface next to small cuts. See Figures 8-1b-f.

5. Minimal surface stippling blending into open space, adjacent to line, adjacent to small open space areas, signifies

an overall curved surface that contains a cut and exhibits an open hole. See Figures 8-1a, c, and d.

6. Large open space next to line cuts with not stipple work signifies overall surface next to cuts, and no holes. See Figure 8-1g.

7. Continuous stippling terminated with a line of ink adjacent to empty space indicates a large curved surface pierced with a hole. Or, continuous stippling with a section of linework adjacent to open space signifies a curved object interrupted with an angular cut ending with an open hole. Open space next to angular line work signifies a generally flat artifact containing angular cuts.

GOUACHE AND WATERCOLOR REPRODUCTION POLYCHROME POTTERY

Polychrome pottery can be effectively reproduced with gouache or with watercolor paints. There is a pronounced advantage in having the added dimension of color to any reconstruction. It permits a truer conception of the artifact for the viewer to examine. Limitations of course exist: colors cannot ever be quite completely matched between all parts of the ancient example and the modern rendering, and even when this goal is very nearly achieved, limitations in the reproduction or printing process involve further changes. Also, the cost of color reproduction is beyond most publication budgets in archaeology.

If the illustrator is working with a painted sherd taken from the once whole vessel, a single projected image is usually sufficient. This necessitates only one frontal photographic projection. Or, if a frontal portrait of the whole vessel is required, a single projected image in exact profile would be the draftsman's working image. However, if a rollout of the design will be painted, new problems present themselves, and another approach is required. A series of photographs encircling the entire vessel following the design need to be taken. This is not an easy task: careful and exacting control must be maintained in the relationship between camera and vessel all around the rotating vessel. The method requires expertise with the camera. Another technique for obtaining a rollout of the design is to trace the image of the original vessel as by Olin and Dillon (this volume). This drawing can then be projected with an opaque machine on the watercolor paper. Penciling on watercolor paper should be done with a light touch since the paper does not react favorably to repeated erasures. It should also be noted that lead will show through the transparent qualities of watercolor or gouache.

Daylight is by far the best light for working with color. If natural light is unavailable, a good lamp of even lighting can provide the next best illumination. The ceramic subject may have to be turned while it is being illustrated so as to examine the progression of color and design. The light should remain stationary.

Before attempting the painting, a careful study of form and design will help to enlighten work on the reconstruction painting. Some understanding of the ancient culture as well as a familiarity with the vessel will combine to produce a sensitive painting. It should be remembered that the archaeological illustrator is really transferring images created by ancient artists. Even if the painted figures are recognizable, the task is often one of reproducing complex and abstract form as well as space. Nothing should be taken for granted. Every form should be carefully examined along with the balance of negative space which is in a sense also form.

Painted areas often take on their own abstract forms within the confines of a recognizable object such as those which can be defined by a limb or fold in the costume. Consequently, one must study the design as a whole and individual element as parts of its natural positioning. Painted areas should be rendered in exactly the same manner as the original artist's brush landed on the surface of the vessel.

The technique of either watercolor or gouache is not quickly mastered and practice is a prerequisite to any polychrome reconstruction. Many examples should be studied before beginning reconstruction on paper. A book of watercolors highly recommended for this purpose is Classic Maya Pottery at Dumbarton Oaks (ed. Michael D. Coe, 1975), which contains excellent works by Diane G. Peck and Felipe Davalos H.

Before beginning the painting, color should be matched to the original with trial applications made on the same paper to be used for the reconstruction. Allow the paper to dry so as to determine actual shade and color value. In the delicate process of gouache or watercolor, allow any light layers of paint to dry completely before continuing with subsequent areas. Adjacent regions of paint are added only after a thorough drying has been reached. Large areas of color are best mapped out on the paper and applied first. Smaller forms of color are next added. The process of adding color continues, allowing time for each color to dry separately.

Finally, more delicate line work is added. It is advisable to work with the lighter shades of color first of all. The white underlying surface of paper will add a brilliancy to lighter colors, and darker colors can then be added in a later stage. Watercolor paints have a transparent quality and should be handled lightly. They do not react well to overworked painting. Gouache has a more opaque quality and also responds well to a delicate approach. Heavy layering or reworking is not suitable for this type of paint. Brushes should be soft and can have a flat edge for broader areas of paint, or they can have a pointed tip for line and fine edging or border work. Cleaning the brush continually in water will help to keep the colors true. It might be helpful to remember that clear and sparking color is a result of patience and care.

Figure 8-2: Museum photograph of polychrome vessel with compicated designs in three horizontal bands or panels. Complete recording of any panel must be done through rollouts.

REDISCOVERY OF ANCIENT RULES OF DECORATION

Ceramic slip painting can be represented entirely with ink (Olin and Dillon, this volume). Here, colors are indicated through standardized shading methods. Slip painting was originally put onto ceramic vessels by ancient artists who often left subtle traces of individuality. Such artists worked within a particular culture bound by artistic canons with perhaps few personal characteristics. It is the task of the archaeological illustrator to discover these rules and then to faithfully delineate the painting in a reconstructive drawing. Any

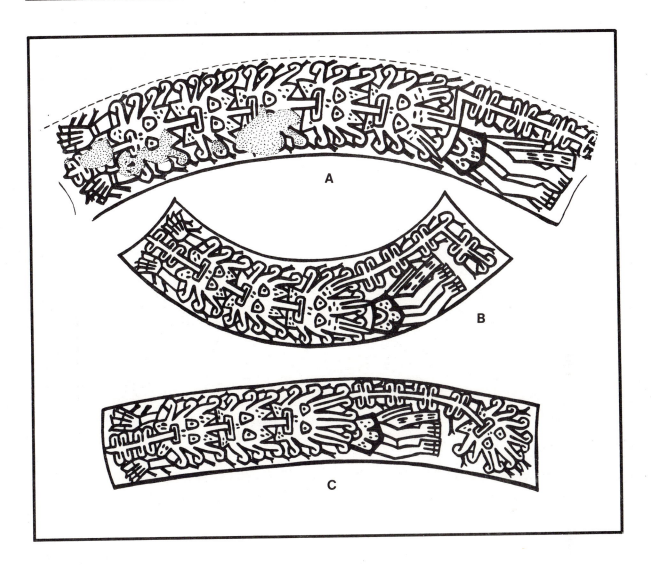

Figure 8-3: Rollout drawings of the three design panels on the vessel in Figure 8-2, with outline painting indicated but fill colors not represented. A: Neck panel; B: Upper body panel; C: Lower body panel. Note how the curvature of each rollout drawing indicates its relative position on the vessel exterior.

decision to ignore a seemingly unimportant element may result in a loss later on. If sometime in the future the pottery is no longer available for study, features chosen to be eliminated in a drawing are forever lost.

As a focus for remarks made for reconstructive ceramic slip painting, a Nasca Collared Jar from Phase Six is reproduced here as an ink drawing (Figure 8-2). The full frontal view of the vessel ex-

hibits three panels to be illustrated. Each of the three divergent forms represent the Rayed Face Mythical Figure. It might be noted that an element as simple as a bounding line may be thought relatively unimportant to the draftsman, but this feature becomes significant in at least two areas. First, it is vital to the definition of negative space, and to decisions made by the original artist about which features are to be included in the design. In other words, the border limits what will fit into the design area. Negative space, the amount of it that exists and how it sets off the adjacent design or form, matters greatly in the balance of a completed work of art. Secondly, it is a way of designating the completeness of a figure. This can have implications for later interpretations of certain assigned meanings attributed to the vessel.

The Nasca Collared Jar exhibits an interesting use of border bands (Figure 8-3). The upper panel terminates on either end with curved lines and with open space. The upper panel is interrupted by a modeled face protruding from the vessel itself. The curved line is the hair line of this modeled face. It appears on the hidden reverse side of the view here shown. The broken line at the uppermost boundary represents the top edge of the jar. Middle and lower panels are bordered entirely in black bands. In fact, each panel is in possession of its own border bands. Since none of these black bands are shared, each is represented in the drawing as a complete individual unit. The black bands are in turn separated by another distinguishing band of color. Because the reverse side of the pot contains a modeled head plus related design, the three Rayed Face Mythical Figures are not repeated on that side, nor do they continue all around the vessel.

Several approaches are best combined to decipher the rules followed by the original artist. Analysis of the sequence of decoration by which the artist proceeded serves to bring the archaeological draftsman closer to an understanding of the painting process. If this is done, a more faithful rendering of the original slip painting will be possible. Since the black slip outline was brushed onto our example, it is useful to identify where the stroke was begun and where it lifted off the vessel surface. If the progression of design construction can be determined, style and nuance will become more approachable in a reconstructed drawing.

When black outlining paint is used it is difficult to see overlapping paint strokes. The beginning and ending of the paint stroke also indicates direction. Use of a hand held or stand supported magnifying glass throughout the entire drawing may be necessary. This is especially true until the draftsman becomes accustomed to seeing certain subtleties. Even then periodic checks through magnification is helpful. Understanding the original slip painting will speed up the process of "reading" the original, and ultimately make the drawing procedure more efficient.

DISTORTIONS

A design that wraps around a three dimensional vessel can never be the same on a two-dimensional piece of paper. Simulation of what the viewer perceives can be represented on paper, but distortion of some sort is inevitable. A decision will have to be made about where that distortion will take place. This problem is not unique to ceramic illustration, as a glance at any Mercator projection will show.

If a drawing is to depict the complete design with the correct proportion of positive design to negative space (background) sustained throughout, and with the design expressed as one entire unbroken unit, the drawing cannot be split up or shown in separated sections. A sectional format may be useful for certain other purposes. In this discussion representing the entire design as one unit is the goal. Negative space, the property that defines positive space or the design itself, is maintained in proper proportion throughout the drawing.

Our goal is to balance the entire drawing and yet to unroll the design and transfer it to a flat piece of paper. Minute distortions are eventually distributed throughout the entire design by any conversion of three dimensions to two: certain regions of the design are expanded while other areas are pulled together. That which is closest to the viewer might be the equator if you were looking at the globe. The small spot will be the place of least distortion. Adjustments to the design will increase when moving to the left or right of the viewer's stance. Adjustment will also be made when moving to

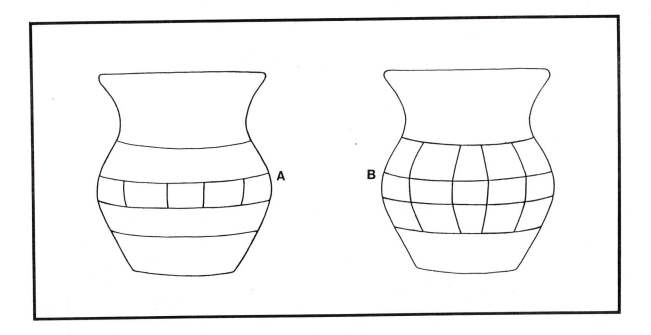

Figure 8-4: Tracing on curved surfaces presents many recording problems, but these can be overcome through cutting the tracing paper or film to fit the vessel being drawn. A: A band of tracing paper cut and fit around the vessel's equator begins the preparation for tracing. B: Additional bands above and below the first are then added so as to incorporate all decorated areas of the exterior.

the top or lower regions of this curved surface. Somehow this must all be unified and pulled together; thus, the design as a whole arches upward on the flat paper instead of encircling the rounded ceramic vessel.

MAPPING THE VESSEL

The simplest way to address this problem is to start with the area of design at the "equator" or the elevation closest to the viewer's eye. Cut shapes of paper that fit this area (Figure 8-4a). Work outward from that central area, cutting and adding adjacent small sections of paper to continue tracing. The form that these small sections of paper will take is determined by the shape of the pot. These may be rectangular sections within the "equator" zone. Pie-shaped sections may be preferred as they are fitted to the upper and lower regions of the pot (Figure 8-4b). It is preferable not to decide on their shape until it is seen how best the paper forms to the pot.

Here it is important to be aware of two matters. First, any tape stuck to the pot holding the paper in place stands a good chance of removing paint with it when pulled off the vessel. Therefore, as difficult as it may seem, with practice one can learn to hold the paper with one hand and draw with the other. Second, be aware of slipping while tracing. The "holding" hand may move unnoticed, thereby altering the traced form without the draftsman knowing this has happened. Continuous checking to see that everything is lined up properly is a necessity. Plastic forceps are the best answer to the problem of holding the paper in place on the pot. These can be clamped to the top open area of the pot, securing the paper in place.

FIRST UNDERDRAWING

The next step is to move from the three-dimensional vessel to the flat, two-dimensional surface of paper. The sequence of

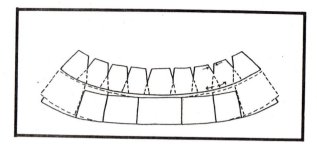

Figure 8-5: Appearance of contiguous strips of assembled tracing paper indicating the nature of line expansion and contraction so as to avoid the "notching" that accompanies Mercator-type projections. A: Lines contracted; B: Lines expanded.

production outlined by Dillon (this volume) is generally followed. Carefully lay out the sections of paper on a flat surface to assemble the design. It will be seen that these pieces of paper do not exactly fit together edge to edge. Certain pieces overlap and at the other end they leave a gap. To preserve positive-negative spatial relationships and at the same time see the entire design, certain alterations are made. In the lower region, the drawing is carefully and minutely expanded, forming an overall arc shape to the design. Near the upper regions, slight contractions are made (Figure 8-5). Alteration of the positive space (design) must be made in proportion to alteration of negative space (background). So it is important to keep in mind the aim of reconstructing slip painting, which is to maintain the original artist's design of negative and positive space.

SECOND UNDERDRAWING

The entire drawing must now be gone over to clarify every detail. This may be done on the first "sectional" drawing if it is made up of relatively few divisions. A new sheet of paper may have to be placed over the "sectional" drawing, however, to complete a clean and clearly drawn reproduction. These are taped together to prevent movement. It is important to draw on the inner side of the line rather than directly on it, or worse yet, on the outside

of the line. This would expand the size of all shapes. Carefully check every area of the original design and proceed to make a new drawing, being true to all detail of shape and line. To capture finishing detail, it may be necessary to hold the paper against the design once again to examine a shape. With practice this can be done with the eye alone, rechecking the design periodically for correct form.

INKING THE FINAL DRAWING

Use a light table to ink the final drawing. Adhere drafting film, vellum paper, or mylar with one side being a matte finish, to the underdrawing. If the latter is used, the drawing should be on the matte side. Dust the paper lightly with a nonabrasive dry cleaning pad. Using a fine point, outline the brush strokes to capture the exact shape. Fill in areas of the brush stroke with a larger pen point. Outlined forms of black may also be filled in with a wider point. Leave other forms open since they may need to be color-coded later on.

Colors can now be represented in the contained forms by designated shading conventions. These are often a series of parallel lines. The wider spaced lines indicate light colors that gradate to denser lines representing darker colors. Always include a key for these colors.

CONCLUSION

Every new ceramic illustrating job presents different problems which may cause the archaeological draftsman either to draw upon his or her stock of experience, canvass the literature for examples, or to experiment with a variety of previously untried techniques. Many such techniques may have to be discarded until a solution is finally arrived at. Throughout every exercise in ceramic illustration, the single most important consideration to be kept in mind is the ultimate destination of the drawing. Three or four days spent on a careful and exact water color reproduction of a polychrome vessel will be wasted if that effort is reduced through half-tones so as to be included in a volume illustrated solely in black and white: more importantly, a line drawing would have been more appropriate in the first place. Exact replication of very small details such as cutaways or tiny modelled appliques may not reproduce if the original drawing is reduced to too small a size in order to fit a page of text. In this situation it is better to show fine detail as a partial view at 100% size or larger in addition to the overall view of the vessel or sherd involved.

The important thing to remember is that for every problem situation in archaeological illustrating there is a simple and straightforward solution; the difficult part is for the draftsman to decide which solution is the most appropriate for the requirements of the job at hand. As more and more new challenges in ceramic illustrating are met and overcome, the store of practical knowledge will increase, so that problems are more easily and rapidly solved as time goes on.

CHAPTER 9: CERAMIC FIGURINES

Jane Becker

1 cm.

CERAMIC FIGURINES

Jane Becker

As in other fields of illustration, reconstruction artistry makes certain technical demands on the draftsman. Additionally, it requires sensitivity to differences in style among individual works of ancient art. Sometimes these differences are conspicuous; sometimes they are subtle. In either case, they are likely to matter to the larger enterprise of archaeology. The reconstruction artist must therefore be able to identify the special aesthetic character of each object he or she reproduces and to highlight that individuality in completed images so that the intention of the original artist is communicated.

Novice draftsmen sometimes illustrate artifacts by using a similar style for objects from many different periods and locations. Often the result is failure to capture distinguishing characteristics of original works of art. The reconstruction artist is aware of the uniqueness of each object in itself as well as its relation to the style or styles from which it emerged. The responsibility of the reconstruction artist is to express an image that is faithful to the physical features and aesthetic qualities of the original object. At another level, the reconstruction artist seeks to communicate the vision of the ancient artist.

PREPARATION: STUDYING THE SOURCE

Close examination of the work of a fine artist in figurine and pottery reconstruction, that of Antonio Tejeda F., is instructive (see his drawings in R. E. Smith 1955). Tejeda is aware of the most inconspicuous features of Mayan art. He executes drawings with a stipple technique, using a fine ink pen to effect form and shape. This technique is especially suitable for illustrating figurines since it makes possible very delicate shading.

There is, however, much more to Tejeda than technique. His work is proof that it is easier to reconstruct artifacts whose style has become visually familiar to the illustrator and whose archaeological significance is understood. The draftsman will find that some study of the culture that produced the object being illustrated is necessary. For example, the reconstruction artist may need to know what is archaeologically significant in an object that might otherwise remain totally obscure; such knowledge obviously may make the difference between capturing the style of an artifact or missing it entirely.

In an instance of the kind just discussed, the illustrator would do well to consult with an archaeologist about the particular object under study. It is useful to become familiar with the entire range of aesthetic variation extending across different periods and locations in the parent culture. Cycles of history often produce rather diverse alterations in style. Changes in geographical location for a group of people can bring about stylistic variation. Other changes in style may occur from site to site within a given location. Certain characteristics may appear in one creative center but rarely, if at all, elsewhere. Clearly, then, study of a wide range of figurines and other art forms incorporating human and sometimes animal forms will help the draftsman become familiar with the style under examination.

INITIAL STAGE OF RECONSTRUCTION: EXAMINING THE ARTIFACT

Before making the first drawing marks, the draftsman should become intimately familiar with physical and stylistic properties of the object to be illustrated. It is worthwhile attempting to understand the intentions of the original work. The figurine carries an expression in face and body stand that should be reflected in the drawing. Among other particulars, the illustrator can observe whether the figurines is able to impart a feeling of line and movement. For the reconstruction artist, knowing such details in advance aids speed and accuracy in drawing.

STYLE

There are many aspects of detail to consider in attempting to "see" an object completely. Any artifact employing the human figure is likely to have individual character of its own. The figurine may be delicate in appearance, or it may appear massive even though actually constructed on a small scale. Larger volumes created by the torso, arms, or legs of the figurine may be prominent, giving the object a heavy, almost monumental bearing. Definition of this nature should be assessed and translated to the drawing. It is one problem to reproduce an accurately-measured figurine and another to prepare a drawing that evokes the character expressed by the original object.

The draftsman can look for several features that may sharpen perception of line, expression, and style in the original. For example, one's first impressions of figurines are often of stance and movement. Energy and movement are suggested through the distribution of weight. Certain parts of the body may receive the weight of the figure distributing the forms in a particular direction. Angle and line conduct a sense of movement as the eye

Figure 9-1: Drawing a complete figurine is no less demanding a task than rendering a large sculpture. Individual peculiarities should be trial sketched prior to their combination into the finished drawing.

follows the path of a fold in the garment or a swing of an arm, or the glitter of ornament as it progresses across the chest.

ELEMENTS OF EXPRESSION

The draftsman may wish to search for prominent forms and dominating shapes - e.g., a smooth area of the face or the rounded form of a leg or torso - that communicate the overall expression of the figurine. Some of the more massive areas on the object may sustain medium light reflection; others may be highlighted by deep shadows. Certain forms may give rise to a variety of light-reflecting effects. The shapes of noses, eyes, mouths, and incised line work may be especially distinctive. In studying the object for its overall expression, the draftsman should consider whether it exhibits soft, flowing lines (which can produce a relaxed, contemplative appearance) or recurring, grooved lines (which can give a feeling of contained energy and ferocity). Certain dramatic peculiarities of the object - for example, an elongated look to the head and torso or the squashed and wrinkled look of an old man - are more easily seen. The draftsman must realize all of these contributions to expression in the illustration.

From larger and more dominating themes in the figure, the draftsman can move to specific details of the object. These can be examined carefully in advance because even though they may be minute in size they will certainly affect adjacent forms. Thus, the illustrator must search for delicate lines that shape the eyes, nostrils, mouth, facial wrinkles, or other finely incised areas. The slightest curve at the end of a line can change the expression entirely. If the draftsman is aware of line and form that contribute to the total expression, an effective drawing is possible.

THE "INCOMPLETE" ARTIFACT

Erosion is a special problem in reconstruction artistry. When eroded areas are found on an object - e.g., lines that disappear into smoothly worn surfaces or forms that are slightly worn away - thorough familiarity with the style of the object will aid in its reconstruction. The illustrator should resist the tendency to complete shapes with lines that seem to be logical. This requires following the line or shape of what is being drawn with meticulous attention. Caution should be taken not to begin imaginatively filling in what might have been, unless the aim of the illustration is actually to reconstruct a missing area of the figurine.

PROJECTION

To speed up the process of illustration, it is helpful to use an opaque projector. The projected image quickly establishes proportion. It does not exempt the illustrator

from drawing directly from the figurine. Projection requires a photograph or slide of the ceramic figurine, in which the piece has been positioned as it will stand for later drawing. Sometimes the object is drawn from a direct frontal view. A more interesting vantage point may be to position the figure in a semi-oblique manner (a slight turn from frontal exposure) which provides a view of the side showing more shape to the nose, arm, and leg positioning, as well as clothing detail.

The figurine should be photographed at fairly close range. Some experimentation with photographing objects and establishing resulting sizes of the images will be useful in later projecting the images onto drawing paper. When the photograph is projected, the image can be adjusted through the projector to 1:1, 3:2, or 2:1 of the original size (or to whatever scale is desired). Some experimentation with the opaque projector or slide projector will be needed until its capacity for correctly sizing the photographic image is known. The image is projected on vellum paper securely fastened to a wall or other stable surface. At this point the desired measurement to scale should be known so that the exact size can be measured off on the projected image on the drawing paper.

PRELIMINARY VELLUM DRAWING

The draftsman will then begin a careful pencil drawing of the projected figure. The best place to start drawing is the outline of the entire form. The next step is to draw a section at a time, beginning with the area inside the head and then progressing down the length of the figure. In each section, draw the main forms such as lips, nose, eyes, headpiece, and ornaments. Then block out shadows and highlighted areas. Continue with the remaining part of the figure in the same way. When the initial drawing is completed, check for areas that might have been missed. It is difficult to see pencil lines with the projected image still on the paper. The initial drawing will look rather crude. In fact, it will be simply a rough drawing to determine the proportion of forms within the object. This entire ini-

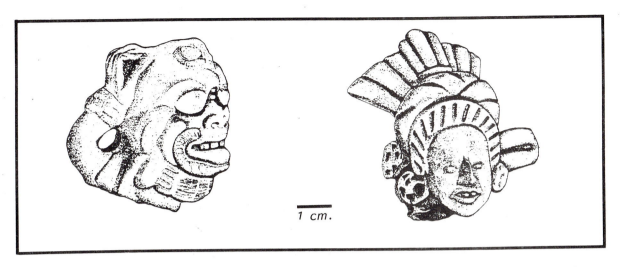

1 cm.

Figure 9-2: Most figurines will be encountered in fragmentary form. Frequently the greatest amount of attention by the original artist is devoted to the head, and consequently the archaeological illustrator should do likewise. Eroded ceramic figurine heads photograph poorly in most cases, and drawings bring out detail that might otherwise be lost.

tial drawing eventually may be erased as the figurine is carefully drawn in its final stage on vellum. This illustration will be the underdrawing on which the final inked drawing will be made.

If an overhead projector is not available, the draftsman can accomplish the same transferral of proportions and scale by using a grid. First, a grid is made on the photograph either by drawing grid lines directly on the photo or by taping black thread to it (Porter, this volume). Then the desired scale of your drawing needs to be determined: if it is to be the same size as the photo, the grid on your drawing paper (transparent vellum or mylar) is the same also; if the drawing is to be larger or smaller, the grid on the drawing paper should be concomitantly enlarged or reduced. For example, if you want the drawing to be twice as large as the photographic image, the lines on the paper should be spaced twice as far apart and the drawing surface itself twice as large as the photograph. The next step depends upon whether the drawing is to be the same size as the photo or larger or smaller. If photographic image and drawing are to be the same size the next step is a tracing.

Place your drawing sheet with its grid over the photograph, preferably using a light table, and trace the general outline and major features. The grid here is helpful only for determining where to draw lines that cannot be easily seen in the tracing process. In the latter case, however, with an enlargement or reduction, the grid is an all-important tool since a direct tracing cannot be made. The procedure is as follows: with the gridded photograph placed where it can be carefully followed, choose a square on the photo and copy those general outlines onto the counterpart square on the drawing sheet, using the bounding lines of the grid as a guide for placement. When you have completed the lines for that particular square, you should have a close, proportionally correct copy of that portion of the photo. Repeat this for all squares in the grid. The result should be similar to that produced by enlargement or reduction via projection: a rather crude underdrawing upon which the final ink drawing is to be made.

If for some reason you are unable to work from a photograph it is possible to build a grid and place it in front of the figurine itself. This is done with small pieces of balsa wood glued together in a frame. Strings are notched into the side of the wood frame to form a grid. The whole arrangement of figurine and grid is put on a platform at eye level. Being careful to keep yourself, that is, your eyes, in exactly the same spot at all times, the figurine is drawn block by block, just as the photo is copied in the process described above. Because of the difficulty in maintaining the same visual vantage point at all times, this procedure should only be followed as a last resort.

POSITIONING

The figurine is positioned exactly as it stands in the photograph. From this point on, all drawing is done from the actual figurine, and the photograph is no longer used. Place a sheet of paper under the figurine. (If the figurine is broken, any kind of prop such as small pieces of wood can be used to hold it firmly in place.) Mark the location of the figurine (and any props) on the paper. If the object is nudged out of position, the mark will help relocate the original stance.

LIGHTING

Lighting must remain constant throughout the process of drawing from the figure. Although natural light gives truest color and probably is best for viewing the artifact, it cannot be used while drawing directly from the figure because it changes hourly. Daylight causes shadows to move across the figurine, making forms within the figure change shape constantly. A good source of light is a movable-arm desk lamp with a 40- to 60-watt bulb or a tensor lamp. Such a source provides strong enough light to permit clear vision, and yet it does not produce light so strong as to obliterate fine lines. Glaring light that is very bright can dissolve fine carving in the figurine. Position the source of light to create the clearest view of the figurine, allowing not too much shadow but retaining some for definition and contrast. Shadows help give shape to all forms within the figure, as do highlighted areas.

After illumination and position of

the figurine have been established, a careful pencil drawing is begun on erasable vellum paper. Again, begin by line-drawing the outside of the figure. Follow the contours very carefully. Then work in sections on the face, arms, torso, legs, and other parts in some sort of progressive order.

DRAWING FROM THE FIGURINE

While actually drawing, it is important for the draftsman to look constantly at the figurine. More details will be seen with continual, intensive examination. As the drawing takes place, stylistic features, curves, shapes, indentations, and certain incised lines will emerge that have not been seen before. This happens because not every nuance is seen until the drawing actually takes place. This means that during the process of drawing, the draftsman will find it useful to examine the surface of the figurine almost as if touching every tiny incised area and form. The importance of continual eye contact cannot be emphasized too greatly. It can make the difference between a sensitive and an inadequate reconstruction of any artifact.

FINAL DRAWING

Place drafting film over the underdrawing and secure it with tape. Trace the outer lines of the figurine with an ink pen. Then work down through the inside of the drawing. Within each section, begin by shading in the main areas in stipple work. For the finest results, it is best to avoid actually drawing more than a few lines. Softer and more realistic definition can almost always be achieved by using stippling in place of actual line. Use of lines may be appropriate when indicating a separate, disconnected piece of clay that has been attached to the main form (a necklace or other added decoration).

The draftsman must be aware of the texture of the artifact's surface. This should be expressed subtly so as not to overcome other features of the object. Variations in depth of carved and incised areas must be handled delicately. There can be a tendency for the novice draftsman to bear down too heavily on the ink. Shadows can become deep valleys, lines great gulleys, and textures grotesque landscapes. Discretion in using the pen will give the drawing a chance to become something like the original. Forms with more light reflection need very sparse stippling, or perhaps none at all. A check can be made on the drawing as it progresses by slipping a small piece of white paper between the first pencil drawing and the inked drawing. In this way, one can evaluate the overall texture and shading.

FINAL CHECK

To examine an illustration for completeness, place it at eye level across the room from the viewer. This will reduce the drawing to approximately printing size. It can then be determined whether the drawing appears clear. If reduction is to take place in printing, it is useful to examine the illustration with a reducing lens while it is still on the drawing table. An indication of scale should be placed near the lower margin of the paper. This is demonstrated by drawing a unit of measure that will correspond to the length of a centimeter on the actual artifact.

CONCLUSION

Rendering ceramic figurines is one of the most demanding but rewarding tasks the archaeological illustrator can undertake. All of the problems inherent in reproducing sculpture in the round are also to be found in making drawings of three-dimensional figurines, and while size and portability sometimes make the physical manipulation of the subject matter easy during the illustration process, showing the complex interplay of mass, curvature and volume is still difficult. Because ceramic figurines are often masterworks of art in miniature and, being created of a completely plastic medium, they often lend themselves to amazingly inventive or original exercises in creativity, the archaeological illustrator must be thoroughly conversant with the stylistic context into which they fit. A correctly executed figuring drawing will in many ways reflect the intention of the creators of the subject matter; it will have a life of its own.

CHAPTER 10: STONE ARTIFACTS
Jennifer Corsiglia & Martin D. Rosen

STONE ARTIFACTS

Jennifer Corsiglia & Martin D. Rosen

Stone artifacts, both utilitarian and ornamental, are perhaps the most widespread kind of archaeological evidence in the world. They have the broadest geographical distribution and the longest known history of use. It is a certainty that any archaeologist, if he or she works in the field long enough, will eventually be dealing with and probably illustrating stone tools. At present, there is no known archaeological culture where stone was available that did not in some way make use of it, and for many of the simpler cultures, lithic artifacts are sometimes the only ones that have been preserved for us to study. Previous chapters have dealt with artifact categories usually associated with sedentary cultures or civilizations; here, examples are drawn from one of the best known hunting and gathering culture areas in the New world, prehistoric California. Mastering the illustration of lithic artifacts from this area will enable the student to draw artifacts from palaeolithic Europe, Oldowan Africa, or prehistoric Australia with equal success.

This chapter is not a "cookbook" for drawing every different kind of stone artifact, for it is up to each illustrator to develop his or her recipes for what works best in specific application. We would like to point out that the techniques discussed are not necessarily the "only" or "right" examples, only those which have worked best for us. Two principles, nevertheless, guide all stone artifact illustration, and these are equally important for any kind of archaeological rendering: practice, and a familiarity with previous conventions of depiction. The former is self explanatory, and no text can take the place of patient trial and error. The latter is obtained through a literature review for the geographical area of analysis and a consideration of how others have drawn similar kinds of artifacts, which attributes are illustrated, and which efforts are successful as opposed to which are not. It is especially instructive to compare illustrations with their corresponding text description to see if the writer and the artist (if these are different) are communicating or even dealing with the same thing.

The simplest idea in stone artifact illustration is perhaps the hardest to conceptualize. Every archaeological site report deals primarily with the artifactual remains recovered, and for clarity of presentation and ease of comparison the assemblage is grouped into functional and/or stylistic categories. Each separate category is then described and illustrated so as to provide an inclusive definition of the group and account for variation within it. The importance of proper description and illustration of the differences between and within artifact categories is paramount, for it is only through this process that the archaeological site can be located in time and space by the direct comparative method.

FORMAL CHARACTERISTICS OF STONE ARTIFACTS

Before proceeding with a discussion of the methods by which stone artifacts are illustrated, it is necessary to define the types of artifacts considered in this section and to place the objectives of stone artifact illustration within the context of formal archaeological reporting. The objects dealt with here are in every case portable. Both utilitarian and "aesthetic" lithic artifacts are produced through similar processes and differ most greatly through presumed function. Production techniques are in every case reductive, and include chipping (pressure or percussion), pecking, grinding, pounding, perforating or polishing (Crabtree 1972, discusses such methods of stone tool production).

"Utilitarian" refers to those objects which served as tools in the maintenance of daily subsistence activities such as the procurement of food, water and other raw materials. Such artifacts may not have been modified prior to use, and might only be changed from their natural state through attrition due to wear resulting from use as tools. If the artifact has wear resulting from use, it is this wear or intentional modification which is important and which the archaeological illustrator depict. "Aesthetic" artifacts are associated with cultural activities not necessarily involved directly with subsistence, and in their simplest form include such objects as beads, pendants, pipes, wand-mounted crystals, and incised stones.

Hunting-gathering societies usually practiced a modified form of seasonal transhumance. Habitation areas would change during the year to enable the population to take advantage of a wide array of food resources ripening over the landscape, and this adaptation is reflected in the nature of the artifacts encountered. Smaller tools were generally carried from place to place, while larger objects would be stored at the seasonal camp to be used when needed.

Illustrations of stone artifacts should attempt to convey a diverse range of information, including (but not necessarily limited to) the material used, production techniques, usewear, and formal style of the finished product. The draw-

ing can serve as graphic evidence for a specific theoretical, technological, or sociological argument, or as a "type" or member of a typological scheme.

CHIPPED STONE

All stone artifacts are produced according to a series of manufacturing stages executed in sequence, although their form may be dependent upon whether they were taken through the entire sequence. The models developed by Collins (1975) and Bradley (1975) assume that flint knapping was not a haphazard art, but rather was a well disciplined technological process. The stages involved include: (1) the acquisition of the raw materials; (2) core preparation and initial reduction; (3) (optional) primary trimming; (4) (optional) secondary trimming and shaping; and (5) (optional) maintenance/modification. "Each of these steps is composed of one or more activity sets and each activity set results in a product group of chipped or ground stone artifact. An activity set may include one or more specific activities and each product group (except the first) consists of two kinds of materials: waste by-products and objects destined for further reduction or for use" (Collins 1975:17). Product groups can be technologically described and inferences made regarding the activities employed to produce the particular manufacturing process.

Step 1: Core preparation and initial reduction. The next step after acquisition is initial reduction of the raw material. This stage can occur at the quarry or raw material source or at some other site. This aspect of lithic reduction deals primarily with chipped stone artifacts. The resulting artifacts would include cores and byproducts such as large numbers of decortication flakes. Since cortex was generally not viewed as a good working surface, its presence on lithic artifacts is important to illustrate.

Step 2: Primary trimming. Once the reduced cores or usable flakes are brought into the site they are thinned and prepared for tool production. Step 2 trimming can occur at any number of locations. Resulting artifacts are larger secondary flakes, blanks, preforms, simple retouched flakes or rejects, and debitage.

Step 3: Secondary trimming and shaping. At this step in tool production preforms are generally worked into their final forms. The resulting assemblage would include finished tools and broken (unfinished) tools, and debitage of thinning flakes and pressure flakes.

Step 4: Optional maintenance and modification. Included in this stage are implements which have been used, broken, reworked and reused. Also included in this assemblage are small trimming flakes as debitage.

The artifact illustration should convey the method in which an artifact was made. It should be evident from the illustration if a stone tool was made by pressure or percussion flaking, or both.

GROUND STONE

An illustration of a grinding implement should indicate how many surfaces of the stone were modified through use, and this might provide information on the motor habits of the tool-user as well, e.g., whether the grinding surfaces of manos and metates were produced through circular, push-pull or side-to-side motions. If this information can be conveyed through an artifact illustration, it will impart more of a realistic idea of the true nature of the object than will dozens of pages of written description.

The surface of ground stone artifacts should be rendered so that the type of material can be determined. Grinding implements tend to be made from materials that are coarse-grained, and the individual stone crystals are usually visible to the naked eye in sandstones, granites, porphyries, and some basalts. A drawing

should exhibit the granular surface appearance of these materials and should indicate how they differ in texture form those used for chipped stone artifacts. For this reason, dots or a stippling technique is generally preferable. Chipped stone artifacts tend to be made from a crystalline or "glassy" substance such as obsidian, crypto-crystalline silicates, fused shale, and fine-grained volcanics, all of which have an extremely smooth appearance after fracturing. In these instances, line work tends to convey a smoother surface and imparts to the observer a better notion of an object's material and method of construction.

Stone artifact illustrations should not be "decorative" for the sake of aesthetic appeal, but neither should they be distorted. It should be kept in mind that simple drawings which communicate well are preferable to elaborate and time-consuming drawings which convey no more relevant information. One should conceptualize an illustration of a lithic implement much like a graph or a chart; its function is to graphically represent an object which can also be described verbally, but more efficiently and conveniently as a drawing.

Anatomical and biological illustration utilizes the illustrator's knowledge gained through previous study. Consequently, it relies on a synthesis of many different details for the illustration of a typical specimen. For example, a drawing of a kidney in a standard anatomy text may not be a specific kidney from a single individual exhibiting the characteristics peculiar to it alone, but rather may be a synthesis of the illustrator's conception of a typical kidney. The archaeological illustrator, conversely, must make accurate and precise "visual comparisons between actual specimens" (Piggot and Hope-Taylor 1965:169) otherwise, falsification of evidence will result. He or she is generally concerned with the individual characteristics that set each artifact apart from all others and render it important or useful for comparative purposes. Only an eye accustomed to the category of evidence being illustrated can decide which features

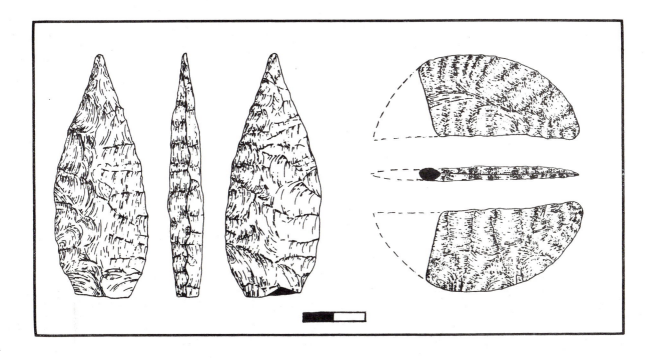

Figure 10-1: Chipped stone artifact illustration utilizing parallel and concentric line shading and limited stippling to indicate facets. Left: projectile point; right: crescent. Note standard convention of illustrating three views (dorsal, ventral, lateral). The glossy surface texture of the material is represented by the fine-line shading.

are necessary versus those that are unimportant and confusing and which should therefore be deleted.

CONVENTIONS OF ILLUSTRATION

The basic division between coarse and fine-grained stone previously noted will directly influence the drawing technique used. Coarse-grained stones common to grinding implements require heavy stipple work (Frontispiece), while chipped stone artifacts tend to have a much smoother surface with well-defined ridges which can be shown by lines (Figure 10-1) as long as the contours and ridges are simple. To avoid confusing many series of lines on a complex piece, fine stippling can be used with care in order to show the ridges and valleys, overall contour, and the smooth or rough texture of the stone, as in Figure 10-2. However, Figure 10-1 does suggest to the viewer a smooth-surfaced material like obsidian, chert or chalcedony, while

Figure 10-2 suggests a grainier material like tuff, rhyolite or andesite.

One should keep in mind the medium of reproduction the illustrations will go through before being published. While preparing camera-ready artwork it is important to know at what scale the objects will be reproduced. The drawing should be labelled accordingly, i.e., "all drawings 100% size," "50% actual size," and so on. Reduced drawings sometimes tend to crowd line work together, but at the same time line thickness is also reduced. Greater contrast between light and dark is needed if the drawing is to be reduced more than 50% so as to assure that the inking does not fade out.

PRELIMINARY PENCIL SKETCH

The initial pencil drawing is more than just an outline, as it locates all the features in proportion to one another within

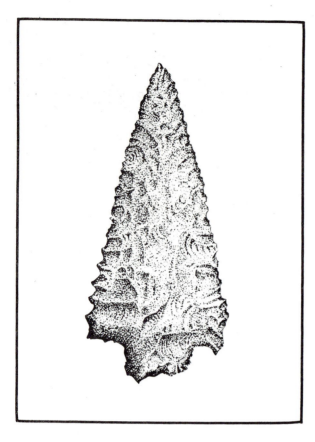

Figure 10-2: Chipped stone artifact illustration utilizing dot-stippling to indicate facets.

the outer borders of the artifact. When its shape is simple, and its size small, an artifact may be placed on the drawing paper and its outline traced directly (Figure 10-3a). Many views, however, will have to be drawn by careful observation, and individual features measured with a ruler and then scaled up or down, depending upon their original size and the size of the final drawing page. Sometimes an artifact may be so intricate that it will have to be drawn one or two times larger than its actual size to allow for a more accurate execution of detail. The normal method of reduction or enlargment using a superimposed grid should be followed here and size changes plotted with the aid of a scaled rule.

SHADING AND FORM

The object to be drawn should be placed

directly in front of the illustrator above the drawing surface. A high intensity light is then directed across the artifact from top left to bottom right, raking it at approximately a 45 degree angle. The light will highlight the object contours and indicate where shading will be necessary, the intensity of the shading and the gradations across the surface of the artifact. The goal is to create a still-life portrait of an artifact under artificial lighting conditions. The direction of light is by standard of convention for technical illustrations, and should be consistent throughout all drawings.

Shading in stone artifact illustration produces the appearance of three-dimensional form on a two-dimensional surface. It can consist of either lines or stippling; texture is suggested in the same manner. As the reproduction of minute details in these drawings is often very important, care must be taken so that shading does not interfere with depiction of detail. Lines or dots should not be spaced so closely together that they merge into a solid dark mass if the illustration is reduced. Different tone values on chipped stone artifacts can be expressed in standard fashion by use of a graduated shading scale (Figure 10-4c) and the different values of dark and light reflected by the separate facets can be plotted after observation on a hypothetical cross-section (Figures 10-4a and b). Shading the artifact in its entirety is accomplished by dividing up all visible facets into specific shading categories and then shading neighboring facets either progressively lighter or darker (Figures 10-4b and c).

Cross-sectional characteristic of certain objects can be used as guides for shading. In artifacts with triangular cross-sections, the plan view will have two main facets and a longitudinal ridge separating them, like the biface illustrations in Figures 10-3a to f. In such situations, the artifact can be divided into right and left halves. The upper left edge, or that portion of the artifact closest to the light source, may not have any shading whatsoever, other than those lines which highlight features (flake scars). As the cen-

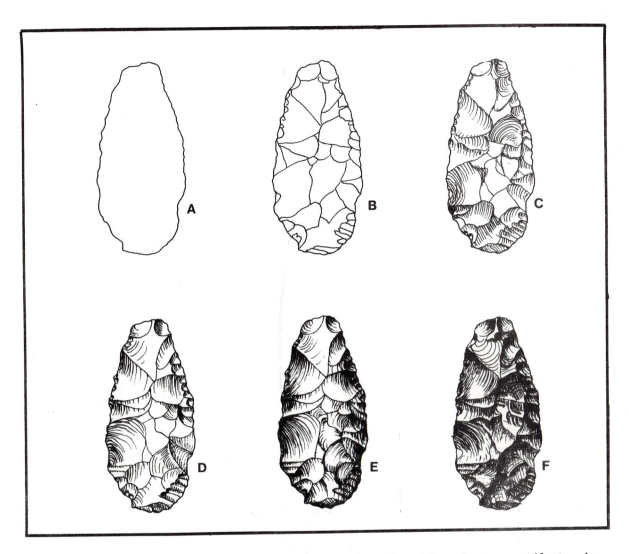

Figure 10-3: Sequential steps in the illustration of a chipped stone artifact. A: inked outline of one side; B: facet boundaries indicated with inked lines; C: trial shading of facets, showing the attempt to set off each neighboring facet through a slightly different shading direction or intensity; D: alternative experimental shading attempt; E: finished drawing, with each facet distinguished; E: example of "overshading", where detail is obscured and facets merge because of similar shading tones.

tral point of the piece is reached, shading may increase slightly. However, since most of the left side faces the light source at approximately the same angle, this side of the object may require very little shading. The cross-section shows how the right half of the artifact facing away from the light source is in shadow and, consequently, requires considerably more shading. Generally, the shading of this side will become progressively darker toward the lower right edge of the piece.

Projectile points are usually illustrated and shaded with lines for clarity, and the curvilinear scars or striations that denote the removal of small flakes during production or use are best shown through line shading that follows the contours or margins of the scars themselves. Figures

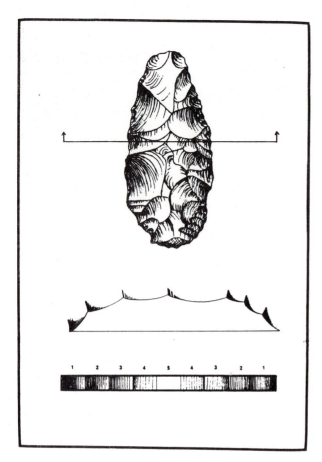

Figure 10-4: Determination of shading values in chipped stone artifact illustration. A hypothetical cross-section of the artifact's surface (A) along the horizontal axis can be analogized (B) into a series of facets of different darknesses. Each facet can then be coded (C) according to a different shading value from 1 (darkest) to 5 (lightest) for ease in inking. Each facet may also be identified by number in non-photo blue pencil prior to inking.

10-3a through 10-3e illustrate the sequential steps in preparing a drawing of a projectile point, from preliminary tracing through to final shading.

The first drawing in the series is simply an exact rendering of the artifact's outlines. This can be made either through direct tracing, use of a 100% scale photograph, or other method. The second in the series locates the ridges between all flake scars which combine to produce the different facets on the piece. The third, fourth and fifth of the series show increasing intensities of shading from light to dark, and culminate in an example that not only appears three-dimensional, but which displays each flake scar clearly and from which the direction of removal can be determined.

In the sixth and final version (Figure 10-3f), we demonstrate how the features of the artifact can be obscured by overuse of line and solid shading, and how the feeling of three-dimensionality might be lost. When using the line technique, never use more lines than minimum necessary to impart information to the viewer. Superfluous shading only confuses the situation and make interpretation of the drawing much more difficult. As shown briefly in these biface illustrations, an important convention in chipped stone illustration is to have the shading line touch the leading facet of the piece, but not the trailing facet. Other examples of this technique can be seen in Frison and Bradley (1980), Kobayashi (1975), Oakley (1972), Semenov (1964) and Tixier (1974).

While it is not necessary to draw everything the eye can see, an accurate and complete picture of the artifact results from careful observation, and what is represented as the final illustration must resemble the original artifact. Light, form and texture are as important as overall contour, and a simple outline drawing is simply not sufficient for the purposes of information communication.

DEFECTIVE DRAWINGS

Figures 10-5a through 10-5g offer a number of examples of bad drawings similar to those that periodically insinuate themselves into the pages of even the most respectable journals. Each is in and of itself an exercise in futility as none provides much visible information about the artifact, or actually misleads the viewer. Drawings such as these can only detract

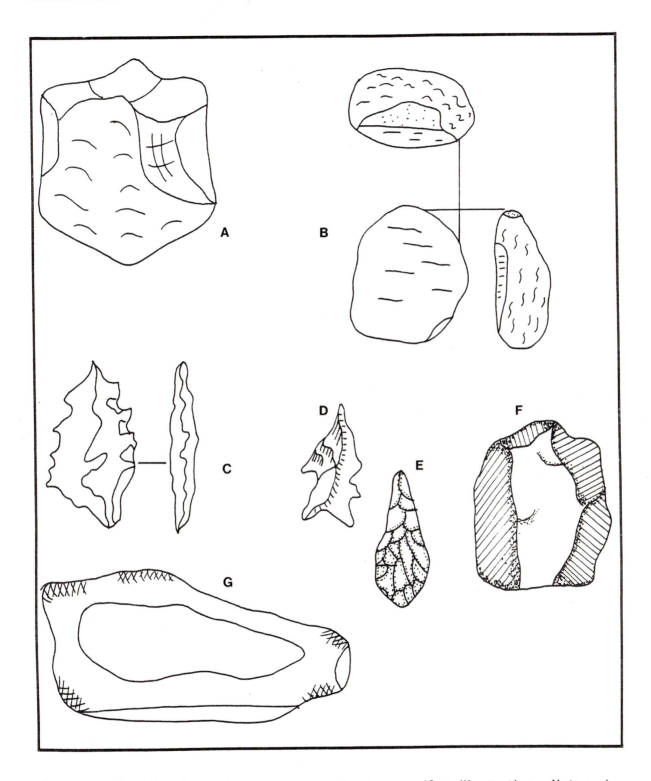

Figure 10-5: Miscellany of common errors in stone artifact illustration. Note uniformity of line in all examples, unconvincing shading attempts, poor positioning on page, and poor proximity of artifact drawings to borders.

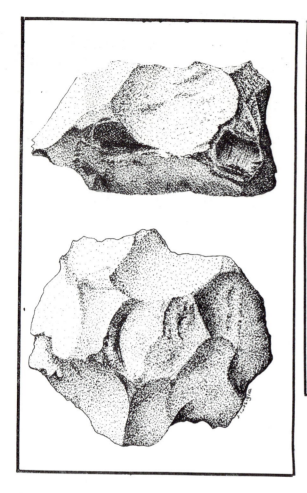

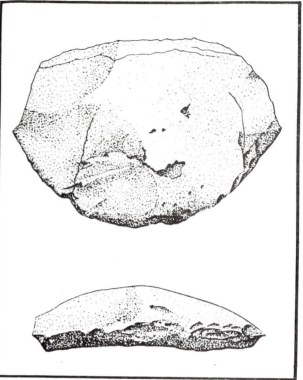

Figure 10-7: Even the simplest kind of stone artifact can be effectively drawn so as to illustrate function. Battering along the edge of this large flake identifies it as a hammerstone.

Figure 10-6: The same general rules governing shading for small, chipped stone artifacts also apply to larger specimens. It is easy to see where flakes have been struck from this core by virtue of shading differences.

from an otherwise worthwhile effort, and do nothing to complement the text. With substantial use of imagination, Figure 10-5a might be seen as a scraper, 10-5b as a trifacial mano, 10-5c and 10-5e as chipped-stone bifaces, 10-5d as a uniface, 10-5f as a core and 10-5g as a metate. In no case does shading indicate anything like three dimensionality, nor is there very good control of line width or direction. The lines, dots and "squiggles" seen in 10-5b are confusing, not recognizable as any kind of standard shading, and nothing concrete is being communicated about the surface texture of the artifact. Figure 10-5c attempts, but fails, at being a two-dimensional contour drawing, and neither 10-5d nor 10-5e have values to indicate form and the shading attempted is inconsistent, leaving us to wonder if the flake scars are concave or convex. In 10-5f and 10-5g, we are not given any clues as to whether the lines and cross-hatching indicate raised, depressed, abraded or shadowed areas.

Figures 10-6 and 10-7 illustrate the point that simply because artifacts are of crude or careless manufacture, they need not be illustrated crudely or carelessly. Cobble/core tools and lightly modified scrapers can be illustrated so that we can immediately visualize the functions that they might have served, and obtain clues

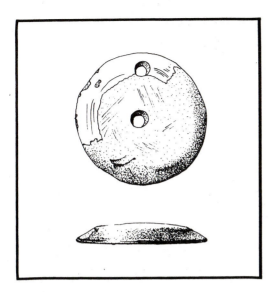

Figure 10-8: In shading ground stone artifacts tones must change gradually and are not set off by lines demarking facets. Note how the stippling on the lower edge of the disk indicates the bevelling, which is understood to also exist under the white pigment at top.

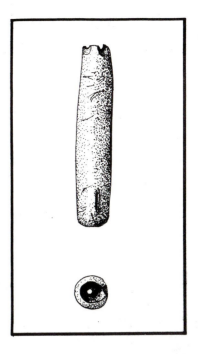

Figure 10-9: Tubular artifacts need not be shown with multiple views unless some design or damage is deemed important. An end view (below) is useful in that it shows the conical nature of the perforation.

as to their manufacture; 10-6 is a core from which flakes have been struck, and 10-7 is a scraper. Note how in both examples the outlines of the artifact are lined in darkly, and major ridges lined lightly, but how each separate facet has been stippled for constant value. Figures 10-8 and 10-9 make use of stippling to indicate the normal rounding of ground stone beads, and line to indicate incisions on the polished surface. The unstippled, upper areas on the flat disk bead indicates white paint added to the outer margin, while the very lightly stippled central area on the tubular bead suggests only the area of greatest highlight.

Chipped stone artifacts should be drawn in architectural perspective, i.e., illustrating three views of the piece. A truly three-dimensional perspective is gained in this fashion while communicating to the observer a maximum of archaeological information about the artifact. While the more usual practice is to provide two views, as in Figures 10-6 to 10-9, an object may be so complex or have so many worked surfaces that three views will be necessary to impart these data to the reader.

CONCLUSION

It cannot be emphasized too strongly that practice is the best instructor. The preceeding discussion recounts ideas and methods by which we have done stone artifact illustration over ten years, and we are still learning new methods and solutions to problems of rendering all the time. The novice lithic illustrator should not expect to be able to perfectly replicate stone tools on paper at the first attempt or even overnight. However, there is no reason why the diligent student cannot attain a high degree of proficiency fairly rapidly through practice and hard work.

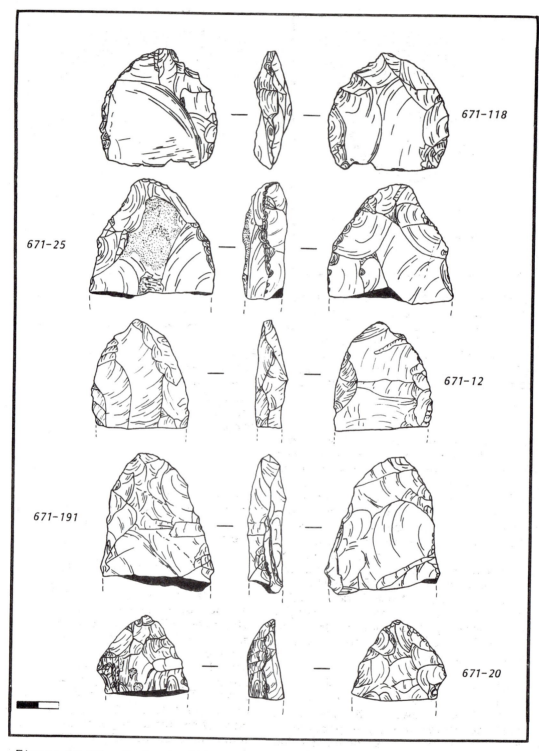

671–118

671–25

671–12

671–191

671–20

Figure 10-10: A standard presentation of chipped stone artifacts may involve multiple artifact drawings on any given page. Here five different biface preforms from the same site are shown in dorsal, ventral, and lateral view. Note stippling to indicate cortex.

CHAPTER 11: BURIAL ILLUSTRATION

Brian D. Dillon and John W. Verano

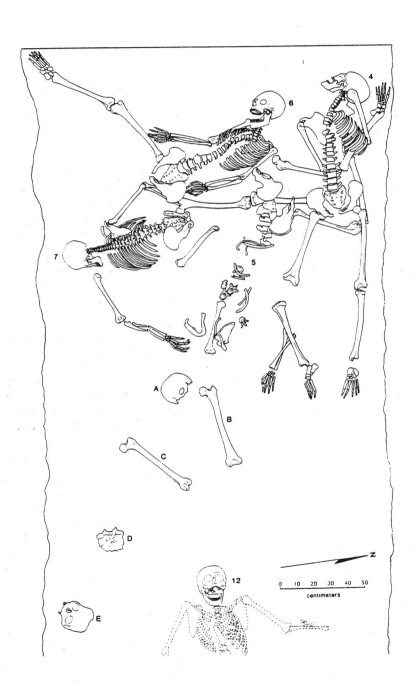

BURIAL ILLUSTRATION

Brian D. Dillon and John W. Verano

If we consider archaeology a humanistic discipline served by scientific methods, then few aspects of research into the past are as rewarding as excavating the remains of human beings themselves. Burial data are often our best evidence for the emotional, religious, and intellectual life of ancient peoples; conclusions about such cultural characteristics may sometimes be inferred but very seldom explained without them. Burials also provide information about what might be called "universal" human concerns or those that are or were important to all human cultures living or dead. These can be demographic, medical, or socio-political in nature and include birth and death rates, life-expectancy health patterns and the incidence of disease, even direct evidence of violence and war.

Of all the kinds of archaeological features which can be excavated worldwide, human burials are the most common. Every human being that ever lived was possessed of a skeleton, and all human populations are, in the eyes of the osteo-archaeologist, also skeletal populations. Depending upon the method of disposal and the degree of preservation, most if not all human populations have left some skeletal trace which can be studied archaeologically.

Regardless of whether he or she is working with hunters and gatherers, agriculturalists, or urban dwellers, any archaeologist who does fieldwork long enough at some time in his career will have to expose and record human skeletal remains. Between the two of us we have excavated or assisted in the excavation of approximately 250 human burials; some of our elder associates estimate they have personally exposed as many as 2,500 to 3,000.

If skeletal information is one of the most basic categories of archaeological evidence, it nevertheless is also one of the most complex and time-consuming to record. Certainly, laboratory renderings of bones owe as much to conventions of depiction in the biological and forensic sciences (Staniland 1953; Zweifel 1961) as they do to archaeological sources. We do not suggest that laboratory recording be done exclusively with drawings, for in the lab all aspects of light, shadow and subject can be controlled. Spectacular results here can be achieved through photography (especially in paleopathological research) that could probably never be equalled through line drawing. Provided the bones survive excavation and the trip to the laboratory, it is much more efficient in terms of time to use photography as a method of recording.

We see little or no conflict between the two recording techniques, for one is most appropriate to field archaeology (burials and burial excavation) while the other is essential for laboratory research (osteology). Accordingly, we find it most interesting to note that two of the most

CHAPTER 11: BURIAL ILLUSTRATION

Brian D. Dillon and John W. Verano

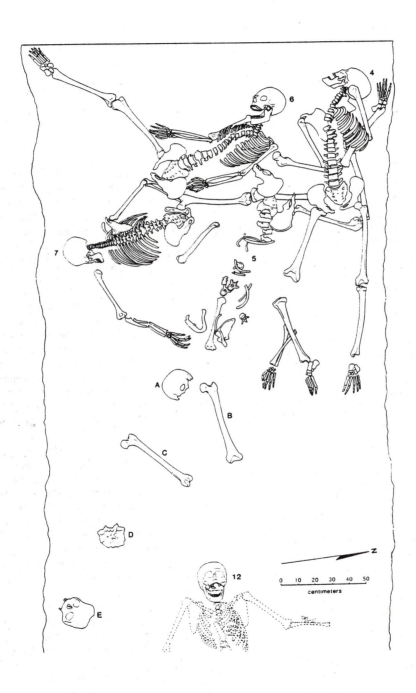

BURIAL ILLUSTRATION

Brian D. Dillon and John W. Verano

If we consider archaeology a humanistic discipline served by scientific methods, then few aspects of research into the past are as rewarding as excavating the remains of human beings themselves. Burial data are often our best evidence for the emotional, religious, and intellectual life of ancient peoples; conclusions about such cultural characteristics may sometimes be inferred but very seldom explained without them. Burials also provide information about what might be called "universal" human concerns or those that are or were important to all human cultures living or dead. These can be demographic, medical, or socio-political in nature and include birth and death rates, life-expectancy health patterns and the incidence of disease, even direct evidence of violence and war.

Of all the kinds of archaeological features which can be excavated worldwide, human burials are the most common. Every human being that ever lived was possessed of a skeleton, and all human populations are, in the eyes of the osteo-archaeologist, also skeletal populations. Depending upon the method of disposal and the degree of preservation, most if not all human populations have left some skeletal trace which can be studied archaeologically.

Regardless of whether he or she is working with hunters and gatherers, agriculturalists, or urban dwellers, any archaeologist who does fieldwork long enough at some time in his career will have to expose and record human skeletal remains. Between the two of us we have excavated or assisted in the excavation of approximately 250 human burials; some of our elder associates estimate they have personally exposed as many as 2,500 to 3,000.

If skeletal information is one of the most basic categories of archaeological evidence, it nevertheless is also one of the most complex and time-consuming to record. Certainly, laboratory renderings of bones owe as much to conventions of depiction in the biological and forensic sciences (Staniland 1953; Zweifel 1961) as they do to archaeological sources. We do not suggest that laboratory recording be done exclusively with drawings, for in the lab all aspects of light, shadow and subject can be controlled. Spectacular results here can be achieved through photography (especially in paleopathological research) that could probably never be equalled through line drawing. Provided the bones survive excavation and the trip to the laboratory, it is much more efficient in terms of time to use photography as a method of recording.

We see little or no conflict between the two recording techniques, for one is most appropriate to field archaeology (burials and burial excavation) while the other is essential for laboratory research (osteology). Accordingly, we find it most interesting to note that two of the most commonly-used English-language textbooks on human osteology (Bass 1971; Brothwell 1972) both employ drawings almost to the exclusion of photographs. Although both are essentially laboratory manuals, the latter includes a section on "Photographing Bones in the Field" (ibid: 7). Yet, despite the excellence of the drawings both books contain, neither explains practical techniques of burial illustration.

The present chapter is offered because there appears to be no detailed, step-by-step exposition of burial drawing techniques readily accessible to the student. Our writing does not attempt to cover every possible burial situation nor to resolve all problems that can arise during the recording and rendering process. Rather, we hope to provide examples and suggestions so that the beginning student can feel confident of accurate results when beginning his or her first burial drawing.

BURIAL PHOTOGRAPHY AND BURIAL ILLUSTRATION

The field situation presents very different kinds of limitations and demands upon the recorder than does the laboratory, and despite some noteworthy contributions (Combes 1964) it is remarkable how little has been published on drafting burial illustrations in the field. The question might be asked, should archaeologists draw burials, or is photography equal to all or most recording requirements? As Collins (1975: 175 paraphrasing Newman and Riddell) states: "Sketches and photographs may seem to duplicate each other but no one can be certain of the quality of a photograph until it is developed and printed". We can attest to the advisability of using both recording methods, for after the close of a recent field season, both project cameras and over 40 rolls of exposed film with documentation of over 30 burials were stolen. If field sketches had not been made, no formal, graphic recordings of these burials would have remained. On the other hand, if burial photographs survive and are found to be objectively correct (see Webb 1946, for exemplary burial exposure, cleaning, and photography) draw-

ings can improve little upon photographic representation and will consume more project time than would really be justified.

While it is essential that human burials, whenever possible, be photographed in situ, some specific limitations of this recording method should be evaluated against drawing. Film, particularly black and white, often cannot distinguish between the soil matrix and the bones themselves, especially if the latter have taken on the color of the former, or disintegration has progressed to the point where only "ghosts" of the bones can be detected. Without adequate contrast of color or texture, only gray tones indistinguishable from each other may be recorded on the negative.

Many burials cannot be photographed because of space or lighting limitations. Burials encountered in tunneling excavations, for example, often can only be viewed from their head or feet, and adequate elevation cannot be obtained for complete coverage on film. Even when a wide-angle lens (35 mm or smaller) allows for burial photography in cramped quarters, distortion often occurs with foreshortening, expansion, and even curvature of some bones depending upon their position and the "fisheye" effect of the lens.

In other cases so many non-essential elements exist to distract the eye that a photograph will reveal more about non-skeletal elements than it will about the osteological material itself. Drawings, on the other hand, allow the archaeologist to "edit out" tree roots that may have penetrated a skeleton's chest cavity and to render less conspicuous gravel or soil of a similar color value as the bones it may be adjacent to (Figure 11-1).

Despite the caveats noted above, when accessibility is not a problem, bone preservation has been good, and the contrast between the bones and their surroundings is clear, photographs should always be attempted. In some cases, these can form the basis for later drawings (see Christensen, this volume). High-quality photographs taken from vertical platforms

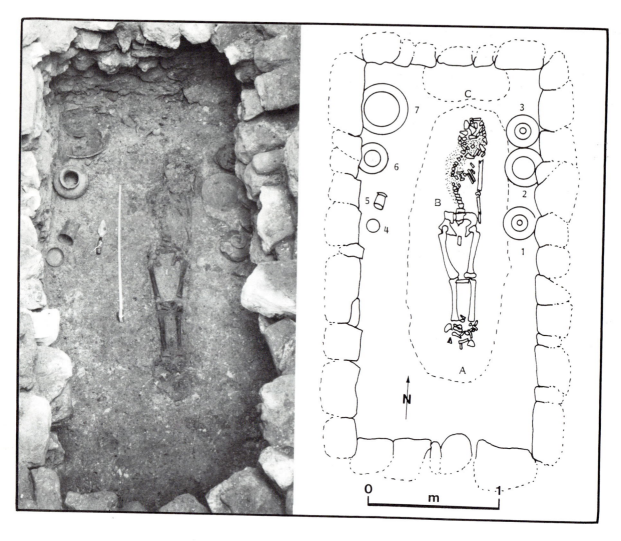

Figure 11-1: The best of both worlds in burial recording, photographs and line drawings side-by-side. Because in many human skeletons excavated in tropical contexts (such as this one) the bones may be in extremely poor condition, a line drawing can often show what a photograph cannot. In photo, tape extended to 1 meter, trowel points north. Note missing bones revealed in drawing not immediately apparent from photograph.

can be enlarged to a standard scale so that drawings of very great accuracy can be made from them: Burial photographs at 20% of natural size have been found to be an excellent working size for the production of finished pen and ink illustrations at the Pacatnamu project of coastal Peru. It should be noted that this system is most successful when the prints are developed in the field, so that the drawings made from them can be compared directly with field maps and notes.

Any representational ambiguities that may have slipped by the illustrator can be corrected through direct reference to the skeletons themselves or through consultation with the project physical anthropologist.

BURIAL DRAWINGS:
SUCCESSFUL AND UNSUCCESSFUL

Anatomical knowledge does not imply good drawing ability, nor does skill at field

Figure 11-2: Calavera cartoon by Jose Guadalupe Posada, ca. 1910. Just as stick figures are not acceptable in skeletal illustration for scientific purposes, neither are generalized cartoons.

Most incorrect illustrations contain errors or oversights which derive from a limited number of problems. These tend to reflect either a lack of anatomical knowledge or attempts to rush matters so that a "shorthand approach" submerges precise details under a kind of symbolic or "part for whole" representation of the skeleton. The important point here is that burial illustrations for archaeological purposes must be scientifically accurate, and simplified or "cartoon" versions cannot by definition be so. Efforts in which "stick figures" are used to indicate burial situations are suitable for rough field notes but should never be offered as final presentations of evidence. Nor should attenuated, abstracted sketches of burials be considered as valid substitutes for carefully measured field drawings. The brilliant early 20th century woodcuts of Posada (Figure 11-2), for example, unmistakably use human skeletons as their subject matter and are completely successful artistic ventures, but were never meant as scientific representations of specific cases. Cartoon representations do have their place, but not in archaeological recording.

Mistakes in measurement or in drafting can create an erroneous impression of the physical characteristics or peculiarities of specific individuals or even of entire populations. Bones drawn too thick might be interpreted as pathological, those too thin as evidence of an extremely gracile body type. Bones missing from a drawing because the draftsman either forgot to include them or found them too hard to draw constitute misrepresentations of evidence and indicate pathological conditions to the objective viewer that do not really exist. Secondary burials are common at many archaeological sites and often are characterized either by missing bones or by impossible articulations occurring from redeposition: evidence for both is somewhat elusive and can often be overlooked. The burial illustrator should not jump to conclusions about "what should be there" but should draw only what can be observed.

A very common error in drafting develops when field measurements are not

drafting necessarily indicate familiarity with the 206 bones of the human skeleton. The ideal combination on any project is, of course, an experienced physical anthropologist who is also a talented draftsman and photographer. In the short term, if such an individual cannot be found, it is preferable to have the best or most accurate illustrator do the most complex work regardless of anatomical training, for details can be corrected through consultation with an osteologist even if the latter cannot draw a straight line. In the long term, however, each student should try to master not only basic human anatomy but illustration skills as well.

taken frequently enough and freehand sketching is substituted for careful re-checking. This can result in inconsistent proportions used for different parts of the skeleton and general distortion. Often the cranium is too large for the post-cranial skeleton, or the feet and hands are too small. The objective observer in such cases might conclude that parts from several different skeletons had been reassembled into a single one, or that severe physical deformity had characterized the individual during life.

Another problem is that of selective attention to specific parts of the skeleton and corresponding inattention to others. Regardless of whether the cranium seems more worthy of study than the postcranial skeleton, both must be depicted with equal accuracy. It sometimes seems that as one works out from the larger, more easily distinguishable (and, often, more complete-ly preserved) bones, less and less attention is devoted to accurate drafting. This is most commonly seen in "shorthand" renderings of phalanges, which often are shown not as individual finger or toe bones but as a kind of inky smear or a blur. Here it is impossible to determine if the corpse had a full complement of fingers and toes or, alternatively, was a polydac-tile or was missing digits.

It is not enough to simply record all bones present, for they must also be re-corded in their specific orientations as dis-covered. Because the body is basically symmetrical, some field recorders presume that if half the illustration job is done correctly, the other half can "mirror" the first part drawn. This may be true for in-dividuals who were healthy in life, but is not if traumatic damage or pathological conditions are present. This is because such afflictions are not usually found in bilaterally symmetrical fashion and must be searched for and recorded on a bone-by-bone basis. Another common problem is that of left and right-handed reversals, which can result in extremities being shown in incorrect positions. These occur where the draftsman, working face-to-face with a basically bilaterally symmetrical skeleton reverses it (left to right instead

of right to left).

Other problems involve anatomical impossibilities, such as where too many bones (or not enough) are shown. Verte-bra, perhaps because there are so many of them and they are so often poorly pre-served, are very frequently misrepre-sented. Many examples can be found of drawings of individuals with only five or six vertebra between occiput and sacrum; perhaps more common are cases in which too many combine to make too long a spinal column. Here, instead of the stan-dard 24 vertebra, 26, 28 or even 30 are shown. Or, freehand drawing allows for a kind of standardized abstraction to creep into the drawing so that the vertebral column ends up looking like a tall stack of peanuts still in their shells. Detailed mapping and careful measurement, label-ing, and constant re-checking against master inventory lists are nowhere more important than in complex situations such as where multiple disarticulated burials (e.g. ossuaries) or cremations are found. In cases such as these it is essential to have a physical anthropologist present who can identify isolated bones or bone frag-ments if the draftsman cannot.

Fortunately, good burial drawings tend to outnumber bad ones by a large margin and numerous examples might be used profitably as models by student ar-chaeologists regardless of their vintage. Donnan and Mackey (1978) provide ex-emplary burial illustrations from coastal Peruvian contexts that should inspire beginners. Earlier this century, abundant work went into shading burial illustrations either through parallel lines or dot stip-pling. Quite impressive examples of the former technique are provided by Lothrop's (1937) Cocle report and have seldom been equalled and perhaps never excelled in New World contexts. Such drawings con-stitute some of the most attractive fea-tures of this landmark study and not only complement the text but provide an en-tirely independent body of evidence that can be much more rapidly assimilated (with captions) than many pages of text.

While some archaeologists at the

present time continue to use elaborate shading for burial illustrations (outstanding drawings in Pendergast 1982, for example, are works of art themselves) the more common trend during recent years is toward unelaborated fine-line drawings which depend more upon precise, understated recording (Smith 1972) than artistic convention or afterthought. Shading can conceal a multitude of errors in burial illustration, and the beginning archaeological draftsman should not presume that unclear aspects of the skeleton undergoing study can be hidden through stippling or cross-hatching. Fine line illustrating requires the clearest possible expression of osteological knowledge yet is relatively rapid; consequently it probably is the best method.

PREPARATION

Valuable experience can be gained by practicing with an articulated laboratory specimen, not only in terms of learning the names of the various bones, but also how they should appear under the most favorable conditions of preservation. The laboratory skeleton can be positioned in a set number of standard poses and drawn in the lab before one goes to the field. Such practice is very important because the number and nature of the distractions involved in day-to-day fieldwork severely limit one's ability to learn not only the parts of the skeleton but how to draw it as well. Working with a laboratory skeleton will be particularly useful for recognizing incorrect articulations in secondary burials; lab specimens are wired so that all articulations are generally correct in most positions unlike some cases the archaeological illustrator may encounter in secondary interments.

Anatomical situations perceived as impossible by a draftsman who only has his or her own body to refer to can sometimes be resolved through posing a fellow student or workman in a living reconstruction of how the burial is thought to have been positioned. If it is unclear how the feet would have appeared after rigor had set in with, for example, a tightly flexed corpse with knees touching but ankles crossed, a mental reconstruction may be entirely in-

correct while visual examination of a living subject will consume only seconds. Peculiar or unique burial positions may be reconstructed in graphic form either through analogies with living models (Agrinier 1978: 12) or with iconographic examples from the same site or area (Dillon 1982).

FIELD PROCEDURES

In the field, associations between bones and artifacts must be recorded before they are altered or basic evidence will be destroyed. The most important rule for rendering burials in the field is sometimes ignored despite being self-evident: the illustration should be made only after the burial has been fully exposed, yet before any bone is moved from its original context of discovery.

Only those bones actually present should be drawn, and any missing bones or portions of bones should be noted in writing as well as left off the drawing. Alternatively, a standard photocopy of the human skeleton may be "filled in" so as to indicate which bones are present/absent, and this should be attached to the burial notes so that no confusion exists later. If this is done, months after fieldwork has been concluded no-one can query "is this a finished drawing or not?".

Hand and foot bones should not be shown if not physically discovered through excavation. Missing finger and toe bones are a common problem in burial excavation since these portions of the body often disintegrate first or are gnawed off by scavenging animals if the corpse is left unburied for any period of time. Fingers in some cultures are occasionally amputated pre- and post-mortem; consequently it cannot be presumed a priori that the absence of phalanges in excavation contexts is always explicable through differential preservation (Dillon, Brunker and Pope, 1985).

Heizer and Graham (1967: 115) suggest that burial drawings should be made from one position only, for perspective and orientation of individual bones will change depending upon the angle of view. It is always best for the burial illustrator to orient himself or herself comfortably in a position where as much of the burial being drawn can be seen. If the skeleton is at the bottom of a pit, planks can sometimes be laid over it and the draftsman can lie or sit directly over the bones. More commonly, the illustrator must sit at one edge of an excavation unit and consequently his or her view of the burial is somewhat distorted; nevertheless, the advantage of elevation is still maintained. In large area excavations accompanying cemetery exposures, a large number of burials may be encountered at the same level and the draftsman may find it difficult to get much elevation above them. In such situations, it may be necessary to climb a tree or a ladder periodically so as to obtain correct vertical perspective even though the drawing is being made literally "at the feet" of the skeletons.

The most time-consuming part of burial illustration is not the drafting itself but measuring the distance and direction of the constituent bones from one or more datum or reference points. The only method by which burial illustration can proceed is through teamwork; the draftsman will not get anything down on paper if he or she is always getting up to check measurements or to move the meter-tape around. Consequently, an assistant whose task is to take all measurements and call them out is an absolute necessity.

Measuring should always begin with metrical data taken from standard landmarks on the skeleton, and all measurements must be taken in relation to datum points or lines. With the measurer guiding the illustrator (or vice versa), the maximum horizontal limits of the skeleton are mapped first. Then the top of the skull, the top of the pelvis, and the farthest extensions of both hands and both feet are measured and transferred to graph paper.

Eventually, all major joints will be plotted, so that as the drawing progresses the long bones will be drawn in from their proximal and distal ends, those ribs pre-served will be drawn from the backbone out to their terminal points, and so forth and so on. Once the most crucial metrical data have been recorded, general characteristics can be filled in through with constant checking and rechecking. It is always preferable to completely finish a burial drawing in the presence of that burial so that the final product can be checked for accuracy against the skeleton itself. Nevertheless, time constraints (usually the availability of sunlight) sometimes prevent this. A useful shortcut is to take a very clear Polaroid exposure of the burial so that many of the more easily drawn elements can be rendered later at night once the most important landmarks have been measured and plotted.

Because many dozens of measurements are necessary in order to illustrate a single burial, any method by which these can be simplified will increase the chances for accuracy and allow more work to be completed. The simplest method is for the archaeologist to lay intersecting and perpendicular meter tapes below and to the side of the burial and then measure up and out from them until the bones are reached, or to scribe measured lines in the soil surrounding the burial if only one tape is available.

The best method of creating standard points of reference to measure against (as well as to orient the drawing itself) is to string guidelines (Joukowsky 1980: 193) along north-south and east-west axes above the burial. The intersection of these two axes becomes the primary datum from which the distance and direction of all bones are determined. An improvement on this system is to affix a 360 degree compass arc with its center at the baseline intersections and attach a tape to that intersection as well. The person measuring the burial simply holds a plumbline above the skeletal landmark to be recorded and then measures with the tape to the vertical line; distance as well as direction from the burial datum is provided in one easy action, and these data can be quickly plotted on graph paper by the illustrator.

Some archaeologists prefer to use a portable grid made by stringing wires or brightly colored twine between eyehooks on a square wooden frame. Most grids are a meter square and the individual internal divisions 10 cm square. Because most burials are larger than this, it will be necessary to reposition the grid at least once, and some possibility of error is consequently introduced. This can be prevented by aligning the end of the grid closest to the remaining portion of the burial beyond its coverage to a strung line and then flipping the grid over so that the strung line that formed, for example, the northern limit of the grid now describes is southern limit. An alternative is to "tailor-make" a grid more specific to burial recording. This would best be 1 by 2 meters, and as such would incorporate most extended burials and probably all flexed ones. Disadvantages, of course, are increased weight and clumsiness. If successive seasons are to be spent at a given location or if many dozens or hundreds of burials are to be recorded, even more elaborate measuring devices might be constructed (Winans and Winans 1982).

When grids are used they should be elevated above burials preferably by corner stakes so that no strings are touching the bones. If the grid with its heavy wooden frame is accidentally kicked off its supports, serious damage to the burial can result, so it is a good idea to drill holes in each corner that can accept pegs driven into the tops of the stakes. The grid squares should be labelled in alphanumeric fashion (letters north to south and numbers east to west) and the graph paper squares coded in identical fashion. If this is done, when the person taking measurements calls out "distal end of left femur, square P-13, 10 cm south, 7 cm west" no confusion about which square the measurement is being taken in will occur.

CASE STUDIES

The beginning student may initially encounter single burials and consequently be faced only with determining how the bones of a single person relate to each other.

Yet it is equally likely that multiple burials or cemetery situations will be confronted. Cemeteries, by definition, are places where human burials are concentrated and where repeated interments are often made over a long period of time. Expectably, two of the most characteristic features of cemeteries are disturbance of early burials by later ones (with burial pits cutting through earlier interments and mixing of bones), and the discovery of individuals with either too many bones or too few. Similar situations occur when a great many individuals are buried simultaneously, most frequently in the context of pandemic desease, mass sacrifice or massacre. Here the problem of chronological position is lessened, but unraveling the precise sequence of events and what happened to each person included in the burial is no less difficult than in cemetery contexts.

The frontispiece shows a portion of a mass burial from Pacatnamu, Peru, that is somewhat typical of such situations. Note that individual number 12's postcranial skeleton is drawn in dashed lines; this is because his body extends into an adjoining excavation unit and is drawn more completely in that corresponding illustration. Isolated bones in the frontispiece are indicated by letters (A through E) because it is not clear to which numbered individual they belong - it is certain, however, that more than one person is involved. In addition to isolated bones, evidence for mutilation or partial dismemberment is found in articulated skeletons 6 and 7, both of which are missing the left leg; an isolated (possibly severed?) left forearm found beneath the right leg of individual number 4 may in fact belong to him, as this extremity is missing. Careful attention to detail allows us not only to identify individual bones, but their orientation as well. It can be seen, for example, that isolated bone B is a left femur lying ventral side up while bone C is a right femur lying dorsal side up.

Extended and simple flexed burials are relatively easy to represent in a two-dimensional illustration. Seated burials, however, present significant problems both

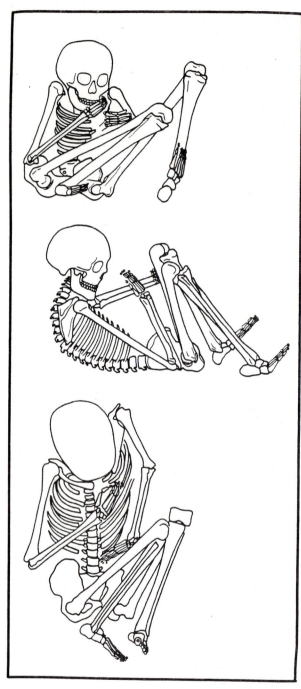

Figure 11-3: Seated burials present a series of drawing problems, and may require multiple views from different angles. Above note front, side, and three-quarter overhead views of the same seated skeleton.

in mapping and in drawing. Because of the complexity of limb position and the superpositioning of skeletal elements when viewed from above, illustrations of seated burials are best done from several different perspectives (Figure 11-3). Field mapping of seated burials and the transfer of information on specific bone positions from the field to the final illustration can be a frustrating process. Here the laboratory skeleton or the plastic model (Combes 1964; Donnan, personal communication) can be used to great advantage if made to approximate the position of the seated burial and referred to constantly while the drawing is being made. Even more useful are photographs made of the model or laboratory skeleton in a variety of poses taken from different angles which can be easily carried to the field and referred to when necessary by the illustrator. These will be much more informative than scrawled notes about bone position or rough sketches of individual articulations.

ILLUSTRATION CONVENTIONS

Burial drawings are usually done in plan or "bird's eye" view, as if the illustrator were on a platform some ten feet above the excavation and able to look down from directly over the center of each skeleton. Because of the nature of the human skeleton and owing to specific kinds of burial practices, which often include flexing of the body, some bones will be obscured or covered by others. These lower bones should never be drawn as if the upper ones were transparent; if they need to be illustrated, sequential drawings taken at various stages of removal should be made. When necessary, side views should also be made in addition to plan views, even though this may entail much more excavation than that required for simple overhead views.

Human skeletons in archaeological sites are often fragmentary and may be very poorly preserved. The archaeological illustrator must decide whether to illustrate poorly preserved burials as if they were complete and intact, or to depict their actual appearance as found. We have experimented with both methods; an

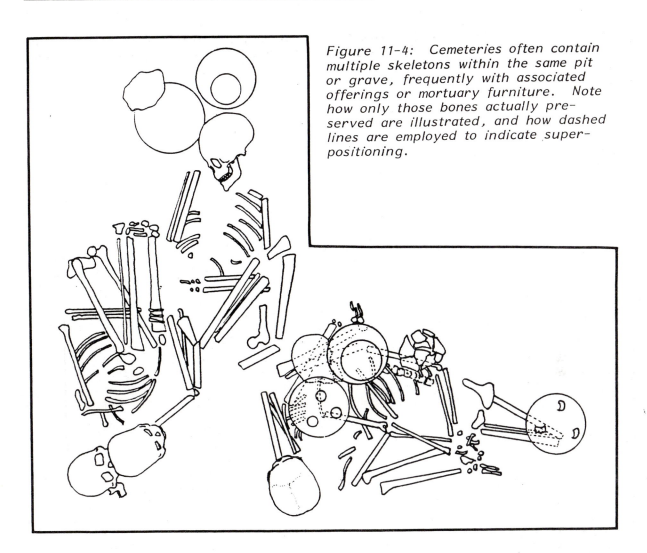

Figure 11-4: Cemeteries often contain multiple skeletons within the same pit or grave, frequently with associated offerings or mortuary furniture. Note how only those bones actually preserved are illustrated, and how dashed lines are employed to indicate superpositioning.

example from Nacascolo, Guanacaste, Costa Rica (Figure 11-4) shows only those bones preserved, and where portions are missing, they are not drawn. It is always better from the standpoint of conveying information to draw burials as if they were complete, that is unless the absence or poor preservation of skeletal parts is believed to reflect some specific cultural activity. Ribs commonly are incompletely preserved, and phalanges, as previously noted, tend to vanish or "wander". The illustration of bones displaced by tree roots, rodents or land crabs, erosion or other naturally disturbing factors sometimes adds too much "noise" to burial illustrations, and sometimes it might be decided to make intelligent reconstructions instead of strictly objective drawings. If this is

done, it should be noted in the accompanying text that such a decision was made.

In most cases only those bones present should be drawn. If specific bones are missing, there is usually a very good natural or cultural reason for their absence and the archaeological illustrator should not take upon himself or herself the option of reconstruction. Where cultural features, artifacts, or offerings obscure parts of burials, these should be drawn in as solid lines, but the bones underneath should be represented as dotted or dashed lines. The same holds true for the opposite situation; where bones cover pottery vessels, grinding slabs, etc., the bones are drawn with solid lines while those portions of the artifacts which are covered are shown dashed. Every burial drawing should always include a north arrow, scale, and indication of the burial pit's outline if present.

Field burial drawings should always be made on graph paper. The paper is normally oriented with its lines running NS vertically and EW horizontally. The baselines strung over the burial as measuring guides are lightly scribed in pencil or photoblue pencil so that constant reference can be made to them. The first thing that is put on the paper is the provenience information: the archaeological site name or number, and the burial number within the site. Next comes the north arrow particular to this burial, and a graphic representation of scale, preferably a scale bar, marked off in 10 cm increments. Finally, the field drawing is always done in pencil and never inked. The ink drawing for publication is traced over the field sketch on graph paper so that two copies exist, one "clean", the other still containing the various notes and comments written down during the course of burial recording.

CONCLUSION

Every archaeology student venturing out into the field should be prepared not only to excavate human burials but to record them from Atlas vertebra to Zygomatic arch. Most instructors will agree that accurately recording a human burial is one of the best training exercises there is for understanding the nature of archaeological associations. The 206 bones of the hu-man body all must articulate correctly in an undisturbed, well preserved burial, otherwise some kind of post-mortem manipulation is indicated. Obviously, those cases in which normal articulation does not occur are more interesting than those in which it does, but it takes basic familiarity with the human skeleton and careful illustrating techniques to recognize and demonstrate the difference. Regardless of how important or unusual any particular human burial is, an accurate drawing of it presents a great deal of information in a easily understandable and rapidly assimilable fashion.

Accurate field recording is the first essential step in producing the finished drawing, and this unfortunately entails many hours of hard work. Dozens of pages of notes, measurements, photos, or standardized "checklists" may be required during field recording to establish the nature and number of bones and articulations present in any given burial. Yet, these can be dispensed with in the final publication if accurate burial drawings have been made. This is because a successful burial drawing reveals at a glance what is present and what is absent, and how it all fits together. We do not suggest that drawings, no matter how exemplary, obviate the need for other forms of recording such as photography, written description, or metrical data. We are convinced, however, that all of these primary means of recording can and should be combined so as to achieve a goal of cumulative scope: illustrations reflecting the application of archaeological science to field data.

CHAPTER 12: SHELL AND BONE ARTIFACTS
Susan M. Hector

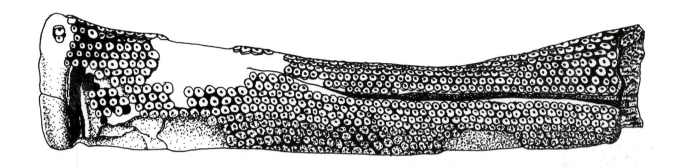

SHELL AND BONE ARTIFACTS

Susan M. Hector

The illustration of shell and bone artifacts requires a combination of the skills of a biologist and an archaeologist. As a biologist, the illustrator must render skeletal remains in anatomical detail. The archaeologist, by contrast, is interested in calling attention to any modifications made in the shell or bone. By integrating these two approaches, it should be possible depict the artifact so that one can determine the type and species of bone or shell as well as place the artifact into a typology or other cultural classification. There are several technical points unique to the illustration of shell and bone artifacts.

1. Profiles of artifacts. Despite the usual rule for other classes of artifacts, in many cases it is not necessary to show the profile of the bone or shell artifact. This is because of the relatively high degree of uniformity between known examples of a single species. If use wear or intentional modification appears on the sides of an artifact, however, this should be noted and a drawing from this view made; otherwise, if the object can be seen plainly and identified from one view, a profile is a needless expenditure of time.

2. Shading techniques. Shading of bone or shell artifacts should be effected through stippling. Cross-hatching or other methods tend to clutter up the illustration and obscure details.

3. Scale of rendition. Most shell artifacts should be drawn at 100 percent of actual size, if not enlarged somewhat, as should most bone artifacts. Only the largest bone artifacts need to be reduced. Therefore drawings to be reproduced at the same size as drawn have to be as precise and blemish-free as possible. All the examples included in this section were rendered at 100 percent size except for one (Figure 12-2c), which was slightly enlarged, and the recording of basic dimensions was facilitated by direct tracing of outlines onto paper.

SHELL ARTIFACTS

Illustrations of shell artifacts should depict two types of information: which species of shell is being used, and the kind of modification made. The shape and size of the shell often dictate the type of modification possible. In ancient California different parts of *Olivella* sp. shell were used to make specific types of beads; the natural shape of the shell was used to formulate these types (i.e., the curve of the lip for "cup" beads, the midsection for "barrel" beads, and so forth). Figure 12-1a is an example that emphasizes the shell species, in this case *Anadara formosa*, originating from a midden site in Okinawa; the shell has been modified slightly by the grinding of its beak. Figures 12-1b and 12-2a are also intended to show the species of shell as well as modifications or alterations of interest to the archaeologist. In Figure 12-1b, a *Conus californicus* from San Nicolas Island (off the southern California coast) is identifiable, while its spire has been removed so as to create a bead; this bead may in turn have

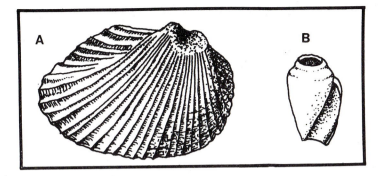

Figure 12-1: An accurate drawing of modified shell should not only allow for species identification but for representation of intentional changes. Note ground bead in A, lopped spire in B.

specific geographical or chronological significance. Figure 12-2a, a *Haliotis* sp. pendant also from San Nicolas Island, shows characteristic abalone shell sculpturing although the piece has been greatly altered. In this case, an end-on profile view was warranted, as it was not possible to establish the thickness of the artifact from only one perspective.

Figures 12-2b through 12-2e concentrate on the exposition of a series of particular artifact types rather than on

shell speciation. The species may or may not have been known, but there are other features more important for the determination of cultural use and typological ordering, and these are given greater attention in the illustrations. Figure 12-2b, a *Haliotis* sp. fishhook from San Nicolas Island, can be identified as abalone, yet the altered morphology of the shell is more important to the archaeological eye. Figures 12-2c through e, from the Medea Creek Village (Ca-LAn-243) demonstrate the use of illustration primarily for typo-

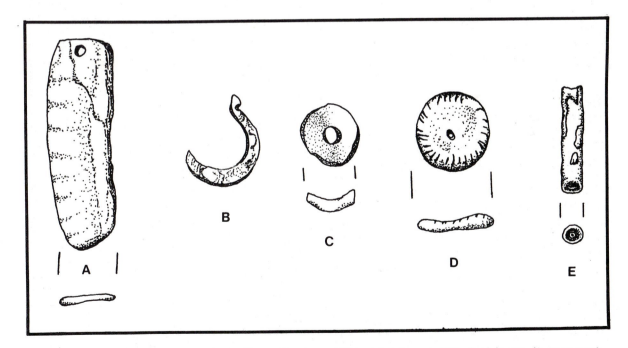

Figure 12-2: Miscellany of shell artifacts. With highly modified objects it may not always be possible to identify the original species, although the pendant (A), and fishhook (B) are of abalone, the enlarged wall bead (C) is of Olivella, the disk bead (D) is of clam, and the long tubular bead (E) is from a bivalve.

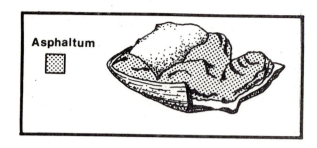

Figure 12-3: A composite shell artifact consisting of two mussel shell fragments cemented together with asphaltum. Note use of transfer shading.

logical purposes. Figure 12-2c is an enlarged *Olivella* sp. "wall and callus" bead and is intended for use in the comparative identification of this type. A profile was added in this case to indicate the thickness and shape from the edge so as to aid comparisons. Both sides of the bead could be illustrated to show the method of perforation (i.e., conical or biconical, or hyperbolic), or this could be done by means of a cross-section.

The shell bead illustrated in Figure 12-2d is so extensively modified that it cannot be identified beyond family classification (*Veneridae* or Venus clams), but the placement and number of incised lines present on the artifact are precisely delineated, which may allow a future student to assign a similar piece more successfully within a known species. In figure 12-2e, an end-on view is an absolute necessity, for the artifact illustrated is actually composed of two bivalve tube beads, one anchored inside the other with asphaltum.

Figure 12-3 is of two *Mytilus* sp. shell fragments attached to each other with asphaltum, deriving from the site Ca-Ven-2, on the southern California coast. In this figure, the utility of standardized transfer shading (Zipatone) is demonstrated to advantage; a key to the left of the artifact indicates native asphaltum used as an adhesive. The key and shading film in this case obviate the need for elaborate ink shading to show different materials in a composite artifact, which is time-consuming and not always productive of clear

results.

BONE ARTIFACTS

The same two dependent goals that govern the illustration of shell artifacts also apply to those of bone: to show which bone was used or possibly which species of animal the bone came from, and to reveal the types of modification the bone was subjected to. When illustrating a bone awl, for example, the archaeologist is most interested in showing the modification of the bone into a sharpened tool, yet the illustrator should pay equal attention to the part of the bone that is left unchanged. If this happens to be an articular end, it is often possible to identify the type of animal, its size, and perhaps even its sex and age. Figures 12-4a through c are bone awls, each similar in modification but from different bones and different animals. Figure 12-4a illustrates an awl from Simomo (Ca-Ven-24; a large coastal village site in southern California), which is identifiable by the clear exposition of the articular end as an *Odocoilus* sp. or deer metapodial. An awl from Medea Creek Village is shown in Figure 12-4b; also from a deer, this tool can be identified as having originally come from a radius. Figure 12-4c, an awl from San Nicolas Island, is made from the humerus of a large sea bird, possibly a pelican.

Figure 12-5a is a pendant from Shemya in the Aleutian Islands and is made from the tooth of a large sea mammal. The illustration conveys not only enough information to allow for a general identification, but also shows the intentional grooving which allowed for either lashing or suspension. Also from Shemya is the toggle harpoon head illustrated in Figure 12-5b, which was made from a sea mammal's rib. Since this bone has been modified to the point at which no identifying details remain, a speciation is not possible, and no attempt has been made to show the surface texture, as this would only clutter the surface and not allow any additional information to be transmitted.

Figure 12-4: Three bone awls from California archaeological sites. A, B: from deer, C: from large sea bird.

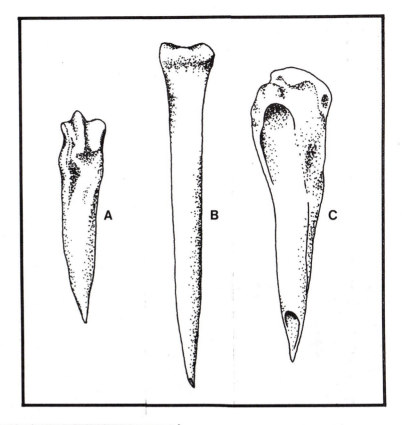

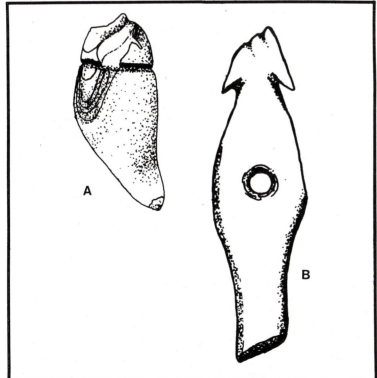

Figure 12-5: Artifacts from the Aleutian Islands. A: Pendant from sea mammal tooth; B: toggle harpoon head from sea mammal rib.

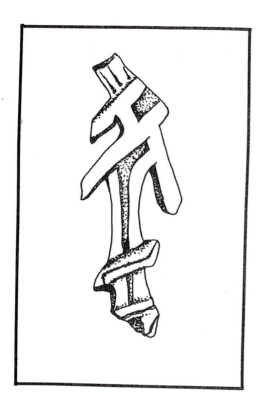

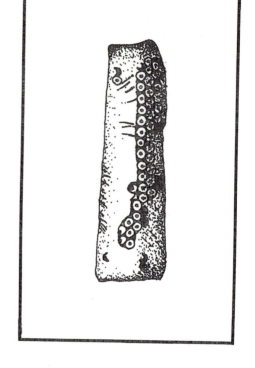

Figure 12-6: Bone pendant from Okinawa, with no portion of the original surface remaining.

Figure 12-7: Bone tube from a California archaeological site. Note the Olivella shell beads cemented over parts of its surface with asphaltum.

The pendant from Okinawa shown in Figure 12-6 has been so highly modified that only a rudimentary guess can be made about the kind of bone from which it was produced, and the primary interest in this illustration is in the precise rendition of the shape and surface configuration of the carved symbol.   The final illustration, Figure 12-7, portrays a compound artifact from the site of Simomo: a tube or flute made from a large sea mammal long bone with *Olivella* sp. beads cemented to it with asphaltum.   The primary interest here is in the piece as an entire composition, rather than as a collection of disparate modified objects that need to be illustrated in precise detail for speciation purposes, and the interrelationship of shell, bone, and asphaltum is shown best without elaborate shading or toning to delineate different materials.

CONCLUSION

In conclusion, satisfactory results can be obtained through simplicity of expression and close attention to details of anatomy and intentional modification, with one being stressed over the other depending on the purposes of the illustration. For typological use, a strict rendition of the human-induced changes is necessary. To show modification and yet clearly indicate the type of bone or the species of animal or shell illustrated, a knowledge of the unmodified structure of the creature is imperative. In either case, a carefully executed drawing should be usable for a variety of purposes, not the least of which is the standard against which newly discovered objects can be compared.

CHAPTER 13: ARCHAEOLOGICAL ILLUSTRATION FROM PHOTOGRAPHS

Wes Christensen

ARCHAEOLOGICAL ILLUSTRATION FROM PHOTOGRAPHS

Wes Christensen

Archaeologists often have only very limited amounts of time to devote to drafting while in the field, yet are often faced with the dilemma of being unable to bring certain kinds of artifacts back to the home laboratory for careful illustration. This is particularly true of non-portable objects such as sculpture and architecture, as it is of artifacts which cannot legally leave the country of origin for further analysis. Making careful drawings from photographs solves both problems, yet it is curious that this method is not more widely employed in archaeological contexts. Possibly, this is because it is very easy to misinterpret a photograph and produce a wildly inaccurate drawing unless correct procedures are followed.

Many otherwise excellent archaeological papers are marred by inept illustrations of artifacts. As subsequent analyses are often based on these initial drawings and, rightly or wrongly, competence in research is sometimes judged by the drawings included in field reports, every effort should be made to produce accurate and professional renderings. This paper is an attempt to demystify the process of producing accurate illustrations of low relief and three dimensional artifacts from photographs. It is not intended for artists but for archaeologists who sometimes freeze up at the thought of any art endeavor.

Mechanical devices which help the draftsman reproduce visual information more exactly have been in use since the Renaissance. The most notable of these devices, the camera obscura, was well developed by the seventeenth century. The device consisted of a darkened chamber with a small opening or lens through which an image was received and then projected onto a facing paper surface; this image could thus be directly traced. The camera obscura facilitated many recording jobs, and broadened the field of draftsmanship. Portable models were used by landscape painters to make quick, accurate sketches outdoors, and were particularly suited to complicated architectural subjects; Canaletto's views of Venice, for example, were produced in this way. The camera obscura was particularly popular with English watercolorists of the nineteenth century and allowed sophisticated amateurs to participate in the landscape vogue (Kelly 1974:74). The most celebrated artist to make use of the device was the Dutchman Johannes Vermeer, whose work achieves an uncanny lifelike quality. His sparkling light, consisting of precisely placed "pointilles," resembles the bright spots in out-of-focus photographs known as "disks of confusion" (Koningsberger 1967:141).

The advent of photography was feared by portrait painters as the ruin of their livelihood and as a danger to art in general. Great realists like Degas, Manet, and Eakins, on the other hand, saw the new invention not as a threat but, like the earlier camera obscura, as a time-saving tool that allowed them to expand their artistic choices. The freedom granted by photography allowed artists to explore the expressive and conceptual innovations that we now know as "modern" art.

"Photorealism", the contemporary art movement, may be instructive for archaeological draftsman. Artists of this school use the photograph itself as their subject matter and translate its information into remarkably illusionistic paintings. Turning away from Romantic notions of the artist's "vision" to an objective aesthetic sense informed in some cases by the philosophy of phenomenology, their work often finds its closest analogy in the records of bank cameras which impartially and honestly translate data without interpretation or emphasis. Richard Martin (Battcock 1975:xxviii), describing these painters, maintains that, "Implicit in the relationship of New Realism (photorealism) to the camera is the passive part played by the camera." Audrey Flack (1981:96) describes the preliminary mechanical process of recording such information as "drawing with the camera." An examination of the working methods of painters such as these can prove useful to the production of scientific illustrations where the artist's style must be subordinated to the artifact itself.

Archaeologists might benefit from studying the work of Chuck Close, whose famous monumental portraits resemble topographic maps in their record of every minute feature of the subject. In more recent graphic work (Figure 13-1), he shows us the underlying structure and how one translates the continuous tonal gradations of the photograph into a graphic medium. Using the standard Kodak photographic gray scale as his vocabulary of 22 shades from black to white, he composed mosaics of these gridded squares "to test the degree of detail necessary to convey the essential information about the (human) face and the original photograph" (Dykes in Battcock 1975:160). This scientific, "just-the-facts-folks" method is precisely the attitude needed for archaeological illustration, where "artistic" improvements are to be avoided. It also provides the beginning illustrator with a mechanical model of creating illusionist effects

Figure 13-1: A mosaic-like collage by Chuck Close of grey-toned squares which shows the structure underlying this photorealist's work and illustrates a way to simplify the kinds of continuous tones present in photographs. (Courtesy of Pace Editions).

needed to make a visual record of his data.

The photograph itself is of primary importance, as are the careful tracings made from it. Figures 13-2 and 13-3 are examples of the "raw material" or photographic starting points for the rendering process. This paper converts the process of illustrating into a step-by-step journey toward the final, camera-ready ink drawing. The following suggestions work for me yet may not for others; in no way are they intended to be the last word on the subject. Their purpose is to relieve artistic anxiety on the part of non-artists and to provide a simple methodological guide that should result in more accurate archaeological renderings.

163

Figure 13-2: Original field photograph of fragmentary, badly eroded sculpture. Note poor contrast, damage from tree-roots and cracking. Stela should be illustrated through a drawing because of poor quality of negative and post-abandonment damage.

PRELIMINARY DRAWINGS

Most defective illustrations result from problems in the first stages of the drawing process. In eagerness to begin the time-consuming process of inking, one is sometimes tempted to shortchange the preliminary tracings. Yet, this initial process of accurately tracing not only the outlines and prominent features of the artifact but the limits of the half-tone shaded areas can often determine the final drawing's overall quality.

After choosing the photographic print or slide that shows the archaeological subject in the clearest detail, a first step could be to do a fast pencil drawing on tracing paper, sketching in the basic outlines and shadows (Figure 13-4). This helps to familiarize the draftsman with the basic planes and overall shape. For this task I use a 314 Berol draughting pencil, which is quite soft, and arrive at shadows by a combination of smearing the drawing with the hand or a pointed paper "stump," and area highlights with a kneaded eraser. This drawing can be used as a control for shaded areas once inking begins. It is, however, only an optional step before careful tracing begins.

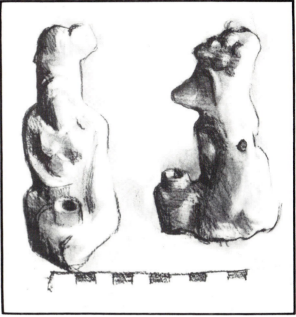

Figure 13-3: Nearly identical pair of figurines cast from the same mold. Poor contrast, eroded and abraded surfaces obscure details of headdress, anthropomorphized face, fan and brazier.

Figure 13-4: Trial drawing of the two figurines. A rapid initial sketch on tracing paper is a good means of familiarizing oneself with basic outlines and forms. Shadows created with soft pencil will be stippled in later drawings.

Quality materials enhance the finished product and are not the areas in which to economize. Papers should be chosen for a smooth, white surface--a preferred type is Strathmore Bristol plate finish. This favorite of illustrators comes in varying thicknesses (from one to three ply), and if care is taken, ink can be erased or scraped away with a razor. A paperlike plastic material combines the qualities of Bristol with the advantage of transparency. Called "Dura-lene" (Seth Cole TM), this product accepts india ink well and can be erased with a regular pencil eraser without damaging the surface. It is very susceptible to grease, however, and will reject ink if you allow sweat from your hands to touch it. Always rest your hand on another piece of paper to prevent this. To guard against this problem on hot days, some artists use cloth gloves with fingertips cut off. A dry cleaning pad (a soft cloth, filled with a grit-free powder) cleans smudges without removing pencil or ink lines.

There is no real substitute for india ink and the hollow-point (RapidoGraph) pen for illustration. This is frustrating because, like your car, this combination inevitably breaks down. Problems can be minimized by, first of all, keeping the pen clean when not in use (and for that matter, periodically when in use), and making sure the ink is fresh and well shaken. India ink does not last much longer than six months and must be discarded and replaced when it gets too old. If the ink flow stops, disassemble the pen and clean it thoroughly with water and a little ammonia--a drop or two in the ink container also helps. One geologist places his pens in a mechanical shaking devise every night to loosen accumulated sediment. Art stores offer a variety of technical pen cleaners. After refilling with ink, gently

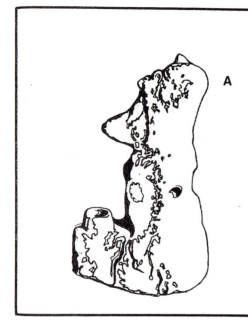

A

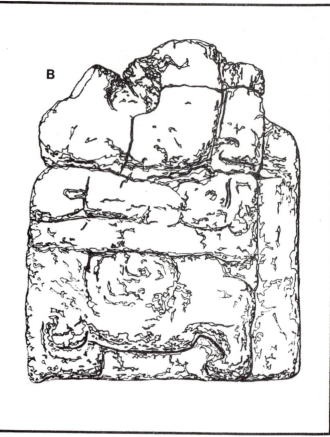

B

Figure 13-5: The first step in production of the ink drawing is creating a guide for shading via a "topographic map" technique. The same method is used for the figurine in the round (A) as well as for the low relief sculpture (B). While these examples are inked for reproduction, in reality the "contour line" effect is done with lightly-pencilled guide lines.

(and patiently) shake the pen up and down, tapping the point on a clean piece of paper to stimulate the resumed flow of ink. Do not do this over artwork, however, because these touchy pens will invariably leak ink while being shaken.

Preliminary tracings should begin in pencil on tracing paper, or in ink or stabilo pencils on acetate. Transparent acetate allows an exact tracing, but ink tends to spread on it, making detail work difficult. The beginner might find its transparency in fact confusing when working on complicated patterns, as it is easy to lose one's place. Tracing paper's semi-opaque scrim allows one to more easily view the lines already drawn as well as the photograph underneath it. Moreover, when drawing on acetate it is easy to lose one's place.

Although I prefer to work from photographic prints, projecting slides onto vertically-mounted paper can eliminate the need for tracing paper altogether. When working from slides, however, special care should be taken that the projected image is parallel to that of the slide. The corners of the frame should be checked with a 90-degree triangle before beginning work and, once begun, do not change the position of the projector until all drawings are completed; otherwise, the image will be altered. Another important limitation of drawing from slides, besides the high cost of replacement projector bulbs, is the influence of the angle of the artist's eye, vis-a-vis the angle of the projected image. On detailed designs try not to move from side to side to avoid your shadow, but rather work from below. This side-to-side motion, when its angle is extended to the pencil's point, can lead to unexpected distortions in the drawing itself. The pre-

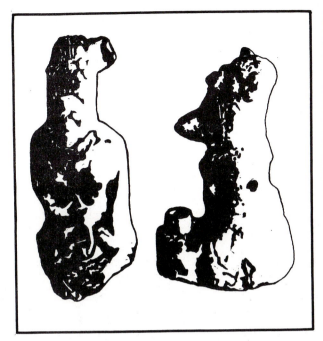

Figure 13-6: *Every ink drawing incorporates highlight areas (white or the very lightest gray) in the finished version. In this tracing these have been isolated while all other tonal gradations have been "blacked out".*

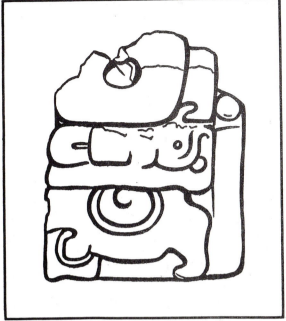

Figure 13-7: *"Police drawing" produced through collaboration between the excavator and the draftsman. Here sculptural details have been sorted out from the effects of erosion, and glyphic and other comparative evidence has been reviewed so as to help make better sense of fragmentary surface areas.*

liminary work in pencil can be erased once it has been inked in.

Preliminary line drawings may be any size--the larger the better--and reduced by xerox or photoprocess to the desired size of the final illustration. Line drawings look better when they are mechanically reduced, for this tends to minimize the effect of a shaky hand and sometimes makes tentative, unsure lines seem more fluid and confident. The format for the stipple shading work itself should be about the size that it is intended to be printed. Such drawings, unlike line work, do not reduce well, and if done severely there is a risk that all the hard work that went into dotting will be reduced to mush if the dot size is too small.

Realistic effects in painting and

graphic arts are achieved not only by additive methods (i.e., making the drawing darker) but by reductive means as well. In a pencil drawing, this is done with the eraser; in a painting, opaque white paint achieves the same effect. One shortcoming of the stipple ink drawings so common in archaeological papers is their lack of this reductive possibility. Opaque white can certainly be used after all other work has been completed, but paint does not take ink well, and the possibilities for further work are effectively terminated. The plastic drawing surfaces (like Duralene mentioned above) remedy this problem to a degree in that they allow mistakes to be erased, but careful application of ink is the best solution. As in traditional watercolor painting, which is also usually executed in an additive fashion, those areas destined to remain white must

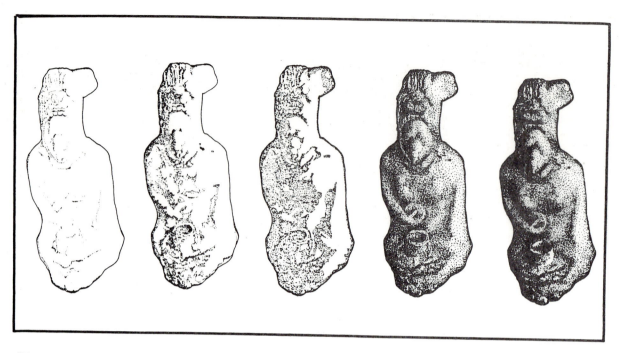

Figure 13-8: Five stages in the development of a stipple drawing taken from a field photograph. Beginning with the outlines and dotted indications of three-dimensional forms (left) note how shadows are expanded or darkened so as to give the proper effect. The fourth drawing in the series may be the correct shade, but depending upon the reproduction method employed (and possible loss of contrast) the fifth may be the best choice.

be carefully isolated at the outset and left alone throughout the entire process.

MAKING THE TRACING

For purposes of clarity, the tracing stage has been broken into three parts: the first involves preparing a contour outline of the artifact which includes all observable carved and modeled features, the second utilizes tracings that follow the limits of the shaded areas (Figure 13-5), and the third requires the careful isolation of the object's highlights (Figure 13-6). Exactly rendering the highlights is necessary for the reductive concerns essential to illusionism. These areas, which are to remain white in the finished drawing, should be as carefully described as the outlines. Though these three stages have been separated in the illustrations to this text, in practice they may be done together on the same piece of tracing paper. Drawing each separately, however, may help rein-

force the need for each and avoids a confusing jumble of lines on the same sheet.

The analogy to a topographic map is helpful in that it forces the recognition of the various layers of shadows that blend in the continuous tone photograph. Try to visualize these shades of gray in terms of graphic dot patterns and separate areas in increments that correspond to the grays available in Letraset tone patterns (i.e., 0-10% and 10-20% for highlights, 80% to solid black for the darkest shadows). Follow this with any other discernible tonal gradations. Like contour lines in a relief map, highlight areas should be described in completed rings with special care taken to avoid isolated or broken lines, for these serve no purpose but to confuse. It is a good idea not to think at this point about what the object is, but to follow the contour lines and the edges of the shaded areas slowly, with an "ant's eye view" unmindful of the overall effect.

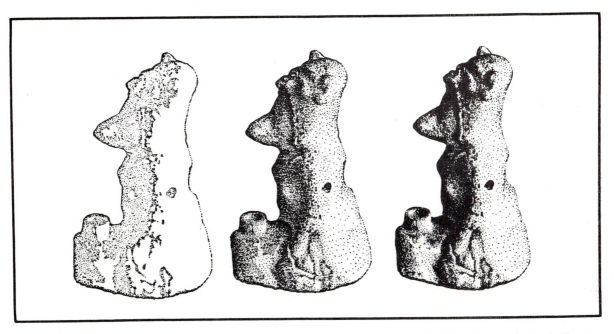

Figure 13-9: Stages in the production of a drawing from field photographs. First, all the middle-to-black tonal areas are covered with an even pattern of dots (left), then dots are scattered over lighter areas and shadows are deepened with heavier dot concentrations (center). Completion of the drawing (right) follows the addition of black ink in solid areas and creation of highlight zones through scraping stipple off with an X-acto knife blade.

No attempt should be made to improve or correct any of the data you see. A careful and complete record of all the photographic information, whether it seems right or not, is essential at this point. This mechanical tracing process can be tedious, but care taken here provides a map which can be continuously consulted during the inking process and produces more confidence when one approaches the final stages of the project. These early tracings are also the key to producing the trompe l'oeil realism associated with the photorealist artists. More time spent at this point means time and errors saved later.

A final preliminary drawing (Figure 13-7) is included to illustrate an important reason for doing the project in the first place. Here we have a collaborative drawing done with the help of the archaeologist who uncovered the monument. In analogy with a police artist's drawing, it combines the evidence from the photograph with the knowledge of the original object derived from first-hand observation. This collaboration was helpful in identifying those features in the photograph that were the result of damage or erosion to the artifact and thus not part of the sculptor's artistic intent. The original excavator and his notes also will describe sculptural details not readily apparent in the photograph alone. Comparisons with similar monuments and reference to the stylistic conventions of the producing culture can be suggested. As James B. Porter (this volume) points out, interpretive alterations or projected reconstructions should be clearly indicated with dotted lines and attempted only after a thorough investigation of the artistic language of the culture of provenience. Unless complete understanding is lessened through their omission, I prefer to omit such reconstructions entirely.

All preliminary drawings for this

paper were made on tracing paper from black-and-white continuous tone photographs enlarged to the desired size. A light box was used almost continuously and is my most valued tool. If one is unavailable, taping the photo and paper to a sunlit window or putting a light under a glass table will do. A basic step to remember while tracing is, tape everything down. Holding tracing paper in place with the hand invites errors due to slippage.

When using multiple tracings, care must be taken in transferring each one to the final drawing surface. Errors may occur at this juncture if the preliminary tracings are not in line with one another, resulting in the out-of-register, "double vision" effect such as that which occurs in bad color printing. (In printing color copy, a large percentage of time is spent checking the register of color separations for precise placement, particularly the angle, to avoid such errors.) Making a precise border around each tracing (whether or not it is used in the finished drawing) is an easy, reliable way to produce registration marks. Be careful to include these marks on each tracing. Remember that small errors are magnified by the transfer process itself.

When transferring the preliminary drawing to a nontransparent surface with chalk or graphite transfer paper, use a hard pencil or fine-point ball-point pen. Art supply stores have transfer paper in all colors including white for "reductive" drawings, but it is easy to make your own with chalk. Use a medium gray over black chalk and avoid messy carbon paper. The distortion described in tracing side to side from projected slides occurs with transfers of this sort and can be avoided by keeping the pencil or pen perpendicular to the drawing surface, or at least at a consistent angle. Be sure to use enough pressure to transfer the final drawing surface.

INKING

A close look at screened photographs is instructive when beginning a stipple drawing in ink. It takes little magnification of the coarse dot screen used on newsprint to reveal the variable concentrations of dots that, from a distance, coalesce into the smooth gradations of the photograph. There are more dots, tightly grouped, in a dark shadow than in a highlight, yet even the brightest areas have a widely spaced scattering of dots indicating the lightest gray. Upon beginning an illustration, it is most prudent to lightly isolate the form and its details with similar dots (Figure 13-8). One can then systematically darken the appropriate areas using the preliminary tracings as a guide--tracing the tracing--using dotted planes instead of lined edges. It is best to avoid lines (except dotted ones) and to save pure black until the very end. You may find that unbroken lines are unnecessary even as outlines. Simple sculptural forms lend themselves to the reversal of this additive approach. A medium density of dots may be regularly placed over the entire surface, while the light areas are left white. The darker shadows are then easily emphasized and lighter ones indicated by more widely spaced dots once again (Figure 13-9).

The stipple technique is time-consuming and is one that invites procrastination. It is the tortoise, not the hare, that wins the illustration race. Yet, dot stippling is a proven graphic means of creating the illusion of three dimensions and results in camera-ready copy. Careful placement of dots in appropriate concentrations creates this realistic impression and, using detailed preliminary tracings as a guide, becomes rather mechanical. Here, a shaky drawing hand is no drawback, for it is the repeated concentration of dots rather than the "one false move" that defines the form. Random, almost haphazard, dotting can describe a rough surface while greater care in adjusting the spacing of dots in a regular pattern is necessary for recreating a smooth surface. Copying successful examples of stipple drawings for practice may help get your feet wet. The technique needed for trompe l'oeil illusionist effects, one author observes, is "basically an applied science rather than an art" (d'Otrange Mastai 1975:15).

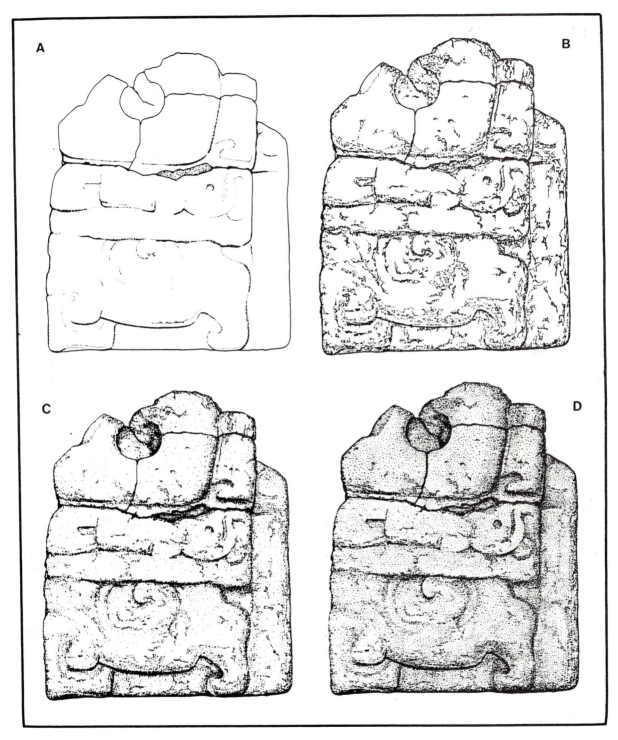

Figure 13-10: Four sequential stages in the production of the final stipple drawing of the low relief sculpture. A: Inked outlines and initial dotted guides for stipple shading; B: "Topographic" contour shading; C-D: The gradually accumulating concentrations of dots deepen shadows and help to identify the planar gradations of different tonal areas.

Figure 13-11:
The completed draw-
ing of the low relief
sculpture made entire-
ly from a single print.
Note how the effects
of erosion, although
indicated, have been
minimized and great-
er attention has been
devoted to carved
areas.

CORRECTIONS

A careful examination of the drawing and the correction of (hopefully) minor errors brings the process to completion. At this point one must shift from the ant's to the bird's eye view. Up to this stage the process of stipple placement and the careful tracings that preceded it has focused attention on small areas, one at a time. Now attention must be turned to the over-all effect. Adjustments for photographic distortions and the addition of what one knows about the artifact are now checked for accuracy or indicated for the first time. An example of this improvement can be seen in Figure 13-10 where the slavish description of the badly eroded relief sculpture's damaged surface has been smoothed and combined with details from the preliminary "police drawing." As the

small circular recesses seen in the photograph were revealed to be damage caused by roots, and not significant iconographic design elements, they were minimized--otherwise too much realism in this case would be misleading.

Showing a completed drawing to peers or experts for critical analysis and advice is important now. Areas of the drawing that are incorrect or awkward, to which the artist may be blind, are often clearly seen by others not so closely involved in the project. This could consist of asking a colleague if the drawing "looks right"; or, where the subtle curvature of a line or the reconstruction of broken areas have bearing on stylistic or interpretive issues, criticism should be sought from an epigrapher or an art historian. Mistakes pointed out now, after all the tedious effort involved in inking, can be disappointing, even embarrassing. One must be objective, however, and remember that the goal is to produce reliable information in the visual record.

Here the art school veteran has the jump on the amateur, having endured countless critiques in studio classes. The realist painter Robert Bechtle made the embarrassing observation in one of these critiques concerning one of my first attempts at photorealism. He said that a figure's hand looked like a donut. While I insisted that I had carefully traced that portion of the composition, and that the painting was "just like" the photo, he reminded me that we must "add what we know to what we see." When I returned to my preliminary tracing it seemed to be accurate, yet it had failed to create the illusion. The lighting used in making the photograph had a flattening effect which obscured the natural curves of the hand. My teacher was indeed correct; my painted hand did resemble a donut.

Though many illustrations approach the standards associated with fine art, their goal is different: the accurate documentation of scientific data. This does not preclude developing a certain style in the course of experience. Style, however, can be dangerous as it casts suspicion on the drawing's factual fidelity. Did the artist impose his style on the artifact? In the process of making a nice drawing, did he "improve" or "clean up" the clumsy original? The "styleless style" of the photojournalist avoids this issue and is the safer ground.

CONCLUSION

Why use an illustration rather than a photograph anyway? When the painter Paul Delaroche first heard of Daguerre's discovery, he said, "from today, painting is dead" (Kelly 1974:75). On the other hand, as M. L. d'Otrange Mastai pointed out in his examination of illusionism in painting (1975:25), "while the camera does not lie and tells 'nothing but the truth,' it does not, however, tell 'the whole truth.'" By the same token, the photographic image

reveals new information invisible to the most careful observer.

The convention of the illustration in archaeological reporting has come to seem almost more authoritative than even the best photographs. The graphic quality of an inked drawing can elevate an otherwise ordinary object by accentuating the often subtle details the camera doesn't know how to look for. In a preclassic boulder sculpture from Abaj Takalik, Guatemala, for example, where the difference between an artifact and another, unaltered stone is a matter of several carefully placed marks (Graham 1982:7-22), one must be careful that the camera "sees" these marks not as another effect of natural erosion but as the handiwork of man. The illustration, by minimizing the random effects of nature and calling attention to important details which make the artifact special, can make us see what the camera cannot.

In the archaeological context, the graphic convention of stippling enjoys an almost archaic prestige. This technique adds an aura of the authentic, seeming to place each new example within a visual record that predates the camera. Engravings of popular paintings were a profitable by-product of art long before the development of photography, and the stipple method of engraving, notes Peterdi (1971:58), made it "possible to achieve effects comparable to fine half-tone reproductions." Given other graphic methods of illusionism, and the fact that the addition of a mechanical dot-screen can make any painting or drawing camera-ready, the old-fashioned stipple process convinced Peterdi "only that some human beings have practically unlimited patience."

Returning to our task of recording prehistoric examples, one of the most illustrious of all archaeological draftsman, Frederick Catherwood, successfully combined the fashionable Romantic mood with the precision of the camera obscura's cousin, the "camera lucida" (von Hagen 1968:35). In some circumstances, Catherwood's original drawings are the only documentary evidence we have left for the appearance of specific sculptures or even buildings that have subsequently been stolen or destroyed; an example of this at Utatlan in the Quichean highlands of Guatemala (Stephens, 1841, Vol. 2: 184-185) shows us how much has been lost since 1839.

These are only a few of the examples of cooperation between the creative artist and the camera's precursors. To-day, photorealism makes use of the most sophisticated darkroom techniques and equipment in its pursuit of illusionism. Scientific illustration can benefit from an examination of the attitudes and techniques of modern photorealists. Archaeologists should learn to read a photograph like a map and, then add a key to it comprised of what they know.

ACKNOWLEDGMENTS

Since this volume first appeared four years ago, many archaeologists, students, and draftsmen have suggested ways to expand and improve it. The editor and authors would like to thank the following persons for their encouragement and advice: Alana Cordy-Collins, George F. Dales, Lawrence Dawson, Christopher Donnan, Helle Girey, John A. Graham, Thomas R. Hester, Patricia Lyon, Clement W. Meighan, John H. Rowe, James R. Sackett, and Norman Thrower.

We are grateful to the following institutions and research projects for permission to use previously published and unpublished artwork: the Lowie Museum, the Bancroft Library, and the Archaeological Research Facility of the University of California, Berkeley; the Archaeological Survey and Museum of Cultural History of UCLA; the Joint American Expedition to Ashara, Syria; the Salinas de los Nueve Cerros Project; the National Geographic Society/University of California, Berkeley Abaj Takalik Project; the UCLA Pacatnamu Project; and the UCLA Nacascolo Project.

ILLUSTRATION CREDITS

Design and layout by Brian D. Dillon.

Cover art by Dana Bleitz Sanburg: Terminal Classic Maya figurine from Operation 8, Salinas de los Nueve Cerros, Guatemala.

Introduction frontispiece by Wes Christensen: pair of Early Classic Maya shell medallions from Tomb 5, Salinas de los Nueve Cerros, Guatemala.

Chapter I frontispiece by Wes Christensen: Late Postclassic Maya carved peccary mandible from Sarteneja, Belize. Previously published in Sidrys, 1983: Figure 126; Boxt and Christensen, 1985: Figure 3.

Figures I-I, 2, 3, 5, 6 by Brian D. Dillon.

Figure I-4 by Wes Christensen: Early Classic Maya jade skull bead from Tomb 5, Salinas de los Nueve Cerros, Guatemala.

Chapter 2 frontispiece by Douglas V. Armstrong, Brian D. Dillon and Ronald Tsuruda: a Late Prehistoric California site from the Southern Sierra Nevada.

Figures 2-I, 2, 3, 4, 6, 7 by Douglas V. Armstrong: Figure 7 previously published in Armstrong, 1980.

Figure 2-5: reproduction courtesy of the British Directorate of Overseas Surveys.

Chapter 3 frontispiece, Figures 3-I, 2, 3, 4, 5, by Timothy Seymour.

Chapter 4 frontispiece by Mark C. Johnson: Classic Period Constructions at Nakum, Guatemala, previously issued by F.L.A.A.R.

Figures 4-I, 2, 3, 4 by Mark C. Johnson.

Figures 4-5 and 6 by Mark C. Johnson: La Venta, Tabasco, Mexico, previously published in Graham and Johnson, 1979: Figure I.

Chapter 5 frontispiece by Brian D. Dillon: Operation 3, Salinas de los Nueve Cerros, Guatemala.

Figure 5-I: adapted from Owner's Manual, Sears Craftsman 22" Lawn Mower.

Figures 5-2, 4 by G. Buccellati: previously published in Buccellati and Kelly-Buccellati, 1978.

Figure 5-3 by Timothy Seymour.

Figures 5-5, 6, 7 by Timothy Seymour: previously published in Buccellati, 1979.

Chapter 6 frontispiece by James B. Porter: Monument 14, Abaj Takalik, Guatemala.

Figure 6-I by James B. Porter: Stela 10, Kaminaljuyu, Guatemala.

Figures 6-2, 3 by Kevin O. Pope: Stela 13, Abaj Takalik, Guatemala.

Figure 6-4 by James B. Porter: Stela 13, Abaj Takalik, Guatemala.

Figures 6-5, 9 by Edgar Luis Torres and

James B. Porter: Stela 13, Abaj Takalik, Guatemala.

Figures 6-6, 7, 8 by James B. Porter: Stela 4, Abaj Takalik, Guatemala.

Figure 6-10 A by Edgar Luis Torres, B by James B. Porter, C after Parsons, 1972: Stela 4, Abaj Takalik, Guatemala.

Figure 6-11 by Edgar Luis Torres: Monument 47, Abaj Takalik, Guatemala.

Figures 6-12, 13, 14, by James B. Porter: Monument 47, Abaj Takalik, Guatemala.

Chapter 7 frontispiece by Joyce Olin: Jorol Plano-Relief: Nueve Cerros Variety vessel from Tomb 1, Salinas de los Nueve Cerros, Guatemala, previously published in Dillon, n.d.: Figure 41c.

Figures 7-1, 3, 5 by Brian D. Dillon.

Figure 7-2 by Brian D. Dillon, Joyce Olin and Patricia Ferber: Lapon Unslipped: Nueve Cerros Variety vessels from Operation 2, Salinas de los Nueve Cerros, Guatemala, previously published in Dillon, n.d.: Figure 13; and Dillon, Brunker and Pope, 1985: Figure 8.

Figure 7-4 by Patricia Ferber and Brian D. Dillon: Rambilin Orange Polychrome: Nueve Cerros Variety from Operation 7C, Salinas de los Nueve Cerros, Guatemala, previously published in Dillon, n.d.: Figure 29c.

Figure 7-6 by Brian D. Dillon: Chaquiste Impressed: Nueve Cerros Variety sherds from Operations 8 and 1, Salinas de los Nueve Cerros, Guatemala, previously published in Dillon, n.d.: Figure 48g-i.

Figure 7-7 by Joyce Olin and Brian D. Dillon: Gkol Resist: Nueve Cerros Variety vessel from Operation 7D, Salinas de los Nueve Cerros, Guatemala, previously published in Dillon, n.d.: Figure 34d.

Figure 7-8 by Joyce Olin: Jorol Plano-Relief: Nueve Cerros Variety vessel from Tomb 1, Salinas de los Nueve Cerros, Guatemala, previously published in Dillon, n.d.: Figure 41a.

Figure 7-9 by Joyce Olin and Brian D. Dillon: Chabil Incised: Nueve Cerros Variety vessel from Tomb 5, Salinas de los Nueve Cerros, Guatemala, previously published in Dillon, n.d.: Figure 36.

Figure 7-10 by Brian D. Dillon: Urita Gouged-Incised: Nueve Cerros Variety vessel from Tomb 4, Salinas de los Nueve Cerros, Guatemala, previously published in Dillon, n.d.: Figure 40a.

Figure 7-11 by Joyce Olin: Puchum Orange Polychrome: Nueve Cerros Variety vessel from Operations 7B and 7D, Salinas de los Nueve Cerros, Guatemala, previously published in Dillon, n.d.: Figure 33a-b.

Figure 7-12 by Joyce Olin: Max Modelled: Nueve Cerros Variety from Tomb 1, Salinas de los Nueve Cerros, Guatemala, previously published in Dillon, n.d.: Figure 47a.

Figure 7-13 by Joyce Olin: Etzunc Composite: Nueve Cerros Variety from Tomb 3, Salinas de los Nueve Cerros, Guatemala, previously published in Dillon, n.d.: Figure 40e.

Chapter 8 frontispiece by Dejon Dillon: from Operation 8 (Beach Cemetery) Nacascolo, Guanacaste, Costa Rica.

Figure 8-1 by Jane Becker: cutware pottery from Mohenjo-Daro, courtesy of George F. Dales.

Figure 8-2 by Eugene Prince: Nazca Vessel, courtesy of the Lowie Museum of Anthropology.

Figure 8-3, 4, 5 by Jane Becker.

Chapter 9 frontispiece by Jane Becker: Late Classic figurine from Salinas de los Nueve Cerros, Guatemala.

Figure 9-1 by Jane Becker: Tomb 5, Salinas de los Nueve Cerros, Guatemala.

Figure 9-2 by Jane Becker: Late Classic figurines from Salinas de los Nueve Cerros, Guatemala.

Chapter 10 frontispiece by Jennifer Corsiglia: a deep basin metate from the Ring Brothers Site Complex, Ventura County, California, previously published in Whitley, McCann, Simon and Drews, 1979: Figure 10.

Figure 10-1 by Helle Girey: artifacts from Coastal California sites. Left: leaf-shaped projectile point from site CA-Sba-1823; right: crescent from site CA-Sba-246.

Figures 10-2, 3, 4, 5, 6, 7, 8, 9 by Jennifer Corsiglia: figure 10-5 after artifact drawings in UCLA Archaeological Survey files; figure 10-7 previously published in Johnson, 1980: Figure 25, upper left; figures 10-8, 9 previously published in Rosen, 1978: Figure 37d, a.

Figure 10-10 by Helle Girey: biface preforms from site CA-Sba-246.

Chapter 11 frontispiece by Galo Cisniegas B.: courtesy of the UCLA Museum of Cultural History and the Pacatnamu project.

Figure 11-1 by Brian D. Dillon: Tomb 5 overhead photograph and plan view, Salinas de los Nueve Cerros, Guatemala, previously published in Dillon, Brunker and Pope, 1985: Figure 7.

Figure 11-2 by Jose Guadalupe Posada: courtesy of the Bancroft Library.

Figure 11-3 by Galo Cisniegas B.: courtesy of the UCLA Museum of Cultural History and the Pacatnamu project.

Figure 11-4 by John Verano: burials 55-59, Operation 8F (Beach Cemetery), Nacascolo, Guanacaste, Costa Rica.

Chapter 12 frontispiece, Figures 12-1, 2, 3, 4, 5, 6, 7 by Susan M. Hector from specimens in the UCLA Museum of Cultural History.

Chapter 13 frontispiece by Wes Christensen: Terminal Classic sculpture from Tilantongo, Oaxaca, Mexico, previously published in Pohl, n.d.: Figure 11.

Figure 13-1 by Chuck Close: "Robert II, 1982", reproduced with permission.

Figures 13-2, 3 by Brian D. Dillon: figure 13-2 of Salinas de los Nueve Cerros Stela 3, previously published in Dillon, 1977: Figure 26b; figure 13-3 of figurines from Salinas de los Nueve Cerros, Guatemala.

Figures 13-4, 5, 6, 7, 8, 9, 10, 11 by Wes Christensen.

REFERENCES CITED

Adams, R. E. W.
1971   The ceramics of Altar de Sacri-
       ficios, Guatemala.
       Papers of the Peabody Museum
       of Archaeology and Ethnology
       63 (1). Cambridge, Mass.

Armstrong, Douglas V.
1980   Shellfish gatherers of St. Kitts:
       a study of archaic subsistence
       and settlement patterns.
       Proceedings, 8th International
       Congress of Caribbean Archae-
       ology. Arizona State Univer-
       sity, Tempe.

n.d.   The Drax Hall slave village: an
       archaeological investigation of
       slavery on a Jamaican planta-
       tion. Preliminary report: part
       I. Documents search and site
       selection.
       Unpublished manuscript.

Aqrinier, Pierre
1978   A Sacrificial Mass Burial at
       Miramar, Chiapas, Mexico.
       Papers of the New World Ar-
       chaeological Foundation, No. 42.
       Brigham Young University,
       Provo, Utah.

Aston, Michael, and Trevor Rowley
1974   Landscape Archaeology: An In-
       troduction to Fieldwork Tech-
       niques on Past Roman Land-
       scapes.
       David and Charles, London.

Bass, William M.
1971   Human Osteology: A Laboratory
       and Field Manual of the Human
       Skeleton.
       Missouri Archaeological Society,
       Special Publications, University
       of Missouri, Columbia.

Battcock, Gregory, editor
1975   Super Realism, A Critical An-
       thology.
       Dutton, New York.

Boxt, Matthew A. and Wes Christensen
1985   A Maya Bone Carving from
       Sarteneja, Belize.
       Journal of New World
       Archaeology, Vol. V, 4: 1-12.

Bradley, Bruce A.
1975   Lithic reduction sequences: a
       glossary and description.
       In Lithic Technology: Making
       and Using Stone Tools, edited
       by Earl Swanson, pp. 5-13. Al-
       dine, Chicago.

Brodribb, Conant
1971   Drawing Archaeological Finds
       for Publication.
       Association Press, New York.

Brothwell, Don R.
1972   Digging Up Bones: The Excava-
       tion, Treatment and Study of
       Human Skeletal Remains (Sec-
       ond Edition).
       British Museum, Natural His-
       tory, Publication No. 704.
       Staples Printers, Ltd., St.
       Albans, Herts.

Bryant, Vaughn M., and Robert K. Holz
1965 A guide to the drafting of archaeological maps.
Texas Archaeological Society Bulletin 36: 269-285.

Buccellati, G.
1979 Terqa Preliminary Reports, no. 10. The Fourth Season: Introduction and the Stratigraphic Record.
Bibliotheca Mesopotamica 10. Undena Publications, Malibu, Calif.

Buccellati, G., and M. Kelly-Buccellati
1978 Field Encoding Manual (Non-Digital).
Aids and Research Tools in Ancient Near Eastern Studies 2. Undena Publications, Malibu, Calif.

Butterworth, Bernard B.
1979 Laboratory Anatomy of the Human Body. 2nd edition.

Clarke, Carl Dame
1940 Illustration: Its Techniques and Application to the Sciences.
John D. Lucas Co, Baltimore.

Coe, Michael D.
1975 Classic Maya Pottery at Dumbarton Oaks.
Dumbarton Oaks, Trustees for Harvard University, Washington, D.C.

Collins, Michael B.
1975a Lithic technology as a means of processual inference.
In Lithic technology: Making and Using Stone Tools, edited by Earl Swanson, pp. 15-34. Aldine, Chicago.

1975b Excavation and Recording of Human Physical Remains.
In Field Methods in Archaeology, by T. R. Hester, R. F. Heizer, and J. A. Graham, 6th edition, pp. 163-182.

Combes, J. D.
1964 A graphic method for recording and illustrating burials.
American Antiquity 30 (2): 216-218.

Crabtree, Don E.
1972 An introduction to flintworking.
Occasional Papers of the Idaho State University Museum 28. Pocatello.

Dennison, Austin D.
1973 Methods of drawing stone artifacts.
Archaeological Survey Association of Southern California Newsletter 20 (2): 7-8, 28-38. La Verne, Calif.

Detweiler, A. Henry
1948 Manual of Archaeological Surveying.
American Schools of Oriental Research, Publications of Jerusalem School, Archaeology 2. New Haven, Conn.

Dever, W. G., and H. D. Lance
1978 A Manual of Field Excavation: Handbook for Field Archaeologists.
Hebrew Union College, Cincinnati.

Dillon, Brian D.
1977 Salinas de los Nueve Cerros, Guatemala: preliminary archaeological investigations.
Ballena Press Studies in Mesoamerican Art, Archaeology, and Ethnohistory, vol. 2. Ballena Press, Socorro, N.M.

1982 Bound prisoners in Maya art.
Journal of New World Archaeology 5 (1): 24-45.

n.d. The archaeological ceramics of Salinas de los Nueve Cerros, Alta Verapaz, Guatemala.
Unpublished Ph.D. dissertation, University of California, Berkeley, 1979.

Dillon, Brian D., Lynda Brunker and Kevin O. Pope
   1985   Ancient Maya autoamputation? A possible case from Salinas de los Nueve Cerros, Guatemala. Journal of New World Archaeology 5 (4): 24-38.

Dittert, Alfred E., Jr., and Fred Wendorf
   1963   Procedural Manual for Archaeological Field Research Projects of the Museum of New Mexico. Papers in Anthropology 12. Santa Fe.

Donnan, Christopher B. and Carol J. Mackey
   1978   Ancient Burial Patterns of the Moche Valley, Peru. University of Texas Press, Austin, TX.

Drucker, Philip, Robert F. Heizer, and Robert Squier
   1959   Excavations at La Venta, Tabasco, 1955. Bureau of American Ethnology, Bulletin 170. Smithsonian Institution, Washington, D.C.

Flack, Audrey
   1981   Audrey Flack, On Painting Abrams, New York.

Frankfort, Henri
   1970   The Art and Architecture of the Ancient Near East. Penguin Books, New York.

Frankfort, Henri, Seton Lloyd, and Thorkild Jacobsen
   1940   The Gimilsin Temple and the Palace of the Rulers at Tell Asmar. University of Chicago Press, Chicago.

French, T. E., and C. S. Svenson
   1957   Mechanical Drawing. McGraw Hill Co, New York.

Frison, George C. and Bruce A. Bradley
   1980   Folsom Tools and Technology at the Hanson Site, Wyoming. University of New Mexico Press, Albuquerque.

Graham, Ian
   1967   Archaeological Explorations in El Peten, Guatemala. Middle American Research Institute, Publication 33. Tulane University, New Orleans.

Graham, John A.
   1982   Antecedents of Olmec Sculpture at Abaj Takalik. In Pre-Columbian Art History: Selected Readings, edited by Alana Cordy-Collins. Peek Publications, Palo Alto, Calif.

Graham, John A., and Mark Johnson
   1979   The Great Mound of La Venta. University of California Archaeological Research Facility Contribution 41: 1-5. Berkeley.

Greene, Merle
   1966   Classic Maya rubbings. Expedition Magazine 9 (1): 30-39. University Museum, University of Pennsylvania, Philadelphia.

Greene, Merle, Robert L. Rands, and John A. Graham
   1972   Maya Sculpture from the Southern Lowlands, the Highlands and Pacific Piedmont, Guatemala, Mexico, and Honduras. Lederer, Street, and Zeus, Berkeley.

Green, Merle, and Eric S. Thompson
   1967   Ancient Maya Relief Sculpture Museum of Primitive Art, New York.

Harris, E. C.
   1979   Principles of archaeological stratigraphy. In Studies in Archaeological Science. Academic Press, London and New York.

Heizer, Robert F., and John A. Graham
   1967   A Guide to Field Methods in Archaeology: Approaches to the Anthropology of the Dead. The National Press, Palo Alto.

Heizer, Robert F., John A. Graham and L. K. Napton
1968   The 1968 Investigations at La Venta.
        Archaeological Research Facility, Contribution 5: 127-154.   University of California, Berkeley.

Hester, Thomas R., Robert F. Heizer, and John A. Graham
1975   Field Methods in Archaeology. 6th edition.
        Mayfield Publishing Co, Palo Alto.

Hodgkiss, A. G.
1970   Maps for Books and Theses.
        Pica Press, New York.

Holmes, William Henry
1895-   Archaeological Studies among
1897   the Ancient Cities of Mexico.
        Field Columbian Museum Anthropological Series I (I).   Chicago.

1919   Handbook of Aboriginal American Antiquities, Part I: The Lithic Industries.
        Bureau of American Ethnology, Bulletin 60.   Smithsonian Institution of Washington.

Hope-Taylor, Brian
1966   Archaeological draughtsmanship: principles and practice. Part II: ends and means.
        Antiquity 40: 107-113.

1967   Archaeological draughtsmanship: principles and practice. Part III: lines of communication.
        Antiquity 41: 181-189.

Isham, L. B.
1965   Preparation of drawings for paleontological publication.
        In Handbook of Paleontological Techniques, edited by Kummel and Raup, pp. 459-468.   W. H. Freeman and Co, San Francisco.

Johnson, Mark
1980   Archaeological investigations at Ven-271.
        In Inland Chumash Archaeological Investigations, edited by D. S. Whitley, E. L. McCann, and C. W. Clewlow, Jr., pp. 187-260.   UCLA Institute of Archaeology Monograph 15.   Los Angeles.

Joukowsky, Martha
1980   A Complete Manual of Field Archaeology.
        Prentice-Hall/Spectrum, Englewood Cliffs, N.J.

Kelly, Francis
1974   The Studio and the Artist.
        St. Martins Press, New York.

Kenrick, P.
1971   Aids to the drawing of finds.
        American Antiquity 45: 205-209.

Kenyon, K. M.
1961   Beginning in Archaeology.
        Phoenix House, London and New York

Kidder, Alfred V., Jesse D. Jennings, and Edwin M. Shook
1946   Excavations at Kaminaljuyu, Guatemala.
        Carnegie Institution of Washington Publication 561.   Washington, D.C.

Kobayashi, Hiroaki
1975   The experimental study of bipolar flakes.
        In Lithic Technology: Making and Using Stone Tools, edited by Earl Swanson, pp. 115-128.   Mouton, The Hague.

Kobayashi, T., and P. Bleed
1971   Recording and illustrating ceramic surfaces with Tahukon rubbings.
        Plains Anthropologist 16: 219-221.

Koningsberger, Hans, and the Editors of Time-Life
1967   The World of Vermeer 1632-1675.
       Time Incorporated, New York.

Kowta, Makoto
1973   An outline guide for the preparation of archaeological line drawings.
       Mimeographed manuscript. California State University, Chico.

Lahee, F. H.
1961   Field Geology. 6th edition.
       McGraw-Hill Co., New York.

Lothrop, Samuel Kirkland
1937   Cocle: An Archaeological Site of Central Panama. Part I: Historical Background, Excavations at Sitio Conte, Artifacts and Ornaments.
       Memoirs of the Peabody Museum of Archaeology and Ethnology, Harvard University. Cambridge, MA.

Maudslay, Alfred P.
1884- Archaeology.
1902   Biologia Centrali-Americana, E. Du Cane Godman & Osbert Salvin, London.

Meighan, Clement W., and Sheldon Rootenberg
1975   A prehistoric Miner's Camp on Catalina Island.
       The Masterkey 31: 176-184. Southwest Museum, Los Angeles.

Monkhouse, F. J., and H. R. Wilkinson
1971   Maps and Diagrams: Their Compilation and Construction.
       Methuen and Co, London.

Napton, Lewis K.
1975   Site mapping and layout.
       In Field Methods in Archaeology, Hester, Heizer, and Graham 1975, pp. 37-63.

Oakley, Kenneth P.
1972   Man the Tool-Maker. 6th edition.
       University of Chicago Press, Chicago.

d'Otrange-Mastai, M.L.
1975   Illusion in Art; Trompe l'Oeil, A History of Pictorial Illusionism.
       Abaris Books, New York.

Parsons, Lee A.
1972   Iconographic notes on a new Izapan stela from Abaj Takalik, Guatemala.
       40th International Congress of Americanists, I: 203-212. Geneva.

Patten, L. M., and M. L. Rogness
1962   Architectural Drawings.
       Kendall/Hunt Publishing Co, Dubuque, Iowa.

Pendergast, David M.
1982   Excavations at Altun Ha, Belize, 1964-1970: Vol. II.
       Royal Ontario Museum, Toronto.

Peterdi, Gabor
1971   Printmaking Methods Old and New, Revised Edition.
       Macmillan, New York.

Piggot, Stuart, and Brian Hope-Taylor
1965   Archaeological draughtsmanship: principles and practice. Part I: principles and retrospect.
       Antiquity 39: 165-177.

Platz, K. A.
1971   Drawing artifacts for identification purposes.
       Missouri Archaeological Society Newsletter 250: 5-8.

Plommer, Hugh
1961   Simpson's History of Architectural Development: Ancient and Classical Architecture.
       David McKay Co, New York.

Pohl, John D.
n.d.   The Earth Lords: Politics and Symbolism of the Mixtec Codices.
       Unpublished Doctoral Dissertation, University of California, Los Angeles, (1984).

Raisz, Erwin Josephus
1962   Principles of Cartography.
       McGraw Hill and Co, New York.

Ridgway, John L.
1938   Scientific Illustration.
Stanford University Press,
Stanford.

Rivard, S.
1964   Technical illustrations applied
to archaeology.
Massachusetts Archaeological
Society Bulletin 25 (2): 44-45.

Robinson, Arthur E., and Randall D. Sale
1969   Elements of Cartography.
J. Wiley and Sons, New York.

Rosen, Martin, D.
1978   Archaeological Investigations at
VEN-294, An Inland Chumash
Village Site.
In The Archaeology of Oak
Park, Ventura County,
California, Monograph V,
Institute of Archaeology,
University of California, Los
Angeles: 7-113.

Ruz Lhuillier, Alberto
1973   El Templo de las inscripciones,
Palenque.
Instituto Nacional de
Antropologia e Historia,
Coleccion Cientifica:
Arqueologia 7, Mexico, D.F.

Sabloff, Jeremy A.
1975   Excavations at Seibal: Ceramics.
Memoirs of the Peabody Museum of Archaeology and Ethnology 13 (2). Cambridge, Mass.

Semenov, S. A.
1964   Prehistoric Technology, an Ex-
perimental Study of the Oldest
Tools and Artifacts from Traces
of Manufacture and Ware.
English translation by M. W.
Thompson. Cory, Adams and
Mackay Ltd, London.

Sharer, Robert J., and Wendy Ashmore
1979   Fundamentals of Archaeology.
The Benjamin/Cummins Publish-
ing Co, Menlo Park, Calif.

Shepard, Anna O.
1976   Ceramics for the Archaeologist.
5th printing.
Carnegie Institution of Washington Publication 609. Washington, D.C.

Sidrys, Raymond V.
1983   Archaeological Excavations in
Northern Belize, Central
America.
Monograph XVII, Institute of
Archaeology, University of
California, Los Angeles.

Smith, A. Ledyard
1972   Excavations at Altar de Sacri-
ficios: Architecture, Settlement,
Burials and Caches.
Papers of the Peabody museum
of Archaeology and Ethnology
62 (2). Harvard University,
Cambridge, MA.

Smith, Robert E.
1955   Ceramic Sequence at Uaxactun,
Guatemala.
Middle American Research In-
stitute Publication no. 20.
Tulane University, New Orleans.

Smith, Robert H.
1970   An approach to the drawing of
pottery and small finds for excavation reports.
World Archaeology 2 (2): 212-
228.

1974   Ethics in field archaeology.
Journal of Field Archaeology 1
(3/3): 375-383.

Staniland, L. N.
1953   The Principles of Line Illustration with Emphasis on the Requirements of Biological and
Other Scientific Workers.
Harvard University Press, Cambridge, Mass.

Stephens, John Lloyd
1841   Incidents of Travel in Central
America, Chiapas and Yucatan.
Harper and Brothers, New York.

Tixier, J.
1974 Glossary for the description of stone tools with special reference to the epipalaeolithic of the Magherb.
English translation by M. H. Newcomer. Newsletter of Lithic Special Publication 1. Washington State University, Pullman.

Tozzer, Alfred M.
1907 A Comparative Study of the Mayas and the Lacandones.
Archaeological Institute of America, Report of the Fellow in American Archaeology, 1902–1905. New York.

Van Riet Lowe, C.
1954 Notes on the drawing of stone implements.
South African Archaeological Bulletin 9 (33): 30–33.

von Hagen, Victor Wolfgang
1968 F. Catherwood, Architect -Explorer of Two Worlds.
Barre Publishers, Barre, Mass.

Webb, William S.
1946 Indian Knoll, Site Oh 2, Ohio County, Kentucky.
University of Kentucky Reports in Anthropology and Archaeology 4 (3): 1.
Lexington, KY.

Webster, G.
1974 Practical Archaeology.
John Baker, London.

Wetherington, Ronald K., editor
1978 Ceramics of Kaminaljuyu, Guatemala.
Monograph Series on Kaminaljuyu. Penn State University Press, University Park.

Whitley, D. S., E. L. McCann, J. M. Simon, and M. P. Drews
1979 Artifacts from the Ring Brothers Complex.
In Archaeological Investigations at the Ring Brothers Site Complex, Thousand Oaks, California, edited by C. W. Clewlow, Jr., D. S. Whitley, and E. L. McCann, pp. 11–100. UCLA Institute of Archaeology Monograph 13. Los Angeles.

Williams, David P.
1974 The body of an archeological report: the illustrations.
In The Preparation of Archaeological Reports, by L. Grinsell, P. Rahtz, and D. P. Williams, pp. 33–57. John Baker, London.

Winans, Melissa C. and Ross C. Winans
1982 Measuring Systems, Techniques, and Equipment for Taphonomic Studies.
In Archaeological Research Tools: Practical Archaeology, Brian D. Dillon, ed., 2: 45–58. Institute of Archaeology, University of California, Los Angeles.

Wood, Phyllis
1979 Scientific Illustration: A Guide to Biological, Zoological, and Medical Rendering Techniques, Design, Printing, and Display.
Van Nostrand Reinhold Co, New York.

Young, K. S.
1970 A technique for illustrating pottery designs.
American Antiquity 35 (4): 488–491.

Zweifel, Frances W.
1961 A Handbook of Biological Illustrating.
University of Chicago Press, Chicago.